DOING HISTORY

Investigating With Children
in Elementary and Middle Schools

ॐ

DOING HISTORY

Investigating With Children
in Elementary and Middle Schools
CREO

LINDA S. LEVSTIK
UNIVERSITY OF KENTUCKY

KEITH C. BARTON
NORTHERN KENTUCKY UNIVERSITY

LEA LAWRENCE ERLBAUM ASSOCIATES, PUBLISHERS
1997 Mahwah, New Jersey

Lawrence Erlbaum Associates, Inc., Publishers
10 Industrial Avenue
Mahwah, New Jersey 07430

Cover illustration by Laura Hughes, eighth grade student in Jeannette Groth's class at the School for the Creative and Performing Arts at Blue Grass, Lexington, KY

Cover design by Kathryn Houghtaling

Library of Congress Cataloging-in-Publication Data

Levstik, Linda S.
    Doing history : investigating with children in elementary and middle schools / Linda S. Levstik, Keith C. Barton.
        p.   cm.
    Includes index.
    ISBN 0-8058-8040-2 (pbk. : alk. paper)
    1. History—Study and teaching (Elementary)—United States.   2. History—Study and teaching (Secondary)—United States.   I. Barton, Keith C.   II. Title
    LB1582.U6L49 1996
    372.89'044—dc20   96-18081
                                                                 CIP

Books published by Lawrence Erlbaum Associates are printed on acid-free paper, and their bindings are chosen for strength and durability.

Printed in the United States of America
10 9 8 7 6 5 4

To our respective spouses,
Frank Levstik and Shaunna Scott,
for putting up with us.

Contents

CR&O

Preface

CRSO

Imagine a group of primary students debating whether Christopher Columbus should be considered a hero, or eighth-grade students producing a video to examine whether a historic document—the Bill of Rights—speaks to current issues. Imagine classrooms where students regularly, and actively, *do* history—frame questions, gather data from primary and secondary sources, organize and interpret that data, and share their work with different audiences. Imagine, too, a history curriculum that reflects the rich diversity of people in the United States and around the world.

We have been fortunate to spend a number of years working with teachers and students in just such classrooms. We have seen powerful historical study in classes where many of the children were recent immigrants, as well as in classes where children's families have lived in the same area for nearly 200 years. Some classes are full-inclusion programs where the special education and "regular" teachers team teach; most include students with special needs, at least for social studies. The classrooms range from urban and suburban to rural settings. But despite their many differences, these communities of inquiry have several things in common. In each one, even the youngest children describe historical study as interesting and important. Moreover, historical study in each of these classrooms deals with important historical content and engages students in authentic historical inquiry. *All* students are invited to be historical participants. Throughout the book, we draw on these classrooms to provide models of instructionally sound, thoughtful, and thought-provoking history teaching with students from a wide variety of backgrounds. Most chapters also begin with a vignette from one of these classrooms.

Many of the teachers cited in this book worked with us on research related to the development of historical thinking. We met others through our work with the field components of our teacher education programs or through professional meetings throughout the country. All of them generously shared their time, ideas, and classrooms. Although we would prefer honoring each of them by using their real names, confidentiality agreements sometimes preclude that possibility. Many appear under their own names—Amy Leigh, Dehea Smith, Jeanette Groth, LeeAnn Fitzpatrick, Rebecca Valbuena, Rhoda Coleman, Ruby Yessin, and Tina Reynolds—whereas other teachers' names are pseudonyms. Similarly, all children's names are pseudonyms except where we had express permission to credit a child for a specific piece of work. Again, we wish we could identify all of the students who so generously indulged our curiosity and answered questions that often must have seemed foolish, who lent us their work, and who shared their time and ideas. Our experience has been that children enjoy discussing their ideas about history and that they want to find out more about how things have changed over time.

As you read the vignettes think of them as snapshots of history in action—including some of the obstacles even good teachers face. As with a snapshot, each vignette is a glimpse of a particular experience teaching and learning history. The rest of the chapter puts the vignette in perspective, explaining why it is sound instruction and sound history and providing examples of activities ranging from the first years of primary school through the end of the middle grades. Although we have not tried to present a complete set of isolated activities, or recommend a specific curriculum, we have tried to suggest a framework for rethinking history instruction at the elementary and middle school levels. Our goal is to stimulate your thinking so that you can decide how to apply the ideas you find here to your own classrooms and your own students. One way to begin thinking about how to adapt these ideas is to refer to the list of related children's literature at the end of each chapter. These lists are by no means exhaustive; rather, selections are specifically intended to represent diversity of perspectives and different levels of difficulty. Other works mentioned in the margin notes are included in the reference section at the end of the book.

The teachers in this book—and others like them—renew our conviction that history *is* relevant to the lives of even the youngest school children, and that disciplined, reflective historical inquiry *is not* the sole province of university historians. We hope this book does justice to the lives and work of these teachers and to the students in their classes. We also hope that their example supports you and your students as you build communities of historical inquiry.

ACKNOWLEDGMENTS

This book grew out of a series of collaborations—with teachers and students, with each other, and with the many colleagues with whom we have discussed and debated the issues surrounding the teaching and learning of history. The teachers and students with whom we work have been incredibly generous, giving us feedback on many sections of the book and always providing a reality check on our theorizing. In addition, we want to thank the administrators who let us observe in their schools, supported our research, and welcomed our university students into their schools. Several people also read and responded to portions of the manuscript. Corinna Hasbach, Terrie Epstein, Raymond H. Muessig, and Noralee Frankel provided encouragement, insightful reviews, and useful suggestions. Lynne Smith provided technical assistance as well as a good "language arts" perspective. Frank Levstik assisted in locating a variety of sources. He and Jennifer Levstik read, listened to, and commented on more drafts of chapters than either probably cares to recall. Marge Artzer also provided valuable assistance, and Larry Newton provided at least one good line. Jenny Smith, Elaine Richardson, and Paula Bayer provided indispensable help in finding good children's literature. We especially want to thank our families for their good humor and patience, and our editor, Naomi Silverman, for shepherding the book to completion.

—Linda S. Levstik
—Keith C. Barton

Chapter 1

The Sociocultural Context
for Studying History

We learn [in history] . . . how people's views change over time. A lot of people's views change, but not everybody. We still have things like the KKK around . . . so obviously their views haven't changed since like the Civil War and stuff, but I think most people's have. Not necessarily everybody. . . . There's definitely still prejudice around, not necessarily just about Blacks and Hispanics, either.

—Caitlyn, Grade 6

You may remember a very different history from the one Caitlyn describes. Too often, history instruction is simply a march through time that never quite connects to the present. History becomes, as one second grader explains, "a main date." The dates may mark interesting stories, but the stories are finished—beginnings and middles established, climax identified, and endings predictable. Figures from a pantheon of heroes and villains step forward briefly, take their bows in stories that often fail to distinguish between myth and history, and disappear back into the pictures displayed above chalkboards. George Washington was the first president, had wooden teeth, and chopped down a cherry tree. Abraham Lincoln was honest, read by firelight, and walked a mile to return a nickel. It is little wonder that children sometimes ask what the point in all this storytelling might be.

Consider the kind of history Caitlyn's comments suggest. She clearly struggles to make sense of the prejudice she sees around her—both to explain how it is that prejudice exists and to separate herself from it. She uses her study of history to identify prejudice as an enduring human dilemma and to understand that "a lot of people's views change, but not everybody . . . there's still prejudice around." In other words, we are still in the middle of the story. The ending isn't predictable, and the story unfolds in our own time and in our own lives. The point of history is that this is, after all, an enormous family drama. Each of us develops the plot twists with which future generations will have to cope. From this perspective, history forces us to consider what it means to be a participant in this human drama.

HISTORY TELLS US WHO WE ARE

"You have Aunt Eliza's laugh," a father tells a child, "and a stubborn streak just like your grandmother!" A second child excitedly investigates a box that is "an old, old, old thing that's crumbling it's so old. [My grandmother] said it's older than her grandmother, so my grandmother's grandmother. It's an old jewelry box from France. We pulled out these old doors and one almost crumbled when we pulled it out." In

Families pass on stories about the past.

1

one classroom, a girl explains that her mother often talks about leaving school as a child in El Salvador to help support her family; a classmate has learned that his uncle was once "the greatest truck driver in all Mexico," able to make it through flooded roads when no one else could; yet another has heard her family recall the homes and businesses they owned before leaving Vietnam.

Holt (1990a, 1990b), Thornton (1987)

In the identification of family characteristics, the passing on of family heirlooms and artifacts, of stories shared and times remembered, we build our personal and family histories and learn something about who we are—or who we would rather not be! Anyone who has listened to family stories grow and change over time, however, also knows that interpretation shifts with the teller. When Uncle Christopher tells the story of Scottish emigration, for example, it is a tale of brave ancestors wrapped in their clan tartans. In Aunt Kathryn's rendering, the tartans are more tattered, and the family roots more humble. As one historian notes, "History is never either a neutral force or a complete world view; history is always *someone's* history." All of us, then, start with our own diverse social histories—the story of who we are as interpreted through the experiences of daily living, family stories, pictures and artifacts.

Appleby, Hunt, & Jacob (1994, p. 11)

Downey (1985)

For much of the 20th century, however, school history derived mainly from the political life of nations and emphasized the study of leaders. History instruction began with the assumption of a unified society, telling a broad story that tended to deemphasize racial, ethnic, gender, and class distinctions. As a result, many of us became invisible in history. If our students are to be visible—able to see themselves as participants in the ongoing drama of history—then we have to rethink the ways in which we conceive of history:

History instruction has traditionally de-emphasized diversity. *Epstein (1991, 1994c, 1994e)*

Barber (1992), Zinn (1990)

- Begin with the assumption of a pluralistic society. All of us belong to many groups that are intricately related to each other. Some of us have exercised more power than others; others have more often been excluded from power.

H. White (1982)

- Recognize that no single story can possibly be our story. Instead, our multiple stories, braided together, constantly speak to and against each other. Each of us is a strand, but not the whole.

Tuchman (1981)

- Remember that history is alive. All our stories are only partially known, always unfinished, and constantly changing as we speak and act.

HISTORY IS ABOUT WHO WE CAN BECOME

History points to some possible paths to the future and forecloses others. *Holt (1990a)*

Because history is a work in progress, it always tells us more than who we were or who we are at the moment. By marking out particular paths to the present, history also points to some possible paths to the future and forecloses others. To the degree that history instruction limits students' views of the multiple paths leading from the past, it also inhibits their perception of the future. Students who do not see themselves as members of groups who had agency in the past or power in the present, who are invisible in history, lack viable models for the future. Consider, for instance, the impact of traditional history instruction that emphasizes the agency of some men—conquering the wilderness, establishing governments, leading social movements—while presenting most women as acted upon—following husbands to new lands, invisible in government, silent on public issues. Particularly when such instruction matches school practice where girls are often taught to be passive and boys active, there is little modeling of alternatives for the future. Of course, similar examples could be used for other groups who have been less visible in traditional history. As a result, history is often perceived as separate from ordinary life, divorced from the puzzles of culture and change that absorb us on a daily basis. On the other hand, shifting the focus of the history curriculum presents a more inclusive and authentic vision of who and what our students can become:

Brophy (1990), Downey (1982), Epstein (1991, 1994a)

Gardner & Boix-Mansilla (1994), Kessler-Harris (1990)

- Focus on enduring human dilemmas. Emphasize that the dilemmas of the present have their roots in the past. Untangling those roots can be both freeing and empowering.
- Focus on human agency. Emphasize the ways in which people have acquiesced to, ignored, or acted against oppression and injustice as well as the ways in which people have worked to build the futures they desired.
- Focus on subjecting interpretations to scrutiny and skepticism. Emphasize the "authored" nature of historical interpretation. Whose voice is heard? Whose is left out? How else might the story be told?
- Connect to the microlevel. Emphasize bringing historical perspective to bear on current issues both in the classroom and the larger society.

Gagnon and the Bradley Commission on History in the Schools (1989), Zinn (1990)

Gordon (1990)

Greene (1993a, 1993b)

Bradley Commission on History in Schools (1989)

HISTORY IS ABOUT SIGNFICANT THEMES AND QUESTIONS

If history tells us who we are and what we can become, then we cannot afford a history curriculum mired in trivia and limited to a chronological recounting of events. Instead, we need a vibrant history curriculum that engages children in investigating significant themes and questions, with people, their values, and the choices they make as the central focus. In the past, we have assumed that students needed "basic skills" before they could engage with big issues. The trouble with this is that timelines, names, and memorized "facts" are not history and they certainly aren't compelling. The enduring themes and questions that humans have struggled with over time are, however, more compelling history (see Table 1.1). In the past, we have reserved these for historians and then wondered why children too often found history insignificant. By shifting the instructional focus from hearing about one historical story to asking questions worth pursuing, children have an opportunity to engage in the real "basics" of history.

National Council for the Social Studies (1994)

Downey & Levstik (1991)

Exploring significant themes and questions is the basic activity of history. Evans (1988)

Table 1.1 provides one set of suggested themes and questions. You would, of course, have to adjust the questions to fit particular grade levels. For instance, a primary class might begin with a question such as "Why do people move from one place to another?" rather than with "How has human movement been encouraged and inhibited?" Their study might begin with the students' own experiences and then expand to consideration of community patterns over time. A middle school class, on the other hand, might consider the question "How have our decisions about the environment changed other communities?" Again, students might begin by analyzing local conditions, then trace them back in time, and finally study the impact of local conditions on the larger community, nationally and internationally. As you look over the themes and questions in Table 1.1, consider how you might adapt them to engage students in thinking about who they are, where they came from and where they might go in the future.

Most of us probably don't remember this kind of history. At worst we may remember a string of isolated dates and questions at the end of a deadly dull textbook chapter. At best we may remember a teacher who told impassioned stories about times long ago. But even at its best, we heard a single story, we already knew how it would come out—and some of us weren't in it. In fact, history always stopped long before it got to us. Therefore, we had no role in history. Always excluded in time, often excluded because we were the "wrong" gender, race, class, or ethnicity, we weren't invited into the story—unless we were willing to identify with the main characters. And we were rarely encouraged to think about why the story was being told that way, or how it might have looked from a different perspective. In other words, we were unlikely to see history as either authored or interpretive.

Many students have been excluded from "the story" of history.

HISTORY IS INTERPRETIVE

No historical account can be entirely objective; historical knowledge always involves interpretation. At the most basic level, anyone interested in knowing what happened in the past faces a problem peculiar to history: the events are already over with, and

TABLE 1.1

Significant Themes and Questions in History

The Development of Human Societies and Cultures

Why have people developed organized societies and cultures?

How have environmental factors influenced social and cultural developments?

How have cultures differed in social, economic, and political organization ?

What elements do societies/cultures have in common?

How have cultures influenced the way people perceive themselves and others?

How have continuity and change been reflected in and across societies over time?

Movement and Interaction of People, Cultures, and Ideas

What forces have created, encouraged, or inhibited human movement?

What factors have enhanced and inhibited the spread of ideas, goods, and cultures?

How has human interaction led to conflict and/or cooperation?

How has the spread of ideas, goods, and cultures influenced societies?

How has the transmission of disease influenced societies?

Human Interaction with the Environment

Over time, how have societies viewed their physical environment?

How have humans changed the environment to suit their needs?

How have humans adapted over time to meet environmental realities?

How have decisions about the environment had cumulative and complex effects on societies?

How have competing interests within a society viewed resource allocation?

Patterns of Economic and Technological Organization and Change

Why have different societies and cultures developed different economic systems?

How and why did some societies develop agricultural economies?

What factors are critical to the emergence of technologically advanced societies?

How have societies with different economic systems included or excluded people/groups from decision making and the allocation of benefits?

How have societies with different economic systems adapted to changing conditions and demands?

How have scientific developments led to technological and/or economic changes?

The Relationships Among Values, Beliefs, Ideas, and Institutions

How have religion and philosophy influenced individuals and groups? How have these influences been expressed in the arts and other institutions?

How have values, beliefs, and ideas shaped culture and social institutions?

What leads some cultures to influence others?

How have some cultures imposed their values, beliefs, ideas, and institutions on others?

How have cultures attempted to maintain their values, beliefs, ideas, and institutions?

How have values, beliefs, ideas, and institutions come into conflict with each other, and how have these conflicts been expressed?

How have cultures defined the relationship between the individual and society?

Note. Adapted from National Council for the Social Studies Focus Group on the NEH History Standards (1993)

P. Bennett (1967)

Historians make decisions that involve human judgment and interpretation.

cannot be directly observed or repeated. As a result, finding out what happened always involves indirect methods (such as using primary sources and artifacts), and this requires interpretation: the historian has to decide which sources to use, how reliable they are, and what to do when they contradict each other. Everyone knows that the same event can be explained differently by different people, and those in the past were no less subject to bias than we are; there are dozens of firsthand accounts of the Battle at Lexington Green, for example, and no two of them are alike. Faced with conflicting sources, the historian must decide which descriptions seem most plausible; such decisions necessarily involve human judgment and interpretation.

The historical record is more often incomplete than contradictory, however, and so the historian has to piece together fragments of information to construct a complete description. Such descriptions inevitably involve speculation, because some facts can never be recovered. Consider, for example, the assassination of President Kennedy. No single source contains enough information to know exactly what happened at the scene, and so the historian has to pull together evidence from films, recordings, firsthand accounts, and medical reports. The fact that this event has spawned decades of controversy indicates just how impossible it is to establish "objectively" what happened: there will always be gaps in the record, and people will disagree over the most reasonable way of filling in those gaps. For many historical events, it is impossible to separate description from interpretation.

The historical record is always incomplete.

HISTORY IS EXPLAINED THROUGH NARRATIVES

Historical accounts also involve an even more important kind of interpretation—not just in establishing what happened, but in showing how events relate to each other. A simple list of events from the past is usually referred to as a *chronicle*. History, however, is something more: historical explanations almost always explain events in a narrative form. A historical account, then, is a story about the past—with a beginning, middle, and end, and a setting, characters, problem (or problems), and resolution. Think, for example, about accounts of the American Revolution. The story begins at the end of the French and Indian War, as Britain imposes taxes to pay for the defense of the colonies. As the colonists become increasingly upset about the unfairness of taxation without representation, they begin a series of protests, which England meets with increasingly repressive responses. The colonists eventually declare their independence, a war results, and the colonists are victorious. This historical episode has a structure similar to any narrative, fictitious or otherwise—a setting, characters, a problem, and a resolution. Several historians have argued that this kind of narrative structure is the basis of all historical explanation.

Historical narratives explain how events are causally related. *Danto (1965), Gallie (1964), M. White (1965)*

But whenever history is told as a narrative, someone has to decide when the story begins and ends, what is included or left out, and which events appear as problems or solutions. As a result, historical narratives always involve interpretation: someone decides how to tell the story. To take a simple example, it would be impossible to tell everything that happened during the American Revolution (even if complete records survived). That would mean explaining how Thomas Jefferson sharpened his pen each time he sat down to write, how Crispus Attucks buckled his shoes each morning, how Abigail Adams lit candles in her home—and millions of other details about every person in the colonies and in England, every minute of every day for decades. No historian tries to write such a "complete" account, and no one would have time to read one. Instead, every historical account is selective—someone decides which events are important enough to include in the story. Deciding which events to include and which to leave out forms one of the most basic aspects of historical interpretation.

Historical narratives are authored. *Danto (1965), Gallie (1964), Ricoeur (1984), H. White (1978, 1982, 1984), M. White (1965)*

No historical account is complete.

At an even more significant level, however, historical interpretation involves deciding not just what events to include, but how they relate to each other. Explaining that "taxation without representation" caused the American Revolution, for example, is an example of interpretation: the historian selects one reason as a more important cause than others. The facts themselves cannot explain why the war took place, only that it did; explaining the war is a matter of interpretation. To take an even more familiar example, what was the nature of American involvement in the Vietnam War? Some would tell the story of a military hampered by weak politicians and ungrateful protesters, while others would tell of the triumph of the Vietnamese people over a brutal dictatorship and a vicious superpower. What appears as failure from one perspective appears as victory to another. The events of the war remain the same, but

5

Historical interpretations vary from one historian to another. *Cohen (1994), Novick (1988), Ricoeur (1984),Shama (1992), Zinn (1990).*

their meaning changes depending on the story being told. Even when the factual events of history can be established firmly, their meaning—their arrangement in a narrative—is always a matter of interpretation.

The historian engages in interpretation, then, whenever she shapes the events of the past into a story. Since no account of the past is ever complete, and since any event can be told as part of more than one possible story, interpretations will vary from one historian to another: one may see progress where another sees decline, one may find the importance of events that others ignore, and so on. Far from being avoided, debates over interpretation are at the very heart of the historical profession. Historians know that more than one story can be told about the same events, and that interpretations will change over time; there simply is not a single, unchanging story of history. Such ambiguity is regarded as an inevitable, productive, and desirable part of the search for historical knowledge. That is not to say, however, that any interpretation is as good as any other. Any story about the past must, for example, account for the available evidence. A narrative of the World War II era that denies that the Holocaust occurred will not garner much respect because the facts of the Holocaust can be conclusively established.

Not all historical narratives are equally valid. *Kansteiner (1993), H. White (1992)*

HISTORY IS MORE THAN POLITICS

Unfortunately, the range of interpretations traditionally found in textbooks and school curricula (and, until recently, academic history) has been extremely small. The historical narratives students encounter at school, for example, focus almost exclusively on the political and diplomatic history of the United States—the history of laws, presidents, wars, and foreign relations. Information that does not fit into these categories is rarely afforded much importance. As a result, those who traditionally have had little access to politics—such as women, people of color, and the poor—have been largely excluded from the narrative interpretation of American history.

School history has usually focused on politics and diplomacy.

Elshtain (1981)

Women often have been omitted from the history curriculum. *Gordon (1990)*

Women, for example, appear only infrequently in the curriculum, because for much of the nation's history they have had only indirect access to politics—and as long as politics remains the focus of history, women will appear only when they influence that predominantly male realm (as, for example, during the abolition or women's rights movements). There is no objective reason, however, for history to concern itself so exclusively with the public political arena. For several decades now, academic historians have been turning their attention to other areas of life—such as family relations, domestic labor, and religion—and not surprisingly have found women to be significant historical actors. Even more recently, historians have explored the connections between the spheres previously regarded as public and private, and again have found that gender has played a much more significant role than was long recognized. As long as these topics remain absent from the study of history, however, so will most women.

People of color often have been omitted from the history curriculum. *Kessler-Harris (1990)*

Deciding to limit one's attention to politics, then, amounts to excluding large portions of the population from American history; it is one way of deciding what is left in and what is left out of the story. Not only women, of course, but many other segments of the population have suffered from this exclusion. African Americans, for example, have been considered an important part of history only when their presence had an impact on European American politics; the political, economic, and cultural developments within African American society have not been considered a part of the story of the country. (And still less have Latinos, Asian Americans, or other people of color been accorded a prominent place within that story.) Again, however, academic historians have been devoting attention to such issues for well over a quarter of a century—but as long as this more inclusive interpretation of American history remains outside the school curriculum, so will most groups other than European Americans.

6

The traditional stories of history have been particularly severe in their treatment of Native Americans. For many years, the history of the United States was roughly equivalent to the triumph of European American settlement. In that story, the presence of Native Americans appeared as an obvious problem, to be solved through their removal or relocation. Native Americans, of course, saw the story very differently: from their perspective, the problem was the forced surrender of their land (and often their way of life), and armed resistance, peaceful settlement, and collaboration all represented attempts at solutions. A historical map showing the expansion of European American settlement, then, has precisely the opposite meaning for Native Americans: it shows the contraction of their own territory. Again, the facts of the encounter between Native Americans and European Americans can in most cases be established, but their signficance changes greatly depending on the story being told.

Put simply, there is not a single story of history, but many stories. Native-European relations, the American Revolution, slavery, changes in domestic labor, immigration, the Vietnam War—all these will look different from varying perspectives. Each point of view will regard some events as more important, others as less so; each will include some details while omitting others; what appears as progress in one story will seem like decline in another, and solutions in one will be regarded as problems in others. Each story, that is, will invariably contain the kind of interpretation that is an inseparable part of historical understanding.

HISTORY IS CONTROVERSIAL

The combination of interpretation and importance makes for a volatile mix. If historical truth were handed down to us on a stone tablet, the meaning and significance of the past would be certain and unchanging, and there would be no room for controversy. Not only would we know what happened in the past, but we would know just what story to tell about it; anyone who suggested alternative explanations could be dismissed as an unenlightened crank. And if history were unimportant, if it were not so central to our individual and collective identity, its interpretive nature would hardly matter; historians and others could be relegated to the remote confines of archives and libraries, where they would be free to argue over their conflicting narratives, out of sight and out of mind. But history has a more vital fate; because many stories can be told about the past, and because those stories powerfully influence our understanding of who we are and where we come from, history is destined to be among the most controversial areas of human knowledge.

Such controversies are nothing new: they have been a constant feature of the public understanding of history in this country throughout the last century, as some groups have struggled to become part of the story of American history and others have fought just as hard to keep them out. Regional tensions produced many of the most impassioned historical debates in the first decades of this century, as Westerners argued that the Eastern United States dominated textbooks and public celebrations, and Southerners maintained that New England received too much attention at the expense of their own section. The legacy of the Civil War lent a particular fervor to debates between North and South, as each strove to establish its own interpretation as the accepted and "correct" one. In 1920, the New Orleans chapter of the United Daughters of the Confederacy warned mothers not to let their children celebrate Lincoln's birthday at school, and other Southerners promoted Robert E. Lee as the country's preeminent "man of honor." Northern veterans, meanwhile, threatened to boycott a joint reunion at Gettysburg in 1938 if Confederate veterans were allowed to display their flag, and they condemned the use of the phrase "War Between the States" instead of "Civil War." Clearly, the symbols of the past had an important and enduring legacy that still produced serious disagreements.

Sectional rivalries may not be completely dead, but it's hard to imagine the memory of Abraham Lincoln inspiring such a high level of feeling these days; the demise of everyone directly involved in the Civil War makes it a much less emotional issue than it was 75 years ago. Other historical controversies seem even more fleeting: In the 1890s, Anglo Americans protested the proposal to make Columbus Day a legal holiday because only "the Mafia" would be interested in celebrating the life of an Italian; in 1915, prejudice against German Americans forced the removal of a statue of Baron Von Steuben at Valley Forge; and the 1920s saw a movement to condemn American history textbooks as full of pro-British propaganda. These debates, of course, just seem silly today: historical controversies always result from contemporary concerns, and now few people care about the issues that inspired such strong feelings against Italians, Germans, or the British. It's hard to imagine anyone getting upset about a monument to Baron Von Steuben anymore.

But as we all know, there are other contemporary issues that still inspire fierce passions. Racial tensions, both spoken and unspoken, permeate every sphere of our society and invariably affect our understanding of how the story of American history should be told. Since the beginning of Black History Week in 1926 (and before), teachers, parents, students, and scholars have argued that African Americans deserve a more prominent place in that story. This perspective has grown even more inclusive in recent years, as it becomes apparent that all racial and ethnic groups—as well as women, working people, and others—should be part of the story of American history, and that they should be included as full and active participants rather than marginal "contributors."

Because issues of race, gender, and class still divide our society, though, every attempt to tell a more inclusive story of American history is met with fierce resistance, as defenders of the status quo argue that these attempts minimize the achievements of the men who made our country great. Ironically, though, it's rare for anyone to admit that this argument is one of interpretation; doing so would lead to controversy, and historian Michael Kammen argues that Americans have never wanted their history to be controversial; he maintains that Americans have always looked to history to provide a kind of comforting and guilt-free nostalgia, and have consistently "depoliticized" the past.

CONCLUSIONS

From our perspective, the desire to avoid controversy leads to one of the most serious weaknesses in the discussion of history—the refusal to admit that all history is interpretive. Those who defend the status quo portray their version as the "real" story (because it's already in the textbooks) and condemn all other interpretations as somehow weakening the "truth" of American history. Given that these arguments are usually made by precisely those people who benefit most from ignoring issues of race, class, and gender, that position is hardly surprising. But if schools are to prepare students for active citizenship in a democracy, they can neither ignore controversy nor teach students to accept passively someone else's historical interpretations. Being a citizen of a demoracy means much more than that. Education for democratic citizenship requires that students learn to take part in meaningful and productive discussion with people of diverse viewpoints. Consequently, throughout this book we portray history as a subject in which students learn how people create stories about the past and how those stories can be told differently. Far from being limited to some select group of students, we think this kind of instruction is practical for all children in the elementary and middle grades, and in the next chapter we explain the principles of teaching and learning that guide our approach.

Kammen (1991)

Contemporary concerns lead to controversies over historical interpretations.

Racial controversies influence our understanding of history.

Attempts to tell a more inclusive story of American history are met with fierce resistance. *Casanova (1995), Cornbleth (1995), Evans (1988), Ravitch & Schlesinger (1990), Thornton (1990)*

Kammen (1991)

Chapter 2

The Theory
Behind Disciplined Inquiry

Understanding theory to me was like "Ah ha!" Teachers hear so much about theory, and when they go to a workshop or an inservice, they usually say, "Skip the theory, just get to the practical stuff." And so much of what I used to do I just did by instinct—I knew what worked, what would bring results, but I never knew why. Theory helped me understand why it worked, why A plus B equals C. I understood how cooperative learning and integrated instruction and sheltered English all went together; it was like the pieces of a puzzle—they all made sense together. I realized the things I was doing weren't just disconnected pieces, but were part of a design. I found out all these practical ideas I was using had a theoretical foundation behind them.

Knowing theory makes my teaching better. I can pick and choose better—I have a better sense of what will work and what won't. A lot of what I used to do was hit or miss; I would try something, and I would never use it again. Now when I consider a new teaching idea, I can filter it through what I know about theory: I can decide whether it adds to my program or whether it's just busy work. When I go to a conference, I can say, "Oh, that helps build schema," or "That's integrated language"—versus some program that's just a hundred questions or something, where I say, "That wouldn't work, it's not authentic." And theory helps me make sure I'm not doing something just because it looks cute, like, "Oh, gee, I'll have them make a scrapbook." Now I might have students make a scrapbook from the point of a view of a character in a novel, because I know it helps them pick out main ideas, develops their ability to understand characters, provides an authentic assessment—it actually teaches something, it isn't just a cute idea. I don't think, "Oh, isn't that cute! Oh, a bear!" I understand why teaching thematically isn't just having a heart or a bear on every handout.

—Rhoda Coleman, fifth-grade teacher, Buford Avenue School, Lennox, California

Rhoda is right: sometimes teachers hear a lot of theory, and usually it doesn't seem as important as the practical ideas—the good stuff. And some theory really *isn't* very useful: we've all heard or read theories that obviously came about in a laboratory or office, developed by people who don't seem to have any idea what real children do in real classrooms. But theory, like teaching, can be good, bad, or somewhere in between. From our perspective, good theory helps teachers make sense of their own experience; it provides them a clearer understanding of what they see in their classrooms every day—the "Ah ha!" Rhoda mentions. Good theory also helps teachers plan more effective and meaningful lessons for their students: just as Rhoda explains, theory allows teachers to separate ideas that teach something important from those that are simply cute, novel, or well-packaged. Rather than devoting years to trial-and-error attempts to find the best lesson ideas, a teacher who understands the theory behind how students learn can more consistently develop effective plans.

Useful theory helps teachers make sense of their own experience.

In this chapter we lay out the basic theoretical principles that guide our understanding of how to teach history. On the one hand, these principles represent our reading of sociocultural perspectives on learning and contemporary cognitive psychology. On the other, they also reflect key aspects of the best history teaching we've seen. Rather than being removed from the realities of the classroom, then, the theory

The research base for much of this chapter is summarized in Bruer (1993), Caine & Caine (1994), Gardner (1991), and Good & Brophy (1994, especially chapter 10)

9

described in this chapter draws on what we know from our experience with teachers and students. We find these ideas useful in understanding what makes for good teaching, and we think they will help teachers plan their own instruction. Without these principles, the activities we describe in the rest of the book are good but isolated lessons, and teachers may or may not be able to use them in their own classes. But by understanding the theory that guides this approach, teachers can apply and adapt these suggestions to meet the needs of their students.

LEARNING MEANS IN-DEPTH UNDERSTANDING

You have to go into a topic in depth, not just see who can get to the American Revolution by May; otherwise, they won't remember it. I may be slow because I'm just on Jamestown, but my students still remember what they learned about Native Americans. It's important that they're actually *doing* history, not just memorizing information.

—Rebecca Valbuena, fifth-grade teacher, DeAnza School, Baldwin Park, California

I don't remember very much about the Revolution, but it doesn't matter. We'll get it again in junior high.

—Fifth-grade student (1 month after studying the topic), Fort Thomas, Kentucky

In any subject, some people achieve more than others. An engineer can build a better bridge than a college undergraduate, for example, and an experienced doctor diagnoses illness better than a first-year medical student. Among younger students, some read better than others, some solve math problems more easily, and some are better dancers, musicians, basketball players, and so on. Psychological research that investigates the difference between *experts* in various fields from *novices* indicates that those who are more capable do not simply know more, nor do they necessarily have any greater general intelligence or reasoning ability; rather, they have a better understanding of the key concepts in their field, and a more developed understanding of when and how to apply those concepts. In the language of cognitive psychology, experts have more organized *schemas*, or mental representations of knowledge, than novices.

From this perspective, simply knowing more facts does not necessarily mean greater understanding; students may learn facts without having any idea what they mean or why they're important. In elementary school, for example, many children memorize multiplication and division tables to perfection but have no idea how to solve real-life problems; even though they know plenty of "math facts," they don't know enough about what the operations mean to use them in real situations: they know facts *about* division without really understanding what division is all about. Similarly, many students memorize the names of state capitals in fifth grade, but few have any idea what a state capital is or what goes on there. They have retained some trivial facts about place-name geography but have no understanding of geographical principles.

Good teaching focuses on helping students learn important organizing ideas, rather than simply covering massive amounts of factual information. Teaching writing, for example, means teaching students to communicate—how to write for an audience, how to organize information, how to revise, and so on—not how to diagram sentences; diagramming sentences simply doesn't have anything to do with becoming a good writer. Similarly, teaching geography means focusing on human–environmental interactions, the movement of people, goods, and ideas through space, and so on—not the names of state capitals; knowing the names of state capitals has nothing to do with the key concepts of geography. The standards issued by national organizations in science, math, and social studies all focus on developing this kind of in-depth understanding.

Experts have more organized and well-developed schemas than novices. *Chi (1976), Chi, Feltovich, & Glaser (1981), Sternberg & Horvath (1995)*

Memorizing facts rarely results in conceptual understanding.

Teachers help students learn important organizing ideas. See especially *Good & Brophy (1994) and Prawat (1989a, 1989b)*

National Council for the Social Studies (1994), National Council of Teachers of Mathematics (1989), National Research Council (1996)

Such learning does not involve the same all-or-nothing mastery as remembering isolated facts: either you know the capital of Wyoming or you don't, but understanding complicated concepts like culture, environment, society, and the like develop gradually over time; students learn more each time they encounter them. In-depth understanding also requires the time for sustained attention: students have to study topics in enough depth to understand them and to reflect on the meaning and significance of what they've studied. While it's certainly possible to cover a great deal of information by going through a textbook one week at a time, students are unlikely to learn anything important from doing so. The study of history, unfortunately, has been one of the worst offenders in this regard; too many students experience history as part of a "race to get to the American Revolution by May," in Rebecca's words. When students rush through dates and events without understanding their reasons or significance, the best they can hope for is to "get it again in junior high," as the fifth grader quoted earlier says.

In-depth understanding requires sustained study. Newmann, Secada, & Wehlage (1995), Wells & Chang-Wells (1992)

To develop an in-depth understanding of history, students have to engage in sustained study of the kinds of topics identified in the first chapter. Instead of moving through the major events of world history chronologically, for example, a teacher might devote a 2-month unit to the history of human interaction with the environment. A unit like that would not mean identifying every time people and the environment have interacted—obviously impossible!—but developing students' understanding of the variety of ways people throughout time have adapted to the environment, changed it to meet their needs, competed for resources, and so on. And rather than learning a list of names, dates, and events (to be forgotten quickly), students would be *doing* history, as Rebecca suggests—questioning, collecting data, interpreting, explaining. Admittedly, a teacher may cover less material that way, but students will learn more of the things that make for expert understanding.

History involves the sustained study of important topics.

INSTRUCTION MUST BUILD ON STUDENTS' PRIOR KNOWLEDGE

You have to start with what the kids already know. Just reading the text and answering the questions at the end of the chapter doesn't work for my LEP [limited English proficient] students, and I really don't think it works for any students. You can't just let them go in and read a chapter cold. If you can't build on something they already know, they can't learn it. They can't understand it if they have no background; they don't get a thing out of it, and you're wasting your time. Students need to put themselves in the place of someone at the time, or read a diary entry—something more personal. A lot of times history is "untouchable," and if I can say, "This is what an 11-year-old girl really wrote," they're like, "Wow!" That really makes it come alive. They like to read about everyday people who lived a long time ago, even more than famous people, because they can compare it more to their own lives.

—Rebecca Valbuena

No one these days seriously believes that children enter schools as "blank slates," or that the purpose of instruction is simply to fill them up with information. Before they ever arrive in a classroom, children have developed an understanding of the world around them: they have their own ideas about language, counting, the natural world, and even social relations. These intuitive theories are based on their direct experiences with people and objects, and often are quite accurate: preschoolers know that fire is hot, that three cookies is more than one, that sometimes people don't tell the truth, and so on. Other times, their ideas are inaccurate, or at least incomplete—as when they believe that the world is flat, that there are no more Native Americans, or that banks store their customers' money in individual boxes.

Children do not enter school as blank slates.

To help students develop their understanding, teachers must directly address the knowledge students bring with them to school, and build on it whenever possible. In order to learn, people have to link new experiences to previous understanding: they

Instruction builds on the knowledge and experience children bring to school.

have to *restructure* their mental schemas. Sometimes people simply add new information; an automobile mechanic who knows how engines work adds to her schema when she works on a model she's never encountered before. Other times restructuring involves more complete shifts in understanding, as when young children start to understand that plants are alive just like animals. In either case, learning is not passive: people have to compare what they encounter to what they already know. As Rebecca notes, if you can't build on what students know, they can't learn.

Unfortunately, textbooks and other materials rarely devote much attention to students' prior understanding. Of course, every child, every class, and every community is different, and no textbook can address their variety of experiences or range of understandings. But research on learning and instruction consistently shows that when school experiences aren't linked to prior understanding, students learn very little: when they can't connect what they're supposed to learn at school to their own schemas, their understanding is notoriously superficial. Every teacher has thought her class learned something new, only to discover they had forgotten it a week later or couldn't apply it in a new situation. This kind of superficial learning occurs precisely because students have only memorized information or procedures, rather than actually modifying their understanding.

To understand information—not simply repeat it—students must connect it to their previous understanding. Textbooks cannot do that; instead, teachers—the people who know students best—have to find out what they know and how to build on that knowledge. In science, having students make predictions before conducting experiments is an obvious way of finding out what they know, and having them compare observations to predictions helps connect new knowledge and old. Other methods for building on students' understanding apply across the curriculum. By making a web of students' ideas about a new topic on a large sheet of chart paper, for example, the teacher can simultaneously find out what students know and alert them to relevant background knowledge they may have; returning to the web throughout the lesson to discuss information that was correct and that needs to be added or revised helps make connections clear to students.

Of course, webs and other graphic organizers are also useful in history. One of the most important ways of connecting history to what students already know, though, is to focus on the lives of *people* in the past. People are one of the subjects children understand best; even from a very young age, they can reason about the beliefs and intentions of others. Margaret Donaldson maintains that for something to make sense to young children, it must make *human sense*: children, she argues, understand situations in terms of how they involve people. Historians also focus on the human sense of situations: much of their work involves studying the beliefs and intentions of people in the past. When the race is on to make it through the textbook, though, the human element is first to get pushed aside, and students wind up studying the things they know the least about—politics, diplomacy, and government. The absence of people in the study of history may account for the lack of enthusiasm which has been attributed to the subject. By focusing on people, teachers can both build on what students know best and give them a better sense of what historians actually do.

PEOPLE LEARN THROUGH DISCIPLINED INQUIRY

There's the synergistic effect of minds working together, hearing what others are doing—it gets *my* neurons sparking, it multiplies what everybody can do. Then there's also the democratic process: everybody having a say, everybody participating, not just the teacher standing up and lecturing. It also gives them a chance to discover, instead of just *telling* them; they get to hear different points of view, and discuss outcomes on their own, rather than just you connecting the dots for them.

—Rhoda Coleman

Carey (1985)

Piaget (1952)

See especially Caine & Caine (1994) and Gardner (1991b)

Teachers help students connect the curriculum to their prior knowledge.

Wellman & Gelman (1992)

Children strive to make "human sense" of the world. *Donaldson (1978)*

Although teachers can activate students' prior knowledge and call attention to the way it relates to new experiences, they cannot directly teach understanding—they cannot do the mental work for their students. Both research on human learning and our own experience as teachers directly contradict the "transmission" model of learning, which assumes knowledge goes directly from one source (whether a teacher or textbook) to another (the student). We cannot simply fill children up with information, no matter how elaborate our system of rewards and punishments; we can't "connect the dots" for them. People learn when they seek answers to the questions that matter to them; their understanding changes only when they become dissatisfied with what they know. The process of asking meaningful questions, finding information, drawing conclusions, and reflecting on possible solutions is known as *inquiry*.

Fortunately, children are naturally inquisitive learners who strive to make sense of their world. Anyone with young children knows the challenge of keeping up with their urge to explore and their ever-present question, "Why?" Older children, meanwhile, often devote their energy to demonstrating just how much they do know. But although humans are naturally inquisitive, most people do not sit around and memorize trivia just for the fun of it. Outside of school, learning almost always takes place within the context of *purposeful* activity: people learn because they need to know how to do something important, and they can see examples of what it looks like to accomplish those tasks. Young children, for instance, learn to talk because they need to communicate, and they continually see people doing exactly that. Similarly, adolescents who hope to become dancers, musicians, or athletes learn the skills necessary to accomplish those goals, and there is no shortage of expert performances for them to imitate. Not surprisingly, people learn best when they know why they are learning, and can see what it looks like to do it successfully.

This kind of purposeful learning always takes place in a sociocultural context: that larger setting determines what knowledge is worth having, how to acquire it, and how to use it. Scientists, for example, do not pursue their investigations in isolation: the questions they ask, the standards they apply, and the way they report their results are all the product of ongoing debate and discussion among a community of scholars—and the concerns and values of the wider society also influence that community. In every field, knowledge has meaning only in the context of the questions, procedures, and debate in which it develops. Nor does any single community have a monopoly on knowledge; understanding of the environment, for example, may come about very differently depending on whether one is a farmer, research scientist, or environmentalist. Meaningful learning, then, involves not just mastering the content of a subject (no matter how deeply) but understanding the nature and purpose of that subject—the diverse ways of thinking and acting mathematically, historically, or scientifically in our society. We use the term *disciplined inquiry* to refer to purposeful investigations that take place within a community that establishes the goals, standards, and procedures of study.

Teachers can capitalize on children's natural enthusiasm for learning by making their classrooms places where students explore important and meaningful questions. For most of the last century, educators have argued for the importance of teaching students how to use and apply knowledge in authentic situations—rather than simply expecting them to learn isolated or irrelevant information. The tasks students encounter at school should be similar to those people face outside school. By engaging in the same kinds of challenges as scientists, citizens, artists, businesspeople, and so on, students will better understand the purpose of their studies and will be more likely to understand, retain, and apply what they learn. Seeing their peers, teachers, and other community members engaged in these processes is a central feature of this approach.

Unfortunately, schools rarely engage students in authentic inquiry; their experiences are usually determined by the content of textbooks or curriculum guides rather than the pursuit of meaningful knowledge. Children have few chances to investigate

See, for example, Brooks & Brooks (1993), Caine & Caine (1994), Duckworth (1987), Taylor (1993), Wells & Chang-Wells (1992)

People learn when they seek answers to questions that matter to them. *Dewey (1933, 1956)*

Inquiry is the process of asking meaningful questions, finding information, drawing conclusions, and reflecting on solutions.

Children are naturally inquisitive learners. *Dewey (1933, 1956)*

People learn best when they understand the purpose of their learning.

Learning takes place within a sociocultural context. *Lave & Wenger (1991), Resnick (1987), Rogoff (1990), Vygotsky (1978)*

Disciplined inquiry takes place within a community that establishes the goals, standards, and procedures of study. *For more on disciplined inquiry, see Newmann et al. (1995)*

Students use and apply knowledge in authentic situations. *Wiggins (1993)*

questions that have meaning for them, or that engage them in realistic challenges. As a result, schools rarely provide students with any clear sense of purpose; many have no idea why they are expected to study math, science, history, or any other subject, since they rarely see what it means to use those subjects. Although students may sometimes be admonished that they will "need this later," they rarely see before them examples of expert performances in science, history, writing, and so on; instead, they see only artificial exercises removed from meaningful application.

Once again, the study of history has been one of the worst offenders. In the middle grades, studying history all too often means reading a chapter in a textbook and answering the questions at the end (or, worse, memorizing the names of presidents). In the early grades, history rarely amounts to more than learning a few isolated facts about famous people connected to major holidays. In neither case do students have the chance to ask and answer questions important to them; in neither case do they learn how historians work; in neither case do they see examples of the authentic use of historical knowledge. In fact, when asked why they think history is a subject at school or how it might help them, students sometimes can think of little except that it might be useful if they were ever on *Jeopardy!*

Barton (1994a), VanSledright (1995)

History involves disciplined inquiry.

See also Seixas (1993a)

Authentic historical study involves the comparison of conflicting ideas.

To get more from history than preparation for a game show, students must take part in disciplined inquiry, not just repeat isolated trivia. The study of history must begin with the concerns and interests of students, and help them find answers. This means that students have to learn what it means to ask and answer historical questions—how to find information, how to evaluate sources, how to reconcile conflicting accounts, how to create an interpretive account. And students certainly must learn what the authentic application of historical knowledge looks like: they must see how history can explain the present, and they must see this in the most authentic of ways—through the comparison of conflicting ideas about the nature and signficance of the past.

TEACHING MEANS SCAFFOLDING

You have to provide them with structure. You don't just say, "Write a paragraph"; you introduce them to some vocabulary, brainstorm about the topic, make comparison charts and graphic organizers, and then help them use them to write a paragraph. If you want them to produce something, you have to provide structure; you have to take them where they are and move them one step further.

—Rebecca Valbuena

People learn through interaction with more knowledgeable members of a community. *Lave & Wenger (1991), Rogoff (1990), Vygotsky (1978)*

Outside of school, learning almost always involves ongoing collaboration among the members of a community, as more knowledgeable members help newcomers become full-fledged participants in activities they both consider worthwhile. Consider, for example, how young children learn to talk. The process extends over many years and involves countless thousands of utterances, as the child tries to speak and the adult accepts and encourages the attempt—while usually also modeling a more fluent way of expressing what the child wants to say. Although the precise kinds of interaction may vary from one culture (or subculture) to the next, a child who has no opportunity at all to interact will not learn to talk; she constructs her understanding of language through interaction with fluent speakers.

To take a somewhat different example, professional schools require prospective practitioners—doctors, teachers, and so on—to engage in extensive field experiences where experts help them learn to deal with real-life situations. No one would trust a doctor who had learned medicine only from a book; in order to treat patients, doctors must undergo a lengthy period of practical training. During this time, experienced practitioners model the practical use of medical knowledge, and novices are gradually given more responsibility for treating patients on their own. Most learning outside the classroom follows a similar pattern. Whether related to traditional economic tasks (farming, cooking, quilting), the work of modern careers, or pursuits such as sports or the fine arts, learning usually involves a kind of *apprenticeship*, in which those who are more knowledgeable gradually help novices develop expertise. They provide them with the structure Rebecca mentions.

In apprenticeships, those who are more knowledgable help novices develop expertise.

Unfortunately, children rarely have the chance to take part in this kind of sustained interaction at school. Most often, they are expected to listen while teachers transmit information to them. Participation is usually limited to the common *initiation-response-evaluation* pattern: the teacher asks a question, a student responds, and the teacher tells her whether the answer was right. The purpose of such interactions is to assess students' retention of information, not to help them pursue questions or issues that interest them. Other times, students may be given independent assignments or expected to "do research," but aren't taught how to go about the process—and few students have the skills necessary to conduct inquiry on their own. Although inquiry is essential to education, simply assigning such tasks won't guarantee meaningful results. Most students need direct help to make the most of their experiences, and one of the teacher's most important responsibiliies is providing them with the structure they need in order to learn—a process known as *scaffolding*. Just as scaffolding on a construction project supports people as they work, scaffolding in the classroom supports students as they learn. Children learn best when they take part in joint activities with teachers (and more knowledgeable peers) who help them go about their studies.

Cazden (1988)

Teachers scaffold students' understanding by providing the structure they need to be successful.

Scaffolding takes many forms. First, teachers have to develop students' interest in accomplishing tasks; although children are naturally inquisitive, they are more likely to follow through with their investigations when teachers help them maintain interest. When students do not meet with immediate success on a project, many quickly become frustrated; teachers, then, have to actively support and encourage them. This support often involves breaking a task down into manageable components. We certainly don't advocate a behaviorist "task analysis" that teaches small and isolated skills; but as Rebecca explains, students can write a better paragraph when they become familiar with vocabulary, engage in brainstorming, and use graphic organizers in preparation for writing rather than simply being told, "Write a paragraph." Similarly, students learn more from inquiry when they develop questions, identify resources, plan a presentation, and so on than when they are just sent to the library and told to "do research." As Rebecca says, if you want them to produce something, you have to provide them with structure.

Teachers help students develop the skills necessary to engage in inquiry.

Another crucial element of this scaffolding is the teacher's modeling of procedures and her feedback to students on their accomplishment. As suggested earlier, teachers must demonstrate what it looks like to do history; just as students need to see their teachers reading and writing, they need to see them grappling with historical questions, collecting information, making generalizations, and so. Not surprisingly, the teacher has to show students what it looks like to accomplish a task successfully; if they don't see examples, they won't know what they are supposed to do. Just as critically, the teacher has to give students feedback on their performances: she must help students understand how their work compares to ideal versions. Without such feedback, many students will not know if they are accomplishing a task successfully or not. The ultimate goal of this scaffolding is to transfer control from teacher to student by enabling students to plan their learning and monitor their own progress—abilities sometimes referred to as *metacognition*.

Teachers model procedures and provide feedback to students.

Metacognition refers to students' ability to plan their learning and monitor their progress.

CONCLUSIONS

In this chapter we have identified the aspects of human learning that we think provide the best guidance for teaching history. Based both on contemporary research in cognitive psychology and on our own experience, we have argued that the best teaching focuses on in-depth understanding of important ideas; builds on what students already know; engages students in collaborative, disciplined inquiry, in which they investigate important questions in authentic ways; and involves extensive scaffolding. Although we have tried to describe these principles separately, they have little meaning in isolation. Teachers will not succeed if they focus on important ideas but do not build on students' prior knowledge, if they require inquiry but don't teach students how to do it, or if they teach problem-solving but never address significant content. By devoting consistent attention to these principles in an integrated way, however, teachers can develop meaningful and effective instruction for students from a variety of backgrounds in a variety of circumstances. As Rebecca explains in our final quote, understanding this theoretical background ensures that good teaching isn't just a mishap.

> I can't tell you how much [knowing about theory] has changed me; it all makes sense. Being a good teacher means you know what to do and you have a purpose for what you're doing. Everything you do has to have a theoretical base, from classroom management on. I think a lot of teachers do things naturally, but if you know the theory beforehand, it's so much more satisfying: it's not just a mishap, you're doing it on purpose. Knowing the theory takes you to a level beyond.
>
> —Rebecca Valbuena

Chapter 3

Building Communities of Historical Inquiry

It is 11:10 on a cool October morning and 26 seven- and eight-year-olds are gathered around their teacher, listening to a story about Johnny Appleseed. At one point, the teacher stops to talk about what is known about the historical Johnny Appleseed:

Teacher:	What kind of a story is this? Remember we said that some stories were tall tales . . .
Jennie:	And folktales!
Teacher:	Right, some are folktales. And Johnny Appleseed is a le . . . le . . .?
Choral:	Legend!
Teacher:	Legend. That means some parts of the story are . . .
Ryan:	True.
CeCe:	But some are just made up.

At this point, the children engage in a general conversation about why parts of stories might be made up. One boy suggests that the real story probably wasn't exciting; others think that people probably didn't know "the real facts" and so simply made them up.

Teacher:	What parts of this story do we *think* are true?
Gabriel:	Well, there *was* a man who planted apple trees. It said so in that other book.
Avram:	Yeah, but his real name wasn't Appleseed, remember!

Several of the children recall that John Chapman was the "real" Johnny Appleseed. The teacher draws them back to the original question: Which parts of the story do we think are true? Again, she puts the emphasis on *think*, and the students begin to discuss "facts" versus "exaggerations." The conversation bogs down as some children repeat suggestions others have already made. Lucy and Gabriel appear to be having an argument over whether "Appleseed" can be a "real" name, since it was a nickname used by Chapman's contemporaries.

Lucy:	See, it says here [in the encyclopedia entry] that he was "popularly known as Johnny Appleseed." I think that's what people called him then.
Gabriel:	Uhuh. That's what's popular *now*.
Teacher:	I'm getting mixed up. Is there some way we can keep track of our ideas here?
Lucy:	We could make a list . . .

Two children get the large pad of chart paper that hangs in the front of the room. Another grabs the plastic cup of magic markers.

Avram: Let's take the story in pieces! We can put each fact we find under "facts" and have exaggerations on another paper.

For the next 20 minutes, the children analyze the story, event by event. They use two other books about Johnny Appleseed, along with a brief encyclopedia entry, but there are several places where they aren't sure if something is a fact. At the teacher's suggestion, they use red markers to circle these items. Someone else suggests underlining "for sure" facts in green and "for sure" exaggerations in black.

CeCe: There sure aren't a lot of "for sure" facts!

Teacher: No, there aren't. We seem to have a lot of questions about this story. What would it look like if we wrote it so that it didn't have any exaggerations? Could we write it so that it only said what we are pretty sure happened?

CeCe: That would be a short story!

Hyde & Bizar (1989), New-mann et al., (1995), Wells & Chang-Wells (1992)

The students in this vignette are members of the kind of community of reflective, disciplined inquiry already described in chapter 2. Such a community encourages participation with others in goal-directed activity, engagement with intellectual problems that cannot be resolved through the routine application of previously learned knowledge, and understanding and resolving problems with the aid of a variety of intellectual tools. Establishing a community of inquiry in a classroom that provides a meaningful, integrative, challenging, and active context for learning history, as Rebecca Valbuena notes in chapter 2, is not just a mishap. Whether primary children are investigating the facts and exaggerations of an American historical legend, fourth graders are writing the history of their school, or middle schoolers are debating the merits of nonviolent protest as a response to colonialism in India, communities of inquiry have certain things in common:

Characteristics of communities of inquiry.

- There is lively conversation and intellectual negotiation among participants who each have varying degrees of expertise in the topic at hand.
- Conversation focuses on questions and tasks worthy of sustained discussion and in-depth study.
- Students use both prior knowledge and newly gathered data to "master perplexity"—to make sense out of what seemed not to make sense when their study began.
- Teachers model and students practice "classroom thoughtfulness"—taking the time necessary to think carefully and thoroughly before responding to questions or attempting to resolve problems.
- Students *do history*—they pose, investigate, and at least tentatively answer historical questions and develop historical explanations and interpretations—they don't just memorize the history others have done.

Scaffolding is necessary for in-depth inquiry.

This chapter introduces the kind of reflective, disciplined inquiry that sustains the communities of inquiry you will meet throughout this book. Well-constructed, integrated instruction presents students with tasks that require engagement with the content and methods of the discipline of history while providing the scaffolding necessary for students to engage in in-depth study. Consider how the teacher in the opening vignette structures her primary students' engagement with historical inquiry. First, because the Johnny Appleseed legend is a common children's story and an example of the kind of historical mythologizing that appears frequently in the elementary curriculum, it provides an appropriate forum for *talking historically*—communally analyzing the legend's historical roots. Second, the teacher scaffolds the historical talk so that it becomes a conversation, not a recitation. She calls children's attention to the genre—a legend—with which they are dealing, and reminds them

"Talking historically" is con-versation not recitation.

Pierce & Gilles (1993)

18

that legends have particular characteristics that are important for readers to know. Note, too, that the teacher does not ask which parts of the story are "known to be true"—known by someone else. Rather, she asks her students to call on their prior knowledge of literary genres and the historical Johnny Appleseed, and consider what parts they "*think* are true." The choice of language is important here. By asking students what they think, the teacher models a more tentative language that invites speculation rather than final answers. She also encourages students to take intellectual risks that keep conversation alive and engaging. Who is Johnny Appleseed, anyway? Is this fiction or history? How can we distinguish between facts and exaggerations? What makes us think that one part of a story is true, but not another? As they participate in the conversation, these children not only think about what counts as history, but consider why people might exaggerate beyond the historical data, and how different genres use historical information—important questions about the ways in which history is used in the larger world. They also learn that some of the most interesting questions don't have single, or easy, answers. These questions are central to reflective, disciplined inquiry, but equally important is the historical talk surrounding them.

Intellectual risks keep conversation alive.

TALKING HISTORICALLY

As we already mentioned in chapter 2, all of us learn how to "mean" in a variety of social contexts. In addition, we learn how to express what we mean through various symbolic forms—literature, art, music, dance, drama, writing, and conversation, among others. Symbolic forms are not, however, simply windows through which meaning shines clearly. Instead, symbolic forms express and shape meaning. A photograph of a family standing beside a covered wagon (Fig. 3.1) shows us, for instance, how small a space early pioneers had for all their possessions. We can analyze other details as well: the military uniform that one man wears, the prairie stretching behind the family. But the photograph also freezes what would otherwise have been a fleeting moment, giving it weight and meaning it might not otherwise have had. The frown on the woman's face comes to represent more than simple weariness with posing or a response to bright sun; instead, we read in her face the rigors of the overland journey.

Lemke (1991)

Arnheim (1981), Levstik & Barton (1996)

FIG. 3.1.   On the prairie: Family with covered wagon, 1886.

Purves (1990)

Shaara (1974), Boatner (1969)

Language shapes history

As do photographs, written texts store, shape, and transmit information, but they use words rather than visual images. The use of imagery and analogy, the choice and arrangement of words, the expectations we have for a particular genre, shape how we interpret written texts. Both of the descriptions in Fig. 3.2 describe the same man, General James Longstreet, a Confederate officer who fought at Gettysburg, but the first is from Michael Shaara's Pulitzer Prize-winning novel *Killer Angels*; the second is from Mark Boatner's *Civil War Dictionary* As you read each description consider how language shapes your image of this historical figure. What are the differences you can identify between Shaara's and Boatner's descriptions?

Longstreet knew himself. There was no fear there. The only fear was not of death, was not of the war, was of blind stupid human frailty, of blind proud foolishness that could lose it all. He was thinking very clearly now. Mind seemed to uncloud like washed glass. Everything cool and crystal.

—Michael Shaara, *Killer Angels* (p. 202)

[Longstreet's] delay in attacking on the second day at Gettysburg, and his lethargy in organizing "Pickett's Charge" on the third exposed him to the most vindictive criticism by Southerners after the war.

—Mark Boatner III, *The Civil War Dictionary* (p. 490)

FIG. 3.2. Contrasting views of a historical figure.

In the first excerpt, Longstreet is willing to lose it all; in the second he is accused of holding back. Shaara's Longstreet is fearless; Boatner's lethargic. The first account has a more personal voice; the second more distanced and impersonal. Yet neither is objective. What if Boatner had described Longstreet's reluctance to send men to certain death, rather than his "lethargy?" Or if Shaara described a man frozen by his fear of "blind stupid human frailty?" In reading each of these passages, you can't ask the authors for further explanation, hear their tone of voice, or read body language. Instead, you negotiate meaning with the text. You rely on your own life experience, including your experience as a reader of other texts, in making sense out of the semantic clues provided by the text. If this seems confusing, think about a book you have read more than once. Perhaps it was a story you read when you were younger and returned to as an adult. You probably found that the book took on new dimensions with a second reading. The words did not change, but you did, and so you understood it quite differently at a second reading. In part, this is what the students in the vignette are learning to do. But they are also shaping their historical understanding through another symbolic form—talk. By talking historically, students *do* have an opportunity to ask for further explanation, hear tone of voice, or read body language. They can negotiate meaning, try out ideas, keep or discard them—jointly making sense of history. This process is at least as challenging and important to historical thinking as learning to read either written texts or visual images.

Sometimes we take conversation for granted. Talk seems so common that we forget how intricate a truly engaging conversation can be. First, the style of talk implies meaning beyond words. Certain styles signal playful engagement. Participants exchange what in other circumstances would be insults, but in this context are not meant seriously. Other styles signal more serious intent—negotiations during a labor dispute, for instance. In addition, different disciplines use different forms of oral discourse. Mathematicians may talk about "proofs," or the application of algorithms, and rely on mathematical concepts in supporting their ideas. History, too, has it own forms of oral discourse, including expositions, explanations, justifications, narratives, and dialogue. Each of these genres uses historical content and processes as the substance of discourse. Making sense in history, then, is at least partially constructed within (or in opposition to) this discourse, as participants test out ideas, listen to other possibili-

Purves (1990)

In discussion, children jointly make sense out of history.

Conversations are intricate social interactions

Different disciplines have their own forms of discourse

20

ties, ask questions, and challenge interpretations. In order for children to learn history, then, they need practice in using these oral genres as well as the written and visual ones we have already mentioned.

Bakhtin (1986), Swales (1990), Todorov (1990)

We are not, however, suggesting that teaching history to elementary and middle school students is simply a matter of inducting them into the professional culture and discourse of historians. While the conversation in the opening vignette certainly has some elements that would be familiar to historians, elementary and middle school children are not—and need not be—full participants in the semiotic communities of professional historians. Instead, they employ meaning-making practices that work in their multiple communities, including the classroom. Some of these practices barely intersect with those of professional historians. In younger children's parlance, for instance, the term history can be a warning: "If you don't watch out, you're history!" Older students may also use the term history in this way, but they tend to be more adept with an academic history genre. Figure 3.3 shows how a fifth grader is learning to employ this genre. As you read Kareem's comments on American history, notice how he talks about history in terms of cause and effect (if not necessarily multiple causation). Note, too, that he introduces a discourse of morality, using the personal pronoun, "we," and passing judgment on the events he describes.

Levstik & Barton (1996)

History has intersecting discourse communities

Levstik & Pappas (1987)

We had established 13 colonies and then the English started taxing us and we got fed up with that, that was after the French and English War. So then . . . we got our own independence and George Wahington was our leader. [Later] people got in wagons and start moving westward to find new lands and settle and stuff because they didn't even know what was back there. . . . I think it's a shame that we tore down all those trees and ran off the Indians, cause it was their land in the first place. . . . We were trying to con 'em—tell 'em that if they signed this petition paper, they'd still have land, this small portion and they did that 'cause the colonists knew that the Indians couldn't read. They could read their signs that they made but they couldn't read the English.

—Kareem, Grade 5

FIG. 3.3 Combining an academic history genre and the discourse of morality.

Kareem's interest in making historical judgments, and the primary students' enthusiastic participation in "deconstructing" the Johnny Appleseed legend both combine elements of literary, historical, and moral discourses as well as classroom protocols. This is rich and interesting talk. It is also the kind of talk that is unlikely to occur if the only experience children have with history is filling in blanks on a worksheet or memorizing presidents in chronological order. Nor is it likely to occur where children are silenced, because either what they have to say or the way in which they say it, isn't valued. This is particularly important in classrooms where the children come from diverse linguistic or cultural backgrounds. Talking historically is more likely to occur where teachers and students value the multiple perspectives that diversity can provide, where conversation revolves around questions worthy of sustained discussion, and where conversation is supported by in-depth study.

Diversity is valued in communities of inquiry.

Hansen (1993), Peetoom (1991)

THE IMPORTANCE OF QUESTIONS

Anything that may be called knowledge, or a known object, marks a question answered, a difficulty disposed of, a conclusion cleared up, an inconsistency reduced to coherence, a perplexity mastered.

—John Dewey, *The Quest for Certainty* (pp. 226–227)

If children are to enthusiastically engage in sustained conversation about history, four things are required:

- Questions that are worth discussing
- Questions that do not have simple or single answers
- Sufficient and appropriate data sources so that students can attempt to answer the questions.
- Imaginative entry into the past.

Collingwood (1961), Degenhardt & McKay (1988), Holt (1990b)

Questions are at the heart of inquiry

Obviously, questions are at the heart of this approach to history. But we are talking about very different questions than the ones many of us are familiar with from textbooks and workbooks. The point of these questions is not to see if students have read a particular text; rather, it is to provide direction and motivation for the rigorous work of doing history. An example of this kind of direction and motivation can be seen in a sixth-grade classroom where the students are studying India. The class has just completed working with an artifact kit, using a variety of resources to compare life in a modern Indian city with life in the students' home town. A guest speaker previously told them that in order to understand some of the differences between India and America, it is necessary to understand each country's history. Mrs. Groth, the teacher, now asks the sixth graders to use their textbooks to identify eight events in Indian history that they consider pivotal. While the students read and take notes, Mrs. Groth places a large time-line on the board that runs from 2500 BCE to 1948 CE. She then asks students to suggest items for the time line. There is debate about whether farming in the Indus valley was pivotal, and whether it could legitimately be considered to have a "main date." Soon, however, students move on to the establishment of the British East India Company, colonization by the British and the eventual British withdrawal. They use time lines developed by the eighth-grade American history class to compare what was happening in each country during each time period. Jason points out that the colonization periods for both India and the American colonies overlap, "but our Revolution came sooner."

CE (Common Era) and BCE (Before the Common Era) are used instead of AD (Anno Domini) and BC (Before Christ) by some historians, anthropologists and archaeologists

Some inquiries are teacher-initiated.

On the surface, this may not look terribly different than a good traditional history class. In fact, however, this activity is crucial for several reasons. First, it asks students to think about what is historically significant. Second, it makes clear that neither American nor Indian history exists in a vacuum. Finally, it establishes the historical background—prior knowledge—needed to raise the next, teacher-initiated question: Were there any similarities in the ways in which the people of India and the people of the American colonies rid themselves of British rule? Iman exclaims, "Well, we kicked their butts!" Ainslie chimes in, "We tried to get the British mad, to get them started in a war, but the Indians tried compromise." The students draw on their fifth-grade experience in reenacting a trial of the participants in the Boston Massacre. They talk about the techniques the rebels used to end British rule, and check dates on the time line to see what was happening in India during the same period. At this point, different groups are asked to develop comparative time lines showing British colonial rule and the independence movements in each country. By the next class, students are ready to compare colonialism and rebellion in India and North America. Their discussion is lively, requiring them to select relevant information, combine pieces of information—even though some of those pieces might at first have seemed unrelated—compare the problem under investigation with problems previously encountered and use skills and concepts previously employed. In other words, their inquiry requires both prior knowledge in the discipline—their fifth-grade study of the American Revolution—and in-depth study—their investigation of British colonial rule in India.

Inquiry requires prior knowledge and in-depth study.

PRIOR KNOWLEDGE

We know that new knowledge builds on the learner's prior knowledge base. This seems self-evident, but it is certainly not simple, particularly in history. First of all, history might more adequately be described as a set of intersecting fields rather than a unitary discipline. Thus, social historians, military historians, archivists, public historians, interpreters at historic sites, and genealogists, to name just a few, all deal with history, but their various fields are marked by sometimes disparate modes of inquiry, styles of communication, and perceived purposes. In addition, students bring much more background knowledge to the study of history than we sometimes credit them with. History is, after all, not confined to historians. Families construct histories as they interpret events through the lens of family involvement. The media also interpret historic events. They create documentaries and news programs that purport to explain—and sometimes make— history, but they also present fictionalized versions of the past. Television shows like *Little House on the Prairie* or *Dr. Quinn, Medicine Woman*, for instance, present current sensibilities in period settings. There are also persistent historical myths and legends held dear by parts of the larger culture—Betsy Ross sewing the first flag, Columbus "discovering a new world," and so forth. For some students, these images are comforting; others may feel excluded by the popular culture's mythologies. In any case, these myths and legends are often part of the historical knowledge base that children bring to school. Once in school, students acquire historical information (and misinformation) from instruction. The sixth graders studying India, for instance, were able to think more clearly about resistance to British colonialism because they could draw on their prior study of the American Revolution. Notice, however, that their teacher did not rely on unassisted recall. Instead, there were prompts to trigger prior knowledge, most notably the American history time lines constructed by her eighth-grade class.

Levstik & Barton (1996)

Students bring background knowledge to their study.

Barton (1995), Seixas (1993b)

History is interpreted publicly and personally, as well as by historians.

Historical myths are part of popular culture.

Because reflective, disciplined inquiry is rooted in what students already know and can do, and gradually moves beyond the known, teachers must take into account the conceptions and misconceptions held by students and supported by popular culture as well as the knowledge base provided by the fields of history. Historical inquiry most easily develops when the creation or discovery of a problem challenges prior knowledge, providing opportunities for students to outgrow what they already know. As they create and test hypotheses, explore variations on initial problems, and reflect on the consequences of answers as well as the process of study, students engage in authentic historical work, building on prior knowledge to *produce* rather than *reproduce* knowledge. While their interpretations may be naive, and are rarely new to the discipline of history, students are not simply reproducing knowledge that others have produced. Instead, they attempt to construct a coherent explanation for a set of historic events. The sixth graders' comparison of Indian and American independence movements, for instance, obviously owes much to prior studies in American history as well as some of the facts, concepts, theories, and discourse that mark history as a discipline or field. In addition, students' attempts to construct this comparison should make them more interested in and thoughtful about other independence movements as well as other historical interpretations of the events they have just analyzed. Clearly, this approach emphasizes in-depth understanding both of history and historical methods.

Inquiry begins with challenges to prior knowledge.

Students *produce* rather than *reproduce* knowledge. *Newmann et al. (1995), Wells & Chang-Wells (1992)*

IMAGINATIVE ENTRY

In a fifth-grade classroom, Tessa discusses the outcome of a class trial based on the events surrounding the Boston Massacre:

Tessa: The British won [in our class], but in the real trial the British didn't win.... But I'm a colonist, I'm a patriot. She (teacher) showed us all the evidence, and she showed us everything that happened and we studied it, but she didn't tell us anything that happened after that, and—and she said alright, are you for the British, because the British, on one hand were taxing the colonists and the colonists had no way of representing. They could not vote for people who were running in England and they had no say in their taxes they were going to do it upon them so that was on the colonists' side, but the British on the other hand, they were being thrown rocks at. My name was Archibald, and I didn't know that I had already broken my wrist on a British officer, so when I got on the stand and they said have you ever assaulted a British officer, then he said we have evidence you broke your wrists off a British officer, and I went OOH! I didn't know, but I shouldn't have said that, because in the book it said, "Beep, you Yankee bloopers."

From Tessa's comments, we can see that she finds history neither boring nor irrelevant. Her interest in the different perspectives of British soldiers and American rebels is generated and supported by the opportunity to act historically—to take on the perspective of a participant in the historic drama. While in-depth understanding in history comes as students assess, organize, and interpret historical data in the ways already described, it is also grounded in the kind of imaginative entry into the past that is part of Tessa's experience. Students might, for instance, participate in simulations and role-plays, or recreate biographies or historical stories that require imaginative entry into a historical era or event. In doing so, they use historical information to help them either assume the role of historical actors or vividly describe historical events or people. We are not suggesting fanciful retellings of history. Rather, students must speculate on the motives, values, and choices of historical actors in order to build supportable, *discipline-based* accounts that explain events. In doing so, they must imagine the perspective of participants from another time and place *without imagining beyond their data*. Tessa, for instance, is well aware of the need for historical evidence. The fact that she missed an important piece of evidence altered the outcome of the trial. If this had been a test, she might have missed the item, taken her grade, and forgotten all about it. Because this was part of a simulation, her error was corrected in a context that made the correction important and memorable. Tessa's experience also pointed out how easily misinformation can alter interpretations—and how important it is both to hold conclusions as tentative and to reevaluate ideas. Finally, Tessa's experience points up another feature of effective group inquiry. Although Tessa's study was done in community with other students, it was not a matter of each student investigating what every other student investigated, searching for a single right answer. Rather, each student's research provided one piece of a larger puzzle and served as at least a partial check against inaccurate or unsupportable interpretations.

Another feature of in-depth study is the application of new learning beyond the classroom. In other words, disciplined inquiry has value and meaning beyond success in school. Remember that we already said that history presents us both with stories of origins and possible destinations. These are not just school stories, left behind when children exit the classroom. Instead, these are stories that have the power to transform students' understandings of themselves and their possible futures. The writer James Baldwin expressed his sense that historical stories could help children "know that just as American history is longer, larger, more various, more beautiful, and more terrible than anything anyone has ever said about it, so is the world larger, more daring, more beautiful and more terrible, but principally larger—and that it belongs to [the children]." In one sense, our lives become more meaningful when we see ourselves as actors within the context of a historical story—we look for the connections among past and current events, the lives of those around us and our own lives. We begin to recognize that no society or group of people is wholly wise or virtuous, that all of us have the capacity for both good and ill. Wisdom develops as much from stories about human failure as from stories of success. In short, in order to see ourselves in historical perspective we need stories about the range of human experience, and we have to learn to evaluate the meaning of those experiences from many perspectives.

While each encounter with history may not be transformative for every child, cumulatively, in-depth historical study is more likely to encourage children to recognize themselves as historical participants rather than passive recipients of the past and unwitting victims of the present. As have others before them, they can change both

Newmann et al. (1995)

Tunnell & Ammon (1993)

Historical accounts are discipline-based and supported by evidence. *VanSledright & Brophy (1992)*

Newmann et al. (1995), Pappas, Kiefer, & Levstik (1995)

History can be transformative.

Baldwin (1988)

Epstein (1993), Griffin (1992)

24

the present and future. Simply telling students the same myths and stories over and over again, however, will not have this effect. As Oscar Wilde once noted, "The one duty we owe to history is to rewrite it." In-depth study invites students to critique the myths, rewrite the stories, and to tell multiple stories. It asks them, not just to memorize someone else's interpretations, but to develop their own; not just to accumulate information, but to ask themselves and each other, "So what?" What difference does this information make in the world? What does it say about what it means to be human in other times and places and right now, in our world? If students cannot enter imaginatively into the past, if they lack in-depth information about the world around them and its myriad possibilities, they are also less likely to understand the people next door. *Wilde (1982)*

Degenhardt & McKay (1988)

History organized around imaginative entry into the past, in-depth studies of enduring themes and questions, focused on tasks that have relevance beyond the classroom, and tied to students' prior knowledge may seem an overwhelming task. Certainly, communities of historical inquiry don't just happen; they require careful planning on teachers' parts, time to build a foundation of mutual trust and respect, and freedom from some of the constraints of "coverage." The following chapters provide specific research-based suggestions, involving a variety of classrooms in magnet schools; urban, suburban, and rural schools, schools where many children are bilingual (or becoming so)—where doing history is intellectually invigorating for both teachers and students.

CHILDREN'S AND ADOLESCENT LITERATURE

Historical Mystery, Myth, and Legend.

Alderman, C. L. (1979). *Annie Oakley and the World of Her Time.* Macmillan.
Barboza, S. (1994). *Door of No Return: The Legend of Goree Island.* Cobblehill.
Baylor, B. (1988). *And It is Still That Way.* Trails West.
Cashford, J. (1993). *The Myth of Isis and Osiris.* Barefoot.
de Paola, T. (1988). *The Legend of the Indian Paintbrush.* G. P. Putnam's Sons.
Edmonds, I. G. (1994). *Ooka the Wise: Tales of Old Japan.* Linnet.
Fritz, J. (1979). *Brendan the Navigator.* Coward.
Hooks, W. H. (1990). *The Ballad of Belle Dorcas.* Knopf.
Irwin, C. (1980). *Strange Footprints on the Land: Vikings in America.* Harper.
Jaffe, N. (1994). *Patakin: World Tales of Drums and Drummers.* Holt.
Kellogg, S. (1988). *Johnny Appleseed.* Morrow. (Kellogg has also written and illustrated other picture book versions of tall tales, including Pecos Bill, Mike Fink and Paul Bunyon.
Kessel, J. K. (1983). *Squanto and the First Thanksgiving.* Carolrhoda.
Koger, E., Sr. (1976). *Jocko: A legend of the American Revolution.* Prentice-Hall.
Lauber, P. (1988). *Lost star: The Story of Amelia Earhart.* Scholastic.
Lester, J. (1994). *John Henry.* Dial.
Manitonquat (Medicine Story). (1994). *The Children of the Morning Light: Wampanoag Tales.* Macmillan.
Osborne, M. P. (1991). *American Tall Tales.* Knopf.
Sanfield, S. (1989). *The Adventures of High John the Conqueror.* Orchard.
Quackenbush, R. (1987). *Quit Pulling My Leg! A Story of Davy Crockett.* Simon & Schuster.
Van Laan, N. (1993). *Buffalo Dance: A Blackfoot Legend.* Little.
Zeman, L. (1993). *The Revenge of Ishtar.* Tundra.

Chapter 4

Personal Histories

On the first day of school, Tina Reynolds asked her fourth graders to complete the sentence "History is . . ." on slips of paper and to discuss their answers. At least half the class wrote, "I don't know," while others gave short answers like "long ago," "antiques and old stuff," or "presidents and other famous people." Tina asked if they had ever learned about history; a few recalled that parents or other relatives had told them about the past, while others couldn't remember having learned anything about the topic.

She then asked if a *person* could have a history: "Could there be a 'History of Christy,' for example?" Some thought yes, some no, but none could explain why. Tina said that she had a history of herself to show them, and asked what they thought it might look like. Again, students weren't sure. She showed the class a poster she had made with a timeline of important events in her life, and students' interest began to pick up; they eagerly volunteered to read out loud each of the milestones in Tina's life—when she was born, started school, got married, and so on. She then told students they were going to make their own timelines to show the most important things that had had happened to them, and that they would use these timelines to create a "History of Me" to share with the class.

After a discussion of what they might include, students began working on a list of the five most important things that had happened to them. Although they were excited about the topic, writing was difficult for many of them; making a list like this took some time. Seated at tables of four and five, though, they continually shared their experiences as they wrote—telling each other about siblings being born, vacations their family had taken, or starting a new sport. Tina, meanwhile, talked to students as they worked, asking them to explain why they chose the items they did, or helping those who were having trouble. After completing their lists, students were to fill in the dates of each event on a blank timeline of the last 10 years. Because most had no idea when each thing had happened, they had to take these home to complete with their parents' help. Tina also asked them to add any new events they discovered in talking with their parents.

The next day, it was obvious that students had not only recorded a set of dates but had learned an entirely new set of stories from their parents. They were eager to share these in class—the time Martin rolled down the stairs on his tricycle, the time Lisa "almost drowned," and so on. Afterward, students began creating their personal histories. They each had to write a narrative essay about their lives, but they could present it to the rest of the class in several different ways—by recording a video- or audiotape, making a poster with photographs (or drawings) and captions, or simply reading their essay. (One student acted as a "museum guide" to the important events of his life.) The next several days were devoted to this assignment, as students wrote essays, designed posters, and planned scripts for tapes. When the time came to share these products with their classmates, even the shyest were proud to present, and students listened with careful attention to the stories of each others' lives.

Barton (1994a), Levstik & Pappas (1987)

In our interviews with children from first grade through middle school, we have found that all of them know something about how life was different in the past. Less often do they have a clear idea what "history" means. Because students usually don't encounter the subject at school before fourth grade, they sometimes don't even know what the word means; those who have heard it may link it with the past generally ("antiques and old stuff"), or may associate it with famous people or events. But rarely do they recognize that they are part of history, or that they have a history of their own.

Barton & Levstik (1996), Levstik & Barton (1996)

A seventh grader trying to explain the difference between science and history observed that he and the other students were *part of* science, since it was about them and the world around them—"We're *in* science," he pointed out, "but we're not *in* history." Because too many students do not see themselves as being "in history," developing a sense of what the subject is all about and how it relates to them must be one of the teacher's first and most important goals.

Students do not always see themselves as part of history.

ASKING HISTORICAL QUESTIONS

Beginning with students' own lives is an obvious way to develop their understanding of their place in history, and also introduces them to key elements of disciplined inquiry. In the example just given, Tina engaged her students in the most basic of historical questions—how has my own past affected my life today? She did this by asking students to think about their past in terms of *significance*: she didn't want them to try to remember everything that had ever happened to them, but to select the five most important things, those that had the greatest influence on their lives today. This seemingly easy assignment thus introduced students to what it means to ask historical questions. Moreover, this was a highly authentic question: as we have already noted, history is concerned first and foremost with explaining how we got to be where we are today, and knowing the story of one's own life is the most basic form of historical understanding. Note also that students became most interested once they moved away from a general and abstract discussion of *history* and began talking about specific *people* they knew.

Understanding history begins with students' own pasts.

History examines the effect of the past on the present.

Students are interested in history that focuses on people. *Barton (1994b)*

Making a list of important events, however, was not something that came easily; it didn't seem to be the kind of question students had ever been asked. Many had trouble deciding what to include on their lists, and a major part of Tina's responsibility was to help them think about how to answer the question; she stayed busy asking students how things in the past had affected their lives today, and how their lives would be different if various things hadn't happened. Some students stared at blank pieces of paper until talking to her; afterward, they were much readier to commit their ideas to paper. The collaborative nature of Tina's classroom also helped students consider the question: although they worked individually, students shared their ideas constantly and heard others explaining their experiences. Many weren't sure what was important until they heard their classmates sharing what was important to *them*.

Students benefit from collaboration among themselves and with their teacher.

COLLECTING HISTORICAL INFORMATION

This exercise also introduced students to the collection of historical data. They began with the most basic source of information, their own memories; by developing a list of events they remembered, they saw how they could serve as a source of data themselves. They also began to notice the limitations of relying on their own memories: although they remembered many of the things that had happened to them, few knew *when* they happened—either the dates or how old they were at the time. By having to combine their own memories with information from relatives, they learned that using multiple sources leads to a fuller picture of the past than relying on any single source—one of the most basic principles of historical research.

Historical inquiry can help students see the need for multiple sources of information.

Even the idea of consulting resources in order to learn something can be a new concept for children; they sometimes claim they couldn't possibly know anything they haven't directly experienced. In helping students develop a list of important events in their lives, for example, Tina asked one group to think about the things that excite parents when their children do them for the first time. One girl suggested getting a new tooth, another mentioned learning to talk, and both added these to their list of things to find out more about. Exasperated at these suggestions, one boy exclaimed, "How would *I* know any of those things happened!?"—he refused to write these down because (he believed) he had no way of knowing that he had ever gotten his first tooth

Many students are unfamiliar
with how people learn
about the past. *Barton
(1994a), Brophy, VanSle-
dright, & Bredin (1992),
Shemilt (1987, 1980), Wineburg (1991)*

Relatives provide a comfortable and accessible way for
students to move beyond
their own experiences.

Souces sometimes disagree.

Some sources are more reliable than others.

Students need structure to
collect information.

or learned to talk. He couldn't remember it, he reasoned, so how could he know that it ever happened? Although it seems obvious to adults that a person can know something about the past without directly remembering it, this is an understanding that has to be developed in children through exercises like these.

Collecting information from relatives obviously gives students a comfortable and accessible way to move beyond their own experience. Even such familiar sources, however, begin to acquaint them with fundamental issues of historical interpretation. Students quickly learned that their sources might disagree, and that they had to make judgments about reliability. Several found that relatives remembered events differently, and in explaining why they believed some sources rather than others, some noted that parents were more reliable because they probably saw the events firsthand, and more distant relatives would have heard about them later. Other students pointed out that mothers would know more about early events than fathers, because they were around them more when they were babies. Still others found that "baby books" were a useful source of information when people disagreed, and one student found that both his parents had been wrong about when he lost his first tooth. His baby book, he explained, was the most reliable source since things were written down in it at the time, but people trying to remember events years later might forget exactly how they happened. In this simple assignment, then, students dealt with fundamental historical issues—how to reconcile conflicting accounts and how to judge the reliability of sources.

Just as students needed Tina's help to develop a list of events, they needed some structure in order to collect information about dates. This was their first exposure to timelines and to collecting chronological data, so Tina did not simply tell them to go home and find out when events had happened; with those instructions, students probably would have brought back papers with a random collection of words and numbers and little idea how they went together. Instead, she gave each student a timeline of the last 10 years and explained exactly how to record the information they collected—using her own life as an example. As a result, students appeared to have little trouble keeping track of their information, and the next day they could easily use their timelines to answer questions about when things had happened (see Fig. 4.1). Collecting data is a fundamental part of all research, yet it is enormously difficult

FIG. 4.1 Student timeline.

for young children; providing them with the structure necessary—in this case, in the form of a printed timeline—is crucial to ensuring their success. The importance of this structure became apparent when students made their presentations. Many of those who created posters of their lives developed larger and more elaborate timelines for them, and several remarked that making them—spacing the years evenly and so on—was the most difficult part of the entire assignment! Without the help of a printed version to begin with, many of them would never have been able to keep their information organized. Because they had that help, though, they not only completed the assignment successfully but tackled the more challenging task of making new timelines for their presentations.

Collecting data is difficult for young children.

Teachers provide the structure that helps students succeed.

DRAWING CONCLUSIONS

As we noted in chapter 2, learning activities should be *authentic*; if students complete assignments only to please their teachers or get a grade, they're unlikely to understand the purpose of what they're doing or be able to apply it in new situations. In their "History of Me" assignments, students were not simply collecting information about themselves and filling it in on a timeline; that would have been more or less a typical school experience (even if a more interesting one than answering questions at the end of a chapter in a history book). Tina, however, required her students to go further and to use this information to create a narrative of their lives for an audience of classmates—and the creation of narratives is one authentic use of historical information. Like the students in chapter 3, Tina's students were not just learning skills or content but were *using* what they learned to create new knowledge.

Creating a narrative is an authentic use of historical information.

Newmann et al. (1995)

Understanding the purpose of schoolwork is also an important element of authenticity. Tina, however, consciously avoided telling students what they were supposed to think—preferring instead to let them develop their own ideas about the purpose of the assignment. Rather than telling them what *she* thought the purpose was, Tina periodically asked students to reflect on what *they* thought. Several times, for example, she began the history portion of the day by reading books like *Family Pictures/Cuadros de familia* and *This Land is My Land*, in which adults reflect on the events of their youth, and asked students why they thought the characters found stories about their past so important.

Students reflect on the meaning and significance of history.

Garza (1990), Littlechild (1993)

Similarly, Tina asked students why they thought they were doing this project. Their answers reflected a range of understanding—"to find out what year we did things and what we did," "to find out things we didn't know about ourselves," and "to find out what history is," for example. Other teachers might justifiably take a more directive approach and explain how a "History of Me" relates to personal identity, the impact of the past on the present, or the gathering and interpretation of data. Tina's approach, though, has the distinct advantage of allowing children to draw their own conclusions from their school experiences. One of the things about this project that most interested students—and surprised Tina—was their realization that each had his or her own unique history, different from everyone else's. Tina hadn't considered that they wouldn't already realize that, and she wouldn't have thought about emphasizing that as a purpose of the assignment—yet for students it turned out to be perhaps its most important purpose. By placing responsibility for creating meaning with the students themselves, Tina thus allowed them to come away with the understanding they found appropriate. Her approach also lays the foundation for developing truly *critical* thinking: instead of waiting to be told why something is important, Tina constantly teaches students to ask themselves, "So what?"

Students have a range of understandings of the meaning and purpose of history.

Students have responsibility for creating meaning.

Producing this kind of knowledge, however, was no simple matter. After completing their initial timelines and discussing their results in class, students began creating written narratives and presentations about their lives. Since they were learning more about writing during other times of the day, they were familiar with the elements necessary for an effective narrative—putting events in order, including details, and

History is integrated with other subjects.

so on (see especially chapter 9). But when it came to taking the information from their timelines and putting it into a new form, many had great difficulty. Several didn't realize that their timelines contained the information they needed to begin, and they displayed an attitude teachers will quickly recognize: they acted as though they were supposed to pluck ideas out of thin air, on a completely unexpected topic. The look and sound of "I don't know what to write" came from several students around the room. Of course, in some classrooms students *are* expected to do assignments that come out of thin air, but Tina had just spent 2 days engaging her class in prewriting activities for this task. Most did indeed see the connection to their previous work and used their timelines to plan their essays. But others needed more explicit help: they needed someone to show them how to use what they had already learned. As Tina (and their classmates) helped them make this connection, the expectant sound of "Oh! Now I get it!" replaced the desultory "I don't know what to write." As always, scaffolding was critical. Teachers cannot simply throw an assignment at students and expect them to learn from it; at one time or another, most will need help figuring out how to use their knowledge and skills in their work.

An even more significant problem for some students was deciding which information from their timelines was important enough to include in their narratives. Although Tina led the class in a discussion of how to choose what to write and modeled the process using her own timeline, many still weren't sure how to go about it. Again, teachers will recognize how difficult it is for students to take information from one form and put it in another; because many elementary children only learn about creative, fictional writing, they often have little understanding of how to use written language in other ways. Tina's students knew they shouldn't just rewrite everything from their timelines, but they didn't know what *was* important enough to include in their narratives. Just as she did when they first began the assignment, Tina had to help students (individually and in small groups) think about how to choose from among a list of events to include those that were most significant; in essence, she was scaffolding their understanding of historical significance.

Of course, students' understanding of significance will not be the same as an adult's. Many chose the events they had enjoyed the most (a favorite vacation, for example), rather than those an adult might think were actually the most important. Given that they hadn't run into this kind of question before (and since they were only 9 years old), that's hardly surprising. But Tina consistently kept their attention focused on the issue of significance rather than simple storytelling. She never told any student, "Don't include that, that's not important," but she always asked, "Why did you include that—what impact has that had on your life?" As a result of this constant probing, students learned that history is a matter of what's important: by the end of the assignment they could be counted on to explain their choices by beginning, "This has had an impact on me because...." Although not all their explanations were equally convincing, they knew that any justification for including an event had to refer to why it was important in the present—and they learned to use the word *impact* along the way.

BALANCING STUDENT CHOICE
AND CURRICULAR REQUIREMENTS

This project also shows how teachers can maintain a balance between giving students choices and making sure they learn the skills that schools and society consider important. All students were required to write a narrative essay about their lives, and they had to complete this assignment before moving on to their presentations. Narrative compositions were a required part of the portfolio assessment system in Tina's state, and like most people, she considered this kind of writing to be an important part of what students needed to learn at school. Writing assignments were a part of all subjects in her class, and she held students to high standards. As they drafted, revised, and published their compositions, Tina worked to make sure they understood what constituted *novice, apprentice, proficient, and distinguished* performances—terms for the levels used in the state's assessment program—and could apply those standards to their own writing. She kept explicit scoring guidelines posted on the wall and expected students to evaluate their work accordingly. Tina spent the largest portion of her instructional time conferring with students, and these conferences focused on helping them understand what they needed to do in order to improve their written assignments.

But Tina did not assume that writing was the only way to display knowledge, or that students who didn't write well yet couldn't learn. Although they were required to write an essay, students had their choice of many different forms for their presentations to classmates—making posters, using photographs, recording videos or audiocassettes, and so on. Academic research on learning styles and multiple intelligences has made it a commonplace observation that not all students learn the same way. Tina recognized that many students would benefit from using information in forms other than writing, and that they were capable of making their own choices about what they wanted to do. Nor did Tina try to pigeonhole students' work into any single "style" or "strength." Most students, for example, chose to create a poster with a timeline, photographs, and captions and to describe their work orally to the class; this required the use of both oral and written language as well as both visual and mathematical understanding. Although some students may be more visual, others more tactile, and so on, all students learn better when they have the chance to combine different modes of understanding.

Giving students a choice of forms for presentation also made the assignment more authentic. Although books and articles are an important source of historical information in our society, so too are museums, documentaries, and oral accounts. The forms available to students for their presentations introduced them to the different ways of presenting historical knowledge and to some of the unique features of each. The popularity of photographs, for example, showed how interesting visual access to the past can be. Students also learned about its limitations, though: they found that they didn't have photographs of many of the events they wanted to include. As a result, they had to make choices about how to represent their lives. Some included whatever pictures they had, and then revised their judgments about significance: the most important events in their lives turned out to be chosen from the photographs they had. Others took a different approach: they used the pictures that were available, but explained how they represented other events in their lives—a photograph of a vacation, for example, might actually represent the birth of a sister, because she was still a baby in the picture. Again, that is exactly what historians do: they decide how the available resources can be used to tell a story. For years, historians based much of their work on letters, diaries, and diplomatic papers, and as a result they had to omit people who didn't leave behind these kinds of documents. In recent years, many historians have attempted to find other sources to represent the lives of people in the past—wills, court proceedings, tax records, and the like. Similarly, some of Tina's students based their ideas about importance on the sources that were readily available, while some used other criteria and employed the sources as indirect representations.

It is also important to note that these presentations were not simply an enrichment exercise or an activity for "early finishers." Too often, only students who do well at standard written assignments get to move on to those that involve creativity, problem solving, or other forms of learning. In Tina's class, though, all students were given the time and support to complete both kinds of task—and the provision of material resources was as important as Tina's instructional help. The class included students from a wide range of socioeconomic backgrounds; many had their own videocameras and cassette recorders at home, while just buying the materials to make posters may have been difficult for others. Rather than allowing students' schoolwork to mirror their families' economic status, the school supplied all the equipment they needed.

Teachers help students understand the standards of achievement.

Students display their understanding in a variety of forms.

Dunn & Griggs (1988), Gardner (1983), Keefe (1987), Reiff (1992)

Students should not be limited to a single learning "style." *Caine & Caine (1994)*

Authentic tasks allow for student choices.

Students learn about historical interpretation and representation.

The choice of sources influences the kind of stories that can be told.

All students are given the time and support to engage in a variety of assignments.

We recognize that not all schools have the technology or supplies that students need to do their best work; fortunately Tina teaches in a state where schools have great flexibility in deciding how to use their limited resources (rather than being hemmed in by regulations forcing them to buy expensive textbooks). In any event, providing students access to appropriate resources is an essential part of equitable and effective education.

Equitable educational experiences depend on equitable access to resources.

THE "HISTORY OF ME" IN THE CONTEXT OF DIVERSITY

Interestingly, the students who can most easily describe how their own pasts have affected the present are often those whose parents have divorced and remarried; they are usually quite ready to explain how changing houses, being adopted, or getting new siblings have influenced their lives. On the one hand, presenting a "History of Me" can be an enormously fulfilling experience for them; we have been impressed with the way some students use this activity to affirm their backgrounds and proudly present their lives to their classmates, and we have been just as impressed with their classmates' readiness to hear about and appreciate differences in family life. As with academic skills, developing these values depends in large part on how well they are modeled by the teacher. A teacher who accepts the differences among students and their families as natural and who shows genuine interest in their uniqueness will find that many of her students do the same. But a teacher who regards deviations from some imagined norm as deficiencies—or who tries to ignore such differences—will rarely have students who demonstrate even basic tolerance. When a teacher develops a supportive and caring environment in her classroom, "celebrating diversity" can become more than a slogan, and investigating personal histories can help children see how their backgrounds both converge and differ.

Personal histories allow students to take pride in their own lives.

Teachers who genuinely value diversity among students do not see differences as "deficiencies."

Mizell, Benett, Bowman, & Morin (1993), Richards (1993)

On the other hand, the purpose of an assignment like this is not to pry into children's personal lives. Most students and their families will readily answer questions about the most important events in their lives, but others will refuse to address the topic. Students will not want to share some events that have had an impact on them—abuse by a family member, for example, or the loss of a loved one. In other cases, parents will resent participating in this assignment; undocumented immigrants often fear that personal questions will lead to deportation or denial of services for their family, for example, while many people of fundamentalist faiths believe schools should not ask questions about children's lives outside school. The solution to these dilemmas—we decline to call them "problems" because we recognize and accept the reasons for them—is not to avoid assignments about personal histories, nor is it to exempt some students and thus highlight what they may think of as an inadequacy. Rather, teachers must make such assignments flexible enough to accommodate the legitimate differences among students and their families in our extraordinarily diverse society.

Some families decline to reveal personal information.

Assignments must be flexible enough to accomodate diversity.

To do this, teachers should never require students to share (with them or the class) anything they don't want to. In essence, a "History of Me" should include the most significant events children *want to share*, not those most significant in any kind of absolute sense. In addition, the teacher should always give students the option of investigating someone's life other than their own; the purpose of the assignment, after all, is to find out how the past affects the present, not to force students into putting themselves on display. Those who don't want to call attention to themselves should have the option of doing a history of a friend in another classroom, a teacher at the school, or someone else in the community. Rather than being forced to take part in an unpleasant assignment, they then have the enriching experience of learning about someone else's life—and classmates are invariably more attentive to these presentations than any other. It is important to keep in mind, though, that *all* students must be given these options, not just those whom the teacher thinks may need them; otherwise the mere presence of an alternative may seem just as unpleasant as the original assignment.

Students should not be required to share personal information.

All students need choices in assignments.

32

EXTENSIONS

A project like the "History of Me" can be extended in several ways to develop further experience with asking and answering historical questions. An obvious follow-up is for students to use historical biographies to investigate the impact of an individual's past on his or her life. Such biographies are one of the most commonly available forms of historical literature, and range from books appropriate for young children—such as *Diego, Mary McLeod Bethune, Malcolm X*, and *The Last Princess: The Story of Princess Ka'inlani of Hawaii*—to those more suitable for the middle grades—such as *Eleanor Roosevelt: A Life of Discovery, Rosa Parks: My Story*, and *Quanah Parker: Great Chief of the Comanches.* (A more complete list follows the end of this chapter.) Using literature like this allows students to move beyond their own experiences, and gives them the chance to examine the lives of people whose race, ethnicity, gender, socioeconomic class, or physical abilities may be very different than their own.

Winter (1991), Greenfield (1977), Adler (1990), F. Stanley (1991)

Freedman (1993), Parks (1992), Gonzales (1987)

Biographies allow students to move beyond their own experiences.

Of course, teachers often assign students to read such biographies and then "do a report"—but as a colleague of ours once noted, it's been a long time since most of us sat down and wrote a report on a book we've read. Book reports simply are not an authentic genre in our society; they're just a traditionally assigned (and traditionally despised) means of assessing whether students have done their work. Outside of school, people may discuss a book with others who have read it or may recommend it to those who haven't, and many teachers pattern their classrooms on these more authentic tasks—assigning students to take part in literature response groups, for example, or to make advertisements or other recommendations for the books they've read. Such assignments develop children's language skills in a much more authentic way than writing a report that has no clear purpose or audience.

Book reports often have no clear audience or purpose.

In literature response groups, students meet together to analyze the works they are reading.

But how can students use biographies in a way that models the use of disciplined inquiry in a more specifically *historical* way? Certainly there's nothing wrong with using them in connection with discussion groups or other such assignments, in the same way any piece of literature would be used; people do read historical biographies for pleasure, they do discuss them and they do recommend them to others. But in addition, using biographies along with projects like those in this chapter can focus students' attention on the specifically historical nature of the genre. Historians do not read biographies and then write reports on them; rather, they do one of two things—either they *write* such works themselves, or they *evaluate* those others have written. Both tasks are well within the abilities of children.

Students can write their own accounts, for example, by using published biographies, encyclopedias, CD-ROMs, and even oral memories or folklore to make a timeline of important events in a famous person's life, and then construct these into written narratives or other kinds of presentations. Just as they did with their own histories, the emphasis would be on establishing the impact of events on the person's life, and explaining how things might have been different if those events had never happened. A 6-year-old would produce a much different work than a 14-year-old, of course, yet both would be engaged in a more purposeful assignment than "doing a report": they would be asking historical questions, collecting and interpreting information, and reflecting on what they had found. In addition, instead of making the teacher the sole audience for these student-created biographies, the class could compile and compare their findings. They might discuss, for example, which of the figures they investigated has had the greatest impact on contemporary society—thus extending their understanding of the influence of events on individuals to the influence of individuals on society.

Students use multiple sources of information to create biographies.

And just as the primary children in chapter 3 did with Johnny Appleseed, students can critically evaluate published biographies or other accounts by examining the basis for authors' claims. What statements are based on evidence? How good is the evidence? Which simply derive from folklore or legend? We mentioned earlier that in doing a "History of Me," students should only be asked to share what they *want* to share, not everything that has happened to them. At first glance, that may have

Students critically evaluate published biographies.

seemed distinctly inauthentic: surely history is about the truth, not about covering things up. But as we explained in chapter 1, any history leaves some things out—that's the very essence of historical explanation. A student who has had to decide what to include and what not to include in her own biography may then recognize (with the teacher's help) that books about famous people do the same thing, and can try to explain why some biographies of George Washington note that he owned hundreds of slaves, while others ignore the topic. They can compare different biographies of the same person and rank their authenticity and believability, just as historians do.

Students examine how conventions of historical writing have changed over time.

Older students can even examine the way in which the writing of historical biographies have changed over time. Most of us probably remember common biography series from our childhoods, and school libraries are still full of dog-eared copies of them. Students in the middle grades could compare those to more contemporary accounts and try to explain what biographical conventions have changed and which have remained the same, and explain how these changes relate to larger changes in society. Biographies from the 1950s, for example, rarely included any consideration of the failings of their subjects; their purpose was less to teach about real historical individuals than to provide role models who were paragons of patriotism and proper behavior. Many contemporary biographies, on the other hand, treat their subjects in a more balanced way; while they may still serve the purpose of providing role models, they are certainly very different models than those of previous generations.

Wilton (1993)

Of course, most popular biographies focus on famous people, but much contemporary historical writing uses the lives of ordinary people to highlight significant aspects of historical continuity and change, and students can do the same. Although information on famous people is more readily available, with a little bit of work teachers and their students can locate the primary sources necessary to construct biographies of everyday people, particularly from their own communities (see chapter 10 for more on constructing narratives).

CONCLUSIONS

From fifth grade through college, history is one of the most securely established subjects in the curriculum, and most students in the country will take the same survey of American history at least three times—in 5th, 8th, and 11th grades, usually—and a fourth time if they go to college. Yet the amount of information they retain from these courses is shockingly small, as national tests and surveys have shown for more than 50 years. How can there be such a mismatch between what students study and what they learn? Tina suggests that part of the problem lies in the inappropriateness of the content of traditional school history. Even in schools in which teachers have great flexibility and control of their curriculum, there are enormous pressures to teach topics like "state history" in fourth grade, and to do so in a way that mirrors the content of history textbooks or curriculum guidelines—having students learn when the state was admitted to the union, who the first governor was, and so on.

Ravitch & Finn (1987), Whittington (1991)

Brophy, VanSledright, & Bredin (1993)

In order for history to be meaningful, students must understand the meaning of "history" as well as their place in history.

Academic researchers have suggested that teaching state history in fourth grade confuses children, but Tina's criticisms are stronger still: "It's ridiculous to go through a book reading about the founding of the state when students don't even have a sense of what history is, of what it *means*. Without knowing what history is all about, the rest of it will just go over their heads." We agree. At some point in their school career—hopefully in the primary grades, but later if necessary—students have to learn what history is all about, that they themselves have a history and that they are in history just as much as they are in the natural world.

CHILDREN'S AND ADOLESCENT LITERATURE

Personal History, Memory, and Identity

Bahr, M. (1991). *The Memory Box*. Whitman.
Bonners, S. (1991). *The Wooden Doll*. Lothrop, Lee, & Shephard.
Bunting, E. (1995). *Once upon a Time*. Owen.
Clifford, E. (1985). *The Remembering Box*. Houghton Mifflin.
Garza, C. L. (1990). *Family Pictures/Cuadros de familia*. Children's Book Press.
Giovanni, N. (Ed.), (1994). *Grand Mothers: Poems, Reminiscences, and Short Stories About the Keepers of Our Traditions*. Holt.
Greenfield, E. (1989). *African Dream*. Crowell.
Johnson, A. (1989). *Tell Me a Story, Mama*. Orchard.
Littlechild, G. (1993). *This Land is My Land*. Children's Book Press.
Myers, W. D. (1993). *Brown Angels: An Album of Pictures and Verse*. HarperCollins.
Nodar, C. S. (1992). *Abuelita's Paradise/El paraíso de Abuelita*. Whitman.
Pomerantz, C. (1989). *The Chalk Doll*. Lippincott.
Ringgold, F. (1991). *Tar Beach*. Crown.
Say, A. (1982). *The Bicycle Man*. Houghton Mifflin.
Schwartz, A. (1983). *Mrs. Moskowitz and the Sabbath Candlesticks*. Jewish Publication Society of America.
Shea, P. D. (1995). *The Whispering Cloth: A Refugee's Story*. Boyds Mill Press
Stevenson, J. (1986). *When I was Nine*. Greenwillow Books.

Biographies

Adler, D. (1990). *A Picture Book of Helen Keller*. Holiday.
Adoff, A. (1970). *Malcolm X*. Harper and Row.
Brown, M. M. (1992). *Susette La Fleshe: Advocate for Native American Rights*. Children's Book Press.
Codye, C. (1990). *Vilma Martínez*. Raintree.
Coil, S. M. (1993). *Harriet Beecher Stowe*. Franklin Watts.
Faber, D., & Faber, H. (1986). *Mahatma Gandhi*. Julian Messner.
Fox, M. V. (1993). *Bette Bao Lord: Novelist and Chinese Voice for Change*. Children's Book Press.
Freedman, R. (1993). *Eleanor Roosevelt: A Life of Discovery*. Clarion.
Garza, H. (1994). *Frido Kahlo*. Chelsea House.
Gleiter, J., & Thompson, K. (1990). *José Martí*. Raintree.
Gonzales, C. T. (1987). *Quanah Parker: Great Chief of the Comanches*. Eakin Press.
Green, C. (1991). *Elizabeth Blackwell: First Woman Doctor*. Children's Book Press.
Green, C. (1992). *Mark Twain: Author of Tom Sawyer*. Children's Book Press.
Greenfield, E. (1977). *Mary McLeod Bethune*. HarperCollins.
Greenfield, E. (1975). *Paul Robeson*. HarperCollins.
Greenfield, E. (1973). *Rosa Parks*. Harper.
Haskins, J. (1992). *I Have a Dream: The Life and Words of Martin Luther King, Jr.* Millbrook.
Haskins, J. (1992). *Thurgood Marshall: A Life for Justice*. Henry Holt.
Kent, Z. (1989). *The Story of Geronimo*. Children's Book Press.
Klausner, J. (1993). *Sequoyah's Gift: A Portrait of the Cherokee Leader*. HarperCollins.
McKissack, P. C., and McKissack, F. (1992). *Sojourner Truth: Ain't I a Woman?* Scholastic.
Meltzer, M. (1986). *Dorothea Lange: Life through the Camera*. Puffin.
Myers, W. D. (1993). *Malcolm X: By Any Means Necessary*. New York: Scholastic.
Neimark, A. (1989). *Che! Latin America's Legendary Guerilla Leader*. Harper Collins.
Parks, R. (1992). *Rosa Parks: My Story*. Dial.
Pinkney, A. D. (1994). *Dear Benjamin Banneker*. Harcourt Brace.
Roberts, M. (1986). *Cesar Chavez and La Causa*. Children's Book Press.
Sabin, L. (1992). *Roberto Clemente: Young Baseball Hero*. Troll.
Say, A. (1990). *El Chino*. Houghton Mifflin.
Selvin, D. F. (1966). *Eugene Debs: Rebel, Labor Leader, Prophet*. Lothrop, Lee and Shephard.
Selvin, D. F. (1969). *The Thundering Voice of John L. Lewis*. Lothrop, Lee and Shephard.
Simon, C. (1991). *Wilma P. Mankiller: Chief of the Cherokee*. Children's Book Press.
Stanley, D., & Vennema, P. (1992). *Bard of Avon: The Story of William Shakespeare*. Morrow.
Stanley, D., & Vennema, P. (1988). *Shaka: King of the Zulus*. New York: Morrow.
Stanley, F. (1991). *The Last Princess: The Story of Princess Ka'inlani of Hawaii*. Four Winds Press.
Thompson, K. (1990). *Sor Juana Inés de la Cruz*. Raintree.
Turner, R. M. (1992). *Mary Cassat*. Little, Brown, and Company.
Uchida, Y. (1991). *The Invisible Thread*. Simon and Schuster.
Wepman, D. (1986). *Benito Juárez*. Chelsea House.
Winter, J. (1991) *Diego*. Knopf.

Chapter 5

Linking Children to the Past Through Family Histories

After students have completed their personal history projects, Tina Reynolds begins a unit on family history by reading *The Patchwork Quilt*, a book in which a girl and her mother discover meaning in the way a grandmother's quilt "tells stories" about the family's past. Tina asks students whether their relatives have ever told them about the past, and nearly every hand is raised: one boy tells about his uncle who was in "the war"; a girl relates how her grandmother talks about the old things she owns; another student explains that his grandmother's World War II factory badge is in an exhibit at a nearby museum. The rest of the lesson focuses on the concept of generation—which relatives are in their own *generation,* which in their parents', and so on. The next day, Tina introduces students to a new assignment, creating a family history based on interviews with their grandparents. Although students can do a "family history chart" as an optional assignment, their primary task is to give a presentation that focuses on the differences between their grandparents' lives and their own. Tina assigns several questions for students to ask in their interviews, and works with them to develop several more of their own. She also spends an entire lesson modeling how to conduct an interview, as well as how to take notes. Sharing the results of these interviews takes several days, as students feel compelled to share as many of the things they've learned as possible.

* * *

Rebecca Valbuena begins a unit on immigration by portraying her grandfather, a Latvian who immigrated to New York as a 10-year-old in 1910. She places photographs of him around the room, plays Latvian music on a tape recorder, and explains why he came to the United States and what he found here. After answering questions about his life, she asks students why their own families—almost all of whom are recent immigrants—came to the United States. They quickly produce a list with a variety of reasons—to find work, to be with relatives, for political freedom, to get away from war, and (the most common) "for a better life." This discussion leads into the first assignment of the unit: interview an immigrant. Working together as a class, they develop a list of questions that would be important to ask an immigrant—What country did you come from? Why did you immigrate? What difficulties did you have when you first arrived? Was the United States what you expected? And, at students' insistence, How much did it cost? Over the next few days, students develop written and oral reports based on their interviews, and then compare their findings to the experience of other immigrants in history—such as the Irish on the East coast in the mid-1800s and the Chinese on the West coast in the late 1800s. At the end of each day's lesson, Rebecca reads aloud a different book about immigrants, such as *Who Belongs Here?* and *Where the River Runs*, and students discuss the feelings and experiences of immigrants.

One of the most crucial challenges in teaching history to children lies in linking the subject to what they already know. As we discussed in chapter 2, people can only make sense of new experiences when they compare it to the knowledge they have. Without such a connection, children are unlikely to understand the history they encounter at school. Yet it's not always obvious just how to make that connection; certainly many of the topics traditionally covered in history textbooks have no clear relation to students' own experiences, and texts rarely suggest how such topics might be relevant. The challenge for the teacher, then, lies in deciding what aspects of important historical content match up with elements of students' lives. Finding that link is the key to broadening students' understanding of history beyond their own experience, and family histories provide one of the most useful ways of doing that. Tina's and Rebecca's classes show how the lives of students' families can introduce them to important and meaningful topics in history.

Teachers decide how to connect students' experiences with important historical content.

CONNECTING STUDENTS TO IMPORTANT HISTORICAL THEMES

Sometimes classrooms are described as being either "teacher-centered" or "student-centered," but we find that most focus neither on the interests of students *nor* teachers, but on whatever is in the textbook. Studies repeatedly find that textbooks are the most consistent influence on the content of instruction at school. In order to link important historical content to children's backgrounds, however, the primacy of texts has to be replaced with teachers' own decisions about instructional content. From our perspective, it is up to teachers to determine what historical content is worth teaching, and which aspects of students' experiences provide the best avenue for doing that.

Pappas et al. (1995)

teachers have to decide which historical contents can be linked to students' experiences

Rebecca's classroom provides a clear example of such an approach. Her school's textbooks don't start with a comparison of contemporary immigration and Irish and Chinese immigration in the 1800s; like most texts, they start with Native American life and early European explorers, and proceed through time in strict chronological order. Given the amount of material to be covered and the limited time that can be spent on the topic, few fifth-grade teachers who base their instruction on textbooks get much further than the American Revolution. Limiting history to events hundreds of years in the past practically guarantees that students will have few opportunities to make connections to their own experiences. Rebecca, however, began not with what was in the text but with her knowledge of history and her students.

Instruction begins with students' interests and experiences.

Rebecca knew that the movement of people is one of the most important themes throughout both United States and world history (see Fig. 1.1), and that students would return to it throughout the year—when they studied the encounter of Native Americans with European settlers, for example, or when they studied the enslavement of Africans. Moreover, Rebecca focused not just on the bare facts of immigration, but on the issues that would allow students to compare these different movements of people—questions like, "What motivated people to migrate?" and "Did they find what they expected?" By beginning the year with the study of an important theme, students were better able to see how the year's topics were related than if they proceeded chronologically through a textbook.

History focuses on important themes.

A thematic approach to history encourages students to make connections across time and place.

Rebecca also chose this topic because of the obvious ways it allowed children to make connections with their families. Nearly all her students immigrated recently to the United States—some from Mexico, some from Central America, some from Southeast Asia—so questions about motivations for immigrating and the consequences of moving were something they and their families were directly familiar with. (In other classrooms, students may not be immigrants from another country, but their families may still have moved from one place to another, and for some of the same reasons—to find a job, to be with relatives, and so on.) But this is not to say that all teachers should begin with the topic of immigration, and interview their relatives about why they have moved; our intent is not to replace the traditional beginning of elementary history ("Early Explorers") with a new one ("Immigration"). Teaching history does not mean relying on a cookbook in which someone else has decided which topics are most appropriate for the children in all classrooms; only teachers can do this, and only by knowing both history and their students.

Teachers know history and their students.

Tina, for example, also followed her "History of Me" projects (see chapter 4) with family histories, but hers had nothing to do with immigration. Tina's students lived in a stable residential neighborhood, and some of their families had lived in the same town for generations. Interviewing their relatives would yield little or no information as to why people move or what they find when they do. (Although her students did study immigration, it came later in the school year, and was based primarily on children's literature.) Instead, Tina's students interviewed their grandparents to find out how life was different in the past: they learned what chores their grandparents did when they were young, what they did for fun, and so on. In Tina's class, this provided students not with an introduction to immigration in U. S. history but to the study of how material and social life has changed over the last century (see also chapters 7 and 11). Despite the differences in topic, though, Tina and Rebecca developed their curriculum in an identical way: they chose important themes and helped students broaden their understanding through their use of family histories.

Family histories can link students' backgrounds to important historical themes.

IMAGINATIVE ENTRY: PERSONALIZING HISTORY

As we discussed in chapter 2, children strive to make *human sense* of the world around them. Rebecca emphasized the importance of *personalizing* history for students, of helping them see how the subject involves real human beings. Her introduction to the immigration unit is a perfect example: just as Tina's students were excited about reading her personal timeline in chapter 4, Rebecca's students listened with rapt attention as she took on the appearance of her grandfather and described his experiences. In such a presentation, history is not about anonymous groups of immigrants, who moved for some vague reason at some distant point in history; it's about the teacher's grandfather, who came to the United States when he was a kid like they are.

Students are interested in the personal, human elements of history.

The multisensory aspect of Rebecca's presentation was also critical. Students did not just hear about or read about an immigrant, they saw photographs of him, saw the way he dressed, and even heard the kind of music he listened to. (Even for teachers who do not have information from their own families, photographs of immigrants are easy to obtain, since this is a richly documented era in American history.) And students themselves can also take part in acting out the experience of immigrants; Tina's students, for example, planned and acted out an encounter between immigrant families and government officials after reading *Immigrant Kids* and *If Your Name was Changed at Ellis Island*. Visual images, music, artifacts, and role-playing are second nature to any teacher whose students do not speak English as a first language, but in teaching history these strategies should become part of every teacher's repertoire. The more avenues to the past available to students, the more likely they are to make connections to what they already know.

Freedman (1980), Levine (1993)

Teachers provide many avenues of entry to history.

The most important way of personalizing history lies in the connections students make with their own families. Simply assigning them to find out how life has changed over the past three generations, for example, is unlikely to inspire much interest. By having them interview their grandparents, however, Tina could be more confident that they would find the topic of change over time personally relevant; and indeed, students came back from these interviews with pages of notes and eager to share their stories with the rest of the class. It quickly became obvious that they had not limited themselves to the list of questions they developed in class, but had a much more personal and wide-ranging discussion of their family's past. Students also took an interest in their classmates' presentations, because they were hearing not just about history, but about each others' grandparents.

Students are usually interested in learning about their families' histories.

Similarly, Rebecca's primary purpose was to develop her students' understanding of the motivations for and consequences of immigration, but instead of starting with experiences remote in time and place and working forward, she began with what students already knew—why their families immigrated—and these reasons were much the same as those that have motivated people throughout history. By making a list of the motivations found within their classroom, students had a starting point that *they already understood* to compare with the motivations of other immigrants throughout history. Similarly, when they interviewed family members they found out what

Students can study history by beginning with the recent past and working backward.

38

kinds of problems they had when they first came to the United States—finding a job, finding a place to live, not being able to speak the language—and this gave them yet another basis for comparing the experiences of other immigrants.

Literature also provides a highly effective way of helping students make personal connections to history. Unfortunately, picture books and other works for reading aloud sometimes fall by the wayside after the primary years, perhaps because they somehow seem too easy or because reading aloud doesn't involve students in the production of a tangible product in an obvious way. Yet children of all ages love to be read to; when the time for reading aloud arrives, the sounds of "Yes!" and "All right!" filled Rebecca's room. As an adult Rebecca could read with much more expression than her students, and she tried to make the voices and dialects in the books as authentic as possible; as a result, her students heard what it sounds like to read fluently. For Tina's students, meanwhile, literature was absolutely essential for studying immigration. With little personal experience related to the topic, her students relied on books—whether short works like *Watch the Stars Come Out* and *Leaving for America,* or longer ones such as *Letters from Rifka*—to provide them with an understanding of the personal dimensions of immigrants' experiences.

Finally, both Tina and Rebecca made history personal by including attention to what children know best—daily life. Having fourth graders ask their grandparents directly about abstract topics such as economics or society would not be effective, because children have only a rudimentary understanding of those concepts. But by asking about changes in chores, entertainment, school, and the like, students developed their understanding of social and economic changes by linking them to their own experiences. When they studied immigration, Tina's students wanted to know about practical matters; discussion often focused on questions like what people ate while on immigrant ships, how they went to the bathroom, and so on. Rebecca's students were also interested in these seemingly routine details—witness their concern with the monetary cost of immigration—although they could readily identify with the hardships of immigration that Tina's students only wondered about.

COLLECTING AND INTERPRETING INFORMATION

Conducting historical research with family members obviously has many of the same advantages discussed in chapter 4. Interviewing relatives is an accessible and comfortable way for students to move beyond their own experiences, and yet allows them to see how accounts differ, how sources vary in reliability, and how conflicting accounts can be reconciled. Tina found that one of the most striking benefits of this project was that students saw that not everything they learned had to come from a book, and that people were a valuable resource for historical inquiry; her students were amazed that they could get so much information from people.

As we have emphasized before and will emphasize again, however, students need explicit help in learning how to collect and interpret information—no matter how familiar the source may be. Both Rebecca and Tina spent entire lessons teaching students how to conduct an interview. Tina, for example, talked to students about how some topics might be personally sensitive, and how their grandparents either might not want to talk about them or might get emotional when they do; her own grandmother, she explained, cries whenever she talks about World War II. Even more importantly, she provided a model for students of how to conduct interviews: she had students from the class practice by asking her questions, she responded as though she were the grandparent being interviewed, and other students took notes on what she said. Note-taking turned out to be a challenge: students wanted to write down every word she said, and Tina had to explain how to focus on the most important points, and how to write down words and phrases that would help them reconstruct the interview later. That lesson was particularly eye-opening for students: they were shocked that they were allowed to write something other than complete sentence and

Family histories help students build on their background knowledge.

Literature helps students make personal connections to history.

Elementary and middle grades students enjoy being read to.

Levinson (1985), Hesse (1992), Bresnick-Perry (1992)

Learning about abstract concepts begins with concrete examples.

Family histories introduce students to important aspects of historical inquiry.

Teachers help students learn to collect information.

paragraphs! Although as adults we recognize that different uses of language call for different conventions, children need explicit instruction on the topic.

Rebecca also worked with students on conducting interviews, but language development was a much more pervasive aspect of instruction in her class than in Tina's. Almost none of her students spoke English as a first language, and thus every aspect of the unit required attention to the use of words. As she portrayed her grandfather, for example, Rebecca called students' attention to vocabulary cards containing key words for the unit—*immigrant, emigrate, motivation,* and the like. And so that they would be able to write comparisons of immigrants' experiences, Rebecca modeled the use of sentences containing "Magic Words"—primarily subordinating conjunctions like *because, although, when, before,* and *after*—to express causal and temporal relationships (see chapter 14 for more information on using "Magic Words"). Explicit modeling of vocabulary and skills in authentic contexts helped students transform their conceptual understanding into more fluent prose.

A significant part of teaching students to collect and interpret information is providing them with ways to keep track of what they learn, and graphic organizers played an important role in both Tina's and Rebecca's classrooms. Sometimes graphic organizers help individual students organize information, as the timelines Tina provided for personal histories did. Other times, graphic organizers are useful as a way of calling students' attention to the themes that emerge from the information they collect. As students reported what they learn from their grandparents, for example, Tina recorded the information on chart paper with headings like *technology, work, leisure,* and *school.* By seeing the information recorded in this way, students not only gained more insight into the meaning of concepts like *leisure* and *technology,* but could also more readily identify the patterns that began to emerge from the interviews (see Fig. 5.1). Similarly, as Rebecca's students studied immigrants throughout history, they recorded what they learned on a chart that identified the motivations of each group and the consequences of their migration. Again, by seeing the information displayed in a visually organized way, students could more easily discern the similarities and differences in the experiences they learned about. Finally, leaving charts like these on the wall throughout the year allowed students to add new information when they encountered it, and thus to see the topics as issues of ongoing importance rather than isolated units of study.

Technology	Clothes
didn't have VCRs	blue jeans
black-and-white TVs	dresses
no computers	angora sweaters
big cars with fins	bobby socks
coal furnace	overalls
no microwave	suspenders
icebox	
bicycles	

Leisure	Work
board games	lots of chores
baseball	cooking
dolls	mowing the grass
going to movies	feeding animals
listening to radio	pulling weeds
fishing	
tag	

FIG. 5.1. Wall charts based on grandparent interviews.

In both classrooms, students also did more than collect information: they used what they had learned to create authentic historical presentations. Tina, for example, set aside time each day for them to share what they were finding out about their grandparents, and Rebecca's students developed formal presentations based on their interviews with immigrants. Both teachers also assigned written compositions: students in Tina's class wrote simulated diaries from the perspective of their grandparents when they were children, and those in Rebecca's turned their interview notes into written essays. Historical inquiry in these classrooms, then, provided an important opportunity for students to develop their ability to communicate through speech and writing, both of which are central to the use of historical information in our society. "Authentic genres" of historical presentation, after all, are no radical educational innovations—learning how to speak in public and write for an audience are among the most traditional goals of learning and are likely to continue to be so for a very long time to come.

Students use information to create authentic historical presentations.

Authentic tasks include writing and speaking for an audience.

LINKING STUDENTS TO LARGER NARRATIVES

Why use family histories to introduce students to these topics? Is it simply because they provide a way of personalizing the past, and give students an easy way of learning how to collect historical information? These are important considerations, but family histories serve a larger purpose as well. We have argued that the central role of history in our society lies in its ability to explain how the past produced the present. The personal histories discussed in chapter 4 may help students understand that they themselves have histories, but those histories become much more meaningful when they are linked to other stories, and students begin to see themselves as participants in narratives larger than those of their own lives.

History helps students see themselves as part of narratives larger than their own lives.

The stories families tell about the past are one of the most important ways of introducing children to history. Nearly all families tell these stories; regardless of race, ethnicity, class, or geographic region, children learn what has happened in their families and where they fit into that picture. Consider the eagerness of Tina's students to explain what they had learned about the past, and the readiness of Rebecca's to share reasons their families had immigrated. These were hardly new topics to students: they had talked about these things with their families before. Passing on family history of one kind or another is a basic part of most (perhaps all) cultural traditions. Using family histories as a part of instruction, then, represents the very height of authenticity: it engages students in precisely the kind of historical understanding that exists outside of school.

Barton (1995), Levstik & Barton (1996), Seixas (1993b)

As with most topics, students in the same classroom will develop different levels of understanding and awareness of this purpose. In Tina's class, for example, some students see little more than that they have it easier than their grandparents did, and so should appreciate what they have—a variation on the "Eat your peas because children are starving in Asia" line many of us heard as children. Others, however, recognize that the way they live is directly dependent on what came before; one student explained that he found history interesting because "I'm always curious, and history just answers zillions of questions, like 'How did we get here?'" Similarly, Rebecca finds that her unit on immigration helps students understand their place within a nation of immigrants, and to see how they are fundamentally like other Americans. That's not always obvious to them: in a culture that rarely celebrates diversity, students may think of themselves as falling short of the American ideal. Moreover, they are often ready to assert their place in society by denying a similar place to others; Rebecca notes that students at her school often pick up on the general prejudice toward immigrants and refer to other students with pejorative racial terms—names they themselves may have been called only a few years earlier. In a basically intolerant culture, students cannot be expected spontaneously to understand the personal and political effects of such prejudice. She finds, however, that after

History explains, "How did we get here?"

Family histories can give students a sense of their place in the broader society.

studying immigration and comparing the experiences of people throughout history, students are much more likely to understand how they and their classmates are alike. History provides them with an expanded perspective on their place—and the place of others—in American society.

FAMILY HISTORY IN THE CONTEXT OF DIVERSITY

Students are given the choice of collecting information from people other than family members.

Most of our recommendations on diversity in chapter 4 apply here as well; in general, it is important to keep in mind that the point of family histories is for students to learn historical content in a meaningful way, not to put themselves or their families on display. Tina, for example, allows students to interview anyone about the same age as their grandparents if they prefer. Similarly, Rebecca simply requires students to interview an immigrant; although most choose their parents, some interview other relatives or neighbors instead. Just as importantly, both teachers approach these assignments with an acceptance of, and respect for, diversity. During their discussion of what constitutes a "generation," for example, Tina's students become very interested in learning exactly how they're related to people in their families; many are just starting to see what makes someone an uncle, cousin, and the like. This discussion invariably turns to questions of biological and step relations—what they are, how to refer to them, and so on. Tina emphasizes that the existence of a variety of families is completely normal; she explains that there have always been plenty of people who don't live with their two biological parents, but that in the past people sometimes regarded that as something to be ashamed of. The "family history chart" she uses (see Fig. 5.2) is a good example of this approach: rather than taking the form of a traditional lineage chart, in which each person has two and only two parents, it divides families into generations—thus allowing students to include only one parent if they want, or two or three or four. Because Tina models respect for the diversity of family relations that characterize our society, her students feel free to discuss their own families without fear of shame or ridicule. Of course, some children still don't want to share such topics openly, and she doesn't require them to.

Teachers who respect the diversity of family experiences do not see differences as deficiencies.

Family history charts can allow for nontraditional family structures.

Our Generation	Parents' Generation	Grandparents' Generation
Name: _____ Date of Birth: _____ Place of Birth: _____ Married: _____	Name: _____ Date of Birth: _____ Place of Birth: _____ Married: _____	Name: _____ Date of Birth: _____ Place of Birth: _____ Married: _____
Name: _____ Date of Birth: _____ Place of Birth: _____ Married:	Name: _____ Date of Birth: _____ Place of Birth: _____ Married:	Name: _____ Date of Birth: _____ Place of Birth: _____ Married:
Name: _____ Date of Birth: _____ Place of Birth: _____ Married: _____	Name: _____ Date of Birth: _____ Place of Birth: _____ Married: _____	Name: _____ Date of Birth: _____ Place of Birth: _____ Married: _____
Name: _____ Date of Birth: _____ Place of Birth: _____ Married: _____	Name: _____ Date of Birth: _____ Place of Birth: _____ Married: _____	Name: _____ Date of Birth: _____ Place of Birth: _____ Married: _____

FIG. 5.2. Family history chart.

Rebecca models a similar respect for her students' family backgrounds. About half of her students' families are undocumented aliens, yet Rebecca makes no distinction between their experiences and those of families who have official sanction for their immigration. Certainly no student is made to feel ashamed of his or her family's background, and as a result they openly discuss and write about their experience hiding under a blanket in the back of a car, using a friend's passport, running across *the line*, or paying a *coyote* $300 only to be caught anyway. As in Tina's class, though, no student is required to share such personal details.

Unfortunately, not everyone is so accepting of diversity. Rebecca taught the unit described here in the months immediately preceding the passage of a state-wide referendum that, if implemented, would deny all government services to undocumented immigrants. The climate of anti-immigrant feeling made some students hesitant to complete the assignment; the one student whose family were not recent immigrants was forbidden by his mother to interview an immigrant—she was afraid her son would "get into trouble." More importantly, Rebecca will never be able to teach this unit in the same way again: the referendum would require teachers to report any undocumented immigrants (so that they can expelled from school) or have their credentials revoked. Rather than face such an intolerable choice, Rebecca will have to avoid any situation that might provide information on how her students came to the United States. Although she will still be able to teach about immigration—by bringing in guest speakers who have immigrated from a variety of countries, and having students interview them in class—she will no longer be able to use family histories in the same way.

Political realities sometimes force teachers to modify assignments.

EXTENSIONS

Because migration is such an important theme in history, there are many possibilities for extending the topic. In addition to studying voluntary migrations to the United States, for example, students could examine migrations that have been coerced; obvious examples in our own past include the trade in African slaves, the Japanese American internment during World War II, and the Trail of Tears. Students could also study migrations that have been means of escape, such as the Underground Railroad in the United States or the movement of political and economic refugees here and throughout the world.

Students study forced migration and the movement of refugees.

Students might also compare the experiences not only of Irish, Chinese, and contemporary immigrants (as they did in Rebecca's class), but of immigrants from Germany, Japan, Italy, Russia, Poland, or any number of other countries. (See the literature list at the end of this chapter.) Such investigations can provide a meaningful connection to local history; students near Cincinnati could examine the violence and discrimination faced by people of German ancestry during World War I; students in California could learn about the extradition of Mexican Americans during the Depression or prejudice against Japanese and Chinese workers in the 19th century; those in the South could study the forced removal of African Americans in their communities in the early part of this century.

Focusing on important themes in history makes the study of state and local history more meaningful.

These are only a few examples; the power of family histories lies in the way they can be adapted to local circumstances. Most students are required to study their state's history at some point (often in fourth grade), but unfortunately the topic usually amounts to little more than temporarily memorizing the names of early political leaders or other "heroes." (And from other perspectives—such as Native Americans'—these leaders are often anything but heroes.) Moreover, the study of state history generally reinforces the misconception that history is synonymous with progress, that the past has been marked by consensus and increasing prosperity. Rarely does state history acquaint students with the conflicts that have had a lasting impact on them. The topic would be much more vital, interesting, and meaningful if it focused on topics—such as immigration and its consequences—that actually help explain the present.

State and local history should include the conflicts that have influenced the present.

43

Similarly, a topic like *communities* in third grade will be more meaningful than learning about "Anytown, U.S.A." if it involves students in investigations of migration in their own communities. Not every community is fortunate enough to have as high a proportion of recent immigrants as Rebecca's, but people everywhere move. Students could collect information on the moves they, their parents, and their grandparents have made in their lifetimes and use the data to answer a variety of questions—Have most people lived in one place all their lives? Have more people moved from one county to another, one state to another, or one country to another? Why have people moved? Students can then post requests on the Internet (or contact pen pals through the mail) to collect similar information on the movement of people in other communities. Rather than an exercise on how to find the post office on a generic map, the study of community could help students develop an understanding of how communities are similar and different throughout the United States. (For a more detailed description of community study, see chapters 8 and 10.)

Community study should include attention to the historical development of specific communities.

Using family members to learn about history, as Tina's students did, also has unlimited possibilities for extensions. Although her students focused on aspects of everyday life and rarely made connections to larger political or economic issues, teachers in the middle grades can help students learn about national and world events through the experiences of their relatives—who often prove to be amazingly rich resources. One eighth grader in a class studying changing patterns of work in the 20th century, for example, had assumed her family would have little insight into the topic. To her surprise, they knew a great deal: her grandfather still had his union card from the International Tobacco Workers Union, and her great-grandfather's union card was in the family Bible; her grandmother had left the farm during World War II to work in a chemical factory; and a great aunt had saved pro- and anti-union pamphlets from the 1940s in her scrapbook. The personal insights of relatives and the further research they inspired led to a level of involvement that no textbook could have stimulated. Similarly, in one class students did research for a "desegregation timeline" that compared significant events nationally to those in their own school and community; information on the latter came primarily from their interviews with local residents.

Family histories can link students to national and world events.

The experience of families provides motivation for learning about modern history.

Collecting this kind of information can also help students understand more completely the evidentiary and interpretive nature of history. We noted in the last chapter that when children ask their parents questions, they quickly see that people disagree on the past. Students investigating truly significant issues will encounter even more fundamental disagreements. Those in the middle grades, then, could compare the perspectives of family members on Vietnam, the Civil Rights Movement, or changing roles for women, and contrast these to accounts found in textbooks or the media. When students see historical interpretations on television or in movies, they may either uncritically accept or uncritically reject what they see—but when they have a chance to compare these interpretations to those of family members, they gain a better understanding of just how complicated history is. Students come away not only knowing more history but coming closer to understanding how history is interpreted and presented.

Family disagreements help students see history as controversial and historical representations as interpretive.

Students in the middle grades can also use their families to learn about historical evidence other than oral histories. Several eighth graders, for example, extensively documented their families' involvement in World War II with draft notices, transfer orders, newspaper clippings, gasoline rationing forms, and factory identification badges. By combining these with the interviews they conducted, they put together a wide-ranging collection of historical evidence. Other students in the class used report cards, school yearbooks, and newspaper clippings to create histories of their parents' school careers. In both cases, students learned about the variety of sources on which historical accounts can be based.

Families may have a wealth of historical source material.

Of course, as with any topic involving families, teachers must provide choices. Rather than expecting that every family will have experience with a war, unions, or any other single topic, teachers must recognize that each family's experience will differ.

Some students may be able to investigate their relatives' involvement in the political events found in textbooks, but many others will benefit from looking at other topics more closely related to social history. The point of involving family members is not simply to provide some gimmick by which students learn more about textbook content, but for them to understand how history is written and interpreted in order to learn how the past has produced the present.

Families have different historical experiences.

CONCLUSIONS

At first glance, history appears to be more remote from students' experiences than subjects like language, math, and science. Although even young children are familiar with talking, counting, and nature, the world of the past seems inherently more abstract and distant; some educators have even argued that the subject is so far removed from children's experiences that they are not ready to study history until high school! Family histories, however, help students make concrete connections to topics that would be less accessible if they were introduced only through readings in a textbook. By learning about their families' experiences moving or the way their grandparents lived when they were children, students both build on the mental schemas they already have and begin to move outward to people further removed in time and place. Tina points to this as one of the most important benefits of the activities described in this chapter: "Students start to get interested in something other than themselves, other than their friends, their clothes, their bubble gum."

Focusing on families is also tremendously motivating for students and parents alike. Tina's students were excited about getting to interview their grandparents and to tell their stories in class; as one girl pointed out, "I learned things that my grandma did that I didn't know. You know what you have now, but you don't know what they had before." In Rebecca's room as well, students shared countless artifacts from their families' backgrounds, and parents sent in photograph after photograph for students to include in their presentations and papers. Successful schools recognize the importance of students' families and try to make them feel comfortable at school; family history projects take this recognition one step further by making family experiences a part of instruction. As Rhoda Coleman points out, "Parents love it, they love the interaction between the school and home. For once, this 10-year-old is asking them about their lives. Their child is asking them, 'Tell me about yourself.'"

CHILDREN'S AND ADOLESCENT LITERATURE

Family History

Belton, S. (1994). *May'naise Sandwiches & Sunshine Tea*. Four Winds.
Cross, V. (1992). *Great-Grandma Tells of Threshing Day*. Whitman.
Flournoy, V. (1985). *The Patchwork Quilt*. Dial Books for Young Readers.
Greenfield, E., & Little, L. J. (1993). *Childtimes: A Three-Generation Memoir*. HarperCollins.
Howard, E. F. (1991). *Aunt Flossie's Hats (and Crab Cakes later)*. Clarion.
Igus, T. (1992). *When I was Little*. Just Us Books.
Johnson, A. (1989). *Tell Me a Story, Mama*. Franklin Watts.
Lasky, K. (1986). *Night Journey*. Viking.
Levoy, M. (1984). *The Hanukkah of Great-Uncle Otto*. Jewish Publication Society of America.
McDonald, M. (1991). *The Potato Man*. Orchard Books.
MacLachlan, P. (1991). *Three Names*. HarperCollins.
Radowsky, C. (1992). *Jenny and the Grand Old Great-Aunts*. Bradbury Press.
Stevenson, J. (1992). *Don't You Know There's a War On?* Greenwillow Books.
Stolz, M. (1991). *Go Fish*. HarperCollins.
Weber, J. E. (1994). *Melting Pots: Family Stories and Recipes*. Silver Moon.

Migration to the United States

Anastos, P. & French, C. (1991). *Illegal: Seeking the American Dream*. Rizzoli.

Anzaldna, G. (1993). *Friends from the Other Side/Amigos del otro lado*. Children's Book Press.

Ashabranner, B. (1991). *An Ancient Heritage: The Arab-American Minority*. Harper Collins.

Ashabranner, B. (1993). *Still a Nation of Immigrants*. Dutton.

Atkinson, M. (1979). *María Teresa*. Lollipop Power.

Bartone, E. (1993). *Peppe the Lamplighter*. Lothrop, Lee, and Shephard.

Beatty, P. (1981). *Lupita Mañana*. William Morrow and Company.

Bode, J. (1989). *New Kids on the Block: Oral Histories of Immigrant Teens*. Franklin Watts.

Breckler, R. K. (1992). *Hoang Breaks the Lucky Teapot*. Houghton Mifflin.

Bresnick-Perry, R. (1992). *Leaving for America*. Children's Book Press.

Brown, T. (1986). *Hello Amigos*. Holt.

Brown, T. (1991). *Lee Ann: The Story of a Vietnamese-American Girl*. G. P. Putnam's Sons.

Bunting, E. (1994). *A Day's Work*. Clarion.

Cazet, D. (1993). *Born in the Gravy*. Orchard.

Chetin, H. (1982). *Angel Island Prisoner, 1922*. New Seed Press.

Coerr, E. (1988). *Chang's Paper Pony*. Harper.

Cohen, B. (1994). *Make a Wish, Molly*. Doubleday.

Choi, S. N. (1993). *Halmoni and the Picnic*. Houghton Mifflin.

Crew, L. (1989). *Children of the River*. Delacorte.

Fisher, L. E. (1975). (1975). *Across the Sea from Galway*. Four Winds Press.

Fisher, L. E. (1986). *Ellis Island: Gateway to the New World*. Holiday House.

Freedman, R. (1980). *Immigrant Kids*. Scholastic.

Garrigue, S. (1985). *The Eternal Spring of Mr. Ito*. Bradbury Press.

Graff, N. P. (1993). *Where the River Runs*. Little Brown.

Harik, E. M. (1988). *The Lebanese in America*. Lerner.

Harvey, B. (1987). *Immigrant Girl: Becky of Eldridge Street*. Holiday House.

Hesse, K. (1992). *Letters from Rifka*. Henry Holt.

Howlett, B. (1993). *I'm New Here*. Houghton Mifflin.

Hoyt-Goldsmith, D. (1992). *Hoang Anh: A Vietnamese-American Boy*. Holiday House.

Katz, W. L. (1993). *The Great Migrations, 1880s-1912*. SteckVaughn.

Kidd, D. (1991). *Onion Tears*. Orchard.

Knight, M. B. (1993). *Who Belongs Here? An American Story*. Tilbury House.

Kraus, J. H. (1992). *Tall Boy's Journey*. Carolrhoda Books.

Kuklin, S. (1992). *How My Family Lives in America*. Bradbury Press.

Lech, J. (1991). *My Grandmother's Journey*. Bradbury.

Leighton, M. R. (1992). *An Ellis Island Christmas*. Viking.

Levin, E. (1993). *If Your Name was Changed at Ellis Island*. Scholastic.

Levine, E. (1989). *I Hate English!* Scholastic.

Levinson, R. (1993). *Soon, Annala*. Orchard Books.

Levinson, R. (1985). *Watch the Stars Come Out*. Dutton.

Levitin, S. (1989). *Silver Days*. Atheneum.

Lim, G. (1982). *Wings for Lai Ho*. East West Publishing Company.

Meltzer, M. (1980). *The Chinese-Americans*. Crowell.

Meltzer, M. (1982). *The Hispanic-Americans*. Crowell.

Mohr, N. (1979). *Felita*. Dial.

Moscinski, S. (1995). *Tracing our Jewish Roots*. John Muir Publications.

Moss, M. (1994). *In America*. Dutton.

Murphy, E., & Driscoll, T. (1974). *An Album of the Irish Americans*. Franklin Watts.

Naff, A. (1989). *The Arab Americans*. Chelsea House.

Namioka, L. (1992). *Yang the Youngest and His Terrible Ear*. Little, Brown.

O'Connor, K. (1992). *Dan Thuy's New Life in America*. Lerner.

Paek, M. (1988). *Aekyung's Dream*. Children's Book Press.

Polacco, P. (1988). *The Keeping Quilt*. Simon and Schuster.

Poynter, M. (1992). *The Uncertain Journey: Stories of Illegal Aliens in El Norte*. Atheneum.

Rosenberg, M. B. (1986). *Making a New Home in America*. Lothrop, Lee, and Shepard.

Sagan, M. (1993). *Tracing Our Jewish Roots*. John Muir Publications.

Sandler, M. W. (1995). *Immigrants*. HarperCollins.

Say, A. (1993). *Grandfather's Journey*. Houghton Mifflin.

Shefelman, J. (1992). *A Peddler's Dream*. Houghton Mifflin.

Siegel, B. (1985). *Sam Ellis's Island*. Four Winds Press.

Stanek, M. (1989). *I Speak English For My Mom*. Albert Whitman.

Surat, M. M. (1989). *Angel Child, Dragon Child*. Scholastic.

Temple, F. (1993). *Grab Hands and Run*. Orchard.

Waters, K. & Slovenz-Low, M. (1991). *Lion Dancer: Ernie Wan's Chinese New Year*. Scholastic.

Yee, P. (1991). *Roses Sing on New Snow: A Delicious Tale*. Macmillan.

Yee, P. (1989). *Tales from Gold Mountain: Stories of the Chinese in the New World*. Macmillan.

Yep, L. (1975). *DragonWings*. Harper.

Forced Migration, Refugees, and the Underground Railroad

Barboza, S. (1994). *Door of No Return*. Cobblehill.

Bealer, A. W. (1972). *Only the Names Remain: The Cherokees and the Trail of Tears*. Little, Brown.

Beatty, P. (1992). *Who Comes with Cannons?* Morrow.

Bergman, T. (1991). *Along the Tracks.* Houghton Mifflin.

Bial, R. (1995). *The Underground Railroad.* Houghton Mifflin.

Fritz, J. (1988). *China's Long March: 6000 Miles of Anger.* Putnam's.

Haskins, J. (1993). *Get on Board: The Story of the Underground Railroad.* Scholastic.

Hopkinson, D. (1993). *Sweet Clara and the Freedom Quilt.* Knopf.

Johnson, D. (1994). *Seminole Diary: Remembrances of a Slave.* Macmillan.

Kushner, A. (1986). *Falasha No More: An Ethiopian Jewish Child Comes Home.* Shopolsky.

Levine, E. (1992). *If You Traveled on the Underground Railroad.* Scholastic.

Lois, R. (1994). *Steal Away Home.* Macmillan.

Rappaport, D. (1991). *Escape from Slavery: Five Journeys to Freedom.* HarperCollins.

Wilkes, S. (1994). *One Day We Had to Run! Refugee Children Tell Their Stories in Words and Paintings.* Millbrook Press.

I think Columbus went to hell!

Chapter 6
Initiating Inquiry into World History

> Name: _____
> Please help your child with this interview.
> Person interviewed _____ **GUS** _____
> How does someone become famous?
> *They do something special for a person.*
> Who do you think is a famous American? Why?
> *President Clinton. Because he's the president*
> *& he does a lot of things that are famous.*
> Can I become famous?
> *Yes*
> How do you know when you are famous?
> *Because the people you talk to when*
> *you're famous tell you so.*
> Once you are famous, do you stay famous?
> *Sometimes, but if you don't want to you don't*
> *have to stay famous anymore but usually you do.*

Oral history is accessible even to the youngest students.

K. Young (1994), Crook (1988)

Twenty-two kindergarten and first graders excitedly share their homework assignment. They had interviewed family members, neighbors, and friends. Some of them wrote their responses independently; others had an adult help them. They were trying to find out how people became famous. Some of their interviewees thought fame came when you were rich, when you did "something real cool," "headturning," "something out of the ordinary." Their list of famous Americans included President Clinton, Michael Jackson, Miss America, Shaquille O'Neal, Jimmy Carter, Abraham Lincoln, and Daniel Boone. Staying famous was, their survey helped them conclude, not a certainty. "Sometimes," Minna Gayle declared, "you can really blow it."

Even young children can deal with historical controversies.

Sosniak & Stodolsky (1993), Thornberg & Brophy (1992)

Emergent readers can conduct disciplined inquiry.

See chapter 1, Fig. 1.1, "themes and questions" for more on the source of

In classrooms across America, children study famous people. Rarely, however, do they consider *how* these or any other people became famous, or what "fame" really means. Teachers sometimes fear that young children will be unable to deal with the controversies that surround some historic figures or events. Others worry that young children are not ready to study people from more distant times and places. LeeAnn Fitzpatrick shared these concerns, and also worried that her students, a number of whom were nonreaders, might have difficulty with disciplined inquiry. With some hesitation, then, she decided to test this approach with her students, but to do it in ways that would provide many links between the familiar and unfamiliar.

Initially, LeeAnn planned to introduce a number of people whose values, beliefs, ideas, or explorations had influenced or changed America. She decided to start with famous people, because fame would be a familiar concept for most of her students.

Starting with something this familiar, she thought, provided a framework for understanding more distant people and events. As she began planning, however, it became apparent that a study of multiple individuals was too complex for her first attempt at disciplined inquiry with young children. There were not enough sources at the right levels of difficulty and the available sources did not represent the diversity of people that she had hoped for. Finally, juggling that many individual studies seemed unmanageable. LeeAnn began searching for a single individual on whom to focus.

Be sure to select manageable topics. (see also Pappas et. al., 1995)

At about this time, the local news began covering a series of protests surrounding the upcoming Columbus Day celebrations. Here was a famous person who had definitely influenced or changed America, and one with whom the children were probably somewhat familiar. It was certainly easy enough to generate interest—in fact, all LeeAnn had to do was bring in one newspaper article and a cartoon pointing out that some Native Americans saw Columbus as a villain, while some Italian American groups viewed him as a hero. The controversy about Columbus was authentic—real, important, and public—well enough known to generate conversation and different viewpoints that were accessible to children, *and* there were an abundance of resources at appropriate levels. Columbus seemed an excellent beginning point both for thinking about whether fame and heroism were synonymous and for considering the differences between "good" fame and "bad" fame. That there was local controversy provided another familiar, current connection that could help students make sense of Columbus and the time in which he lived.

Controversy generates interest and challenges existing schema.

Newmann et al. (1995), Trout (1982)

In the wake of Columbus' explorations, culture contact between people from the Americas, Europe, and Africa altered the continents on which they met and from which they came. LeeAnn thought that studying Columbus might provide an opportunity to introduce history from this more global perspective. Such a perspective is important for two reasons. First, it helps students make better sense out of world history; second, a traditional history curriculum too often presents American history as almost entirely unrelated to the rest of the world. In an international survey, historians complained that American history had become too "insular and inward-looking, not international or comparative enough." We would argue that this is generally true of the way in which national histories are presented. There seems to be a general ethnocentrism that presents history as if each country existed in a historical and geographic vacuum, rather than in an intricate web of world influences. Many of the teachers in this book actively work to alter this approach. Remember in chapter 3, Jeannette Groth made explicit the connections between independence movements in India and the American colonies. She began with India, and then linked events there to more familiar American history. LeeAnn Fitzpatrick began with a current event—the controversy over a U.S. holiday—and moved from there to connect with roots in American, European, and African history. These connections do not happen by chance. Rather, they require that teachers:

Local issues can link students to global issues.

Anderson (1990)

A global context helps make sense of national history.

Thelen (1995)

Making global connections requires teacher facilitation.

- Make explicit the connections between local and global events
- Scaffold students' understanding of more distant times and places through the use of a variety of symbolic forms—pictures, maps, charts, fiction, nonfiction, mathematics, and writing.
- Make explicit the connections between past events that are history and current events that are making history.

Anderson (1990), Levstik (1995), National Council for the Social Studies (1994)

START LOCALLY; CONNECT GLOBALLY

Christopher Columbus

christopher columbus rode on a sail boat called the Santa Maria. He was standing on the ship when a wave splashed over the boat. The ship sinked and he swam to land. He gave the indians fake jewelry and they gave him real gold. He took the indians back with him to Spain across the ocean to the castel.

The king and queen gave him money to make other trips. He brought food like corn, potatoes, beans and tobacco. He also brought back gold. He was famous

—Donte Morgan, age 6

Blyth, (1989,) Downey & Levstik (1991)

World history can make "human sense" even to young children.

Barton (1994b, 1995)

Traditionally, there has been little emphasis on world history with young children. To some extent, this is related to the problem of ethnocentrism mentioned earlier. More generally, however, the lack of attention to world history can be attributed to theories that assume that young children can learn best those things directly experienced and closest in time and place. As we mentioned earlier, recent research on human cognition suggests that these assumptions are not well grounded; understanding is not so much a matter of physical proximity as it is the degree to which children can make human sense out of whatever history they are studying. Certainly Donte, in his story, makes interesting human sense out of Columbus' interactions with Native Americans. As were several of his peers, Donte was convinced that Columbus violated basic rules of fairness—he traded fake jewelry for real gold and he took human beings away from their families just to show them to the king and queen. The class had acted out this part of their study, with LeeAnn declaring that she was going to need "sample school children" to take home with her because her neighbors didn't understand what she did all day. She asked the children how they would feel if she just decided to keep a couple of them. They couldn't go back home, they would have to be put on display for other people to watch, and maybe they could not understand any of the languages or customs of this new place. This was an issue that made clear human sense to the children. It made no difference that the setting was distant in time and place; people should never be souvenirs, nor taken unwillingly from their homes. Columbus had committed a historic wrong. As 5-year-old James declared, "I think Columbus went to hell!"

But even before the children found out that Columbus had, in their view, behaved unfairly, their study was grounded in a familiar concept: fame. First, of course, the survey asked children to find out how other people in their environment viewed fame. These questions generated interest and discussion at home as well as in the classroom. Students compared their own responses to survey questions with those they received when they conducted the interviews, and discussed the differences. Why, for instance, did so many men mention athletes, women name politicians, and children mention singers and actors? And no one had mentioned Christopher Columbus, despite all the newspaper coverage! Did that mean he wasn't famous? Or, maybe he just wasn't very important? The discussion lasted a good 30 minutes, and when LeeAnn suggested that perhaps they could study more about Columbus and answer these questions, the students were enthusiastic. At this point, she introduced a set of questions that encouraged children to consider how a voyage that began in Spain over 500 years ago touched their lives today:

Linking experience, discussion, and substantive questions leads to student inquiry.

> Why do we celebrate Columbus Day?
> Is Christopher Columbus famous?
> Would we be here today in America if there had never been a Christopher Columbus?
> What do you think it was like living 500 years ago?
> How did people travel in those days?
> What would a person need in those days to travel across such a large body of water?
> How long ago was October 12, 1492?
> How long did it take Columbus to make his voyage to America?

START GLOBALLY; CONNECT LOCALLY

So far, we have looked at introducing global connections by beginning with a familiar concept—fame—and a local controversy—celebrating Columbus Day. While this is an effective technique, it is not the only way to make explicit the connections between local and global events. Consider, for instance, Walt Keet's seventh graders' study of South Africa and the transition from apartheid to a coalition government led by

Nelson Mandela. As had LeeAnn Fitzpatrick, Walt had a topic that was current as well as deeply rooted in historic issues of colonialism and human rights. In addition, the history of South Africa is connected to U.S. history both by foreign policy issues and our own struggles with race and segregation. Walt wanted to make connections between his seventh graders in the present day American South, and the struggles of South Africans half way around the world. There were obvious links, from colonialism and *de facto* and *de jure* segregation, to civil war and civil rights, but Walt wanted his students to start with the human sense of apartheid. He began by arranging with his team teachers for a block of time in which to show the film *Cry, Freedom*. This movie, set in South Africa in the 1960s tells the story of anti-apartheid activist Steven Biko and the newspaper publisher who befriended him and who, from exile, wrote about Biko's life and murder at the hands of the South African government. Anticipating that some parents might object to the film because of the violence of some of the scenes, Walt also prepared a list of alternative readings for those students unable to view the film. *Journey to Jo'burg* and its sequel, *Chain of Fire*, were both short enough to be completed in a week, and both dealt with the issues of separation of families because of restrictive housing and homeland laws (see literature list at end of chapter). In addition, the novels were written from the perspective of Black South Africans, while the film was presented from the White editor's perspective.

The film and books generated interesting responses from Walt's students: "How could people *still* let these things happen?" "Why didn't the Blacks just leave?" "Why didn't somebody go over there and stop them?" These students were too young to remember similar forms of legal segregation in their own country. While they were well aware that race was an often divisive issue—there were racial tensions in the wake of a shooting in their own community—most were sure that the Civil War had ended legal discrimination in the United States. With this in mind, Walt showed excerpts from several documentaries dealing with race and civil rights in 20th-century America. "Now," Walt said, "I have a question for you. One of the issues that faces Nelson Mandela and the new South Africa is what to do about the past—about a difficult and often horrible part of history. Mandela's African National Congress has suggested establishing a 'truth commission' somewhat like the Nuremberg Trials we have already studied. deKlerk's Nationalist Party argues that this will lead to revenge rather than reform. They suggest drawing a 'veil across the past'—do not hold a truth commission, do not tell the story of apartheid. People in South Africa also look to the rest of the world to see how we have handled this sort of issue. After all, this is a human, not just South African, problem. What advice would you give to the people of South Africa? Should they learn the history of apartheid, or not?"

This is not a made-for-school question. Nor is it a question with a single, clear answer. Instead, it is a *real* question, actually being asked by South Africans, that touches on the political and social uses of history. By grappling with this as a central concern of their study, Walt hoped his students would come to better understand why history is controversial, and why it is important. While this question is clearly researchable and has real world applications, its controversial nature and the kind of resources necessary for the research, make teacher mediation—scaffolding— absolutely essential.

SCAFFOLDING INQUIRY
INTO DISTANT TIMES AND PLACES

Young children generally haven't the slightest idea what "research" means, and for older students, as most of us remember all too well, research often means poorly disguised plagiarism, and suffocatingly boring reports. It takes specific kinds of scaffolding to support student inquiry; the kind depends, in part, on the age and experience of the learners, but also on the questions asked and the kind of resources

McGinnis (n.d.)

Older students also need to make human sense of historical controversies.

Boner (1995), Cuthbertson (1995)

Naidoo (1986, 1989)

Films and books can initiate inquiry and represent multiple perspectives.

Real questions are worth investigating.

Newmann et al. (1995), Wells & Chang-Wells (1992)

Pappas et al. (1995)

Particular aspects of scaffolding are necessary for in-
depth inquiry.

used. In general, you should consider the following elements of scaffolding as necessary
to disciplined inquiry:

- Building a set of common experiences.
- Building in challenges to prior knowledge that provide models of multiple perspectives
  on and interpretations of data
- Providing specific, in class, help in selecting, collecting, and organizing data
- Providing specific help with how to report to real audiences

Building Common Experiences

LeeAnn Fitzpatrick and Walt Keet were careful to determine what relevant knowledge
students already had and to establish a set of common experiences for their classes.
While children come to school knowing all sorts of historical information, you cannot
rely on their having either sufficient prior knowledge or much enthusiasm for any
particular topic. Before students can or will conduct inquiry, teachers must generate
interest in history, and help students establish a working knowledge base. It is this
continually growing knowledge base from which questions are generated and against
which answers can be tested. Both LeeAnn and Walt used discussion to "prime the
pump." LeeAnn used a KWL procedure (Know, Want to know, Learned). She began
by asking students what they already knew about why there was a Columbus Day. As
the children talked, she recorded their comments on chart paper under the heading
"Know." Later, questions to investigate were recorded on chart paper under the
heading "Want to Know," and the concluding discussion of the study was recorded
under the heading "Learned." As a result, there was a public, running record of student
conversation to which everyone could refer.

Walt, on the other hand, assumed that the movie would generate considerable
discussion. Concerned that everyone would not participate in a whole class free for
all, he broke the class into response groups of three to five participants each. Each
group was to discuss three questions: What most surprised you about the movie (or
book)? Why do you think this movie (or book) was distributed outside South Africa?
What issues in this movie or book do you think the class should discuss further? Next,
the class moved into a circle so that everyone could see the other participants. Because
Walt had several male students who tended to dominate conversations, he used a
more formal model for full class discussion, passing a "talking stick" (a wooden baton)
from speaker to speaker. While students could opt not to speak when it was their turn,
everyone was required to make at least one substantive comment during a discussion.
He also limited comments to 3 minutes each, and forbade interruption, often holding
up his hand for silence to give students time to think before responding. In conducting
class discussion in this way, Walt found that the male students did not monopolize
the conversation, and several female students who rarely commented in general
discussion were more likely to talk when their turn came.

Both LeeAnn's and Walt's approaches to classroom discussion helped establish
what students already knew and got them thinking about the topic at hand. Making
explicit the local connections also helped each teacher capture student attention.
Following these initial discussions, each teacher set up a series of experiences to
provide students with enough background knowledge to shape and motivate inquiry.
With the younger children, for instance, the concept of fame needed a working
definition. By having the children conduct their surveys, LeeAnn modeled one way
to gather and display data, but she also made clear that people could have different
ideas about the same concept. She laid the groundwork for students to feel comfortable about developing their own interpretation of Columbus, and for their peers to
expect that people might have different points of view. From the very beginning of
the unit, then, the students were helped to see that different people had very different
ideas about what constituted fame. Walt, on the other hand, went about things a bit
differently. Rather than define the concept of apartheid for the students, he decided
to let them see what apartheid looked like and felt like to South Africans. The movie

*Harste & Short (1988), Hepler
(1991), Jorgensen (1993),
Ogle (1986), Reardon
(1988)*

Response groups help organize discussion.

*Sadker & Sadker (1994), Stre-
itmatter (1994)*

Discussion helps establish
what prior knowledge is
available to students.

Teachers model data gathering.

Atwell (1987)

Multiple data sources provide
richer background infor-
mation.

and novels captured the emotional weight of a concept with which students would have to grapple, graphically portrayed the clash of ideologies and emotions, and established the background for the organizing question about the place of history in the new South Africa.

LeeAnn also used film, but she chose an old filmstrip without sound or narration. She explained that "the terminology in a lot of the material on Columbus is too hard for an early primary student to understand. If you paraphrase the plot, though, the pictures make a good introduction to the study." The filmstrip provided visual images of the time and place, and some of the people involved in the Columbian-Native American encounter. Now students had information against which they could test new ideas as well as some understanding that different people might have different ideas. In addition, LeeAnn was able to introduce common terminology—names of countries and their leaders and terms such as *cargo, voyage, exploration, encounter,* and *exchange* that would appear throughout the study. As new words were discussed, they were written on large pieces of chart paper so that the children would be able to use them in their writing and editing. Children also selected several of these words for their individual weekly spelling assignment.

Introductory activities such as these are particularly important when children have relatively little prior knowledge about a topic, which is often the case with world history. These activities establish a common vocabulary and generate discussion. But baseline data is meant to be built on, not preserved untouched. It serves as an intellectual seed bed in which new ideas are planted, transplanted, fertilized or weeded out—and in which what might at first have seemed a weed may turn out to be a flower, or the reverse. At its best, reflective, disciplined inquiry both builds and challenges what students think they know about history. It is essential, then, that new information be presented as a beginning, not an end point, and that teachers carefully scaffold the ways in which what is "known" is held up to challenge.

Challenge the Known: Multiple Perspectives and Changing Interpretations

All of us think we know some history, especially about our own country. We recognize, of course, that we could always learn more, but we don't usually look for proof of those things we think we already know. It is troubling, then, when what we *thought we knew* is challenged. Sometimes we reject the challenge—the new information is wrong! Sometimes we want proof—what evidence is there for this challenge? And sometimes we seek out more information—what did I miss before? Challenges to what we thought we knew happen all the time in history. Sometimes they come as the result of new information. More often they come because we are suddenly asked to look at something from a different historical perspective. Think about the controversy over the names of sports teams, for instance—the Braves or Redskins—and the symbols that accompany them—stereotypical images of Native Americans, hatchets and the like. Or consider how you might interpret the battle at Little Big Horn.

Little Big Horn Battlefield National Monument is a historic site and museum in Montana. You may remember it as the site of "Custer's Last Stand." From 1876 until 1976 that was the way the site was interpreted—Custer and the Seventh Cavalry made a last, desperate stand against the Indians who threatened settlement in the American west. The visitor center at the site was located close to where Custer died, and visitors viewed the battlefield from the perspective of the cavalry. Few visitors went to the site of the Indian village, or were introduced to Native American views of the battle. Beginning in the 1960s, however, the U.S. Park Service began to change its interpretation. What happened? Well, Native American protests and changing ideas about a more inclusive history made people "see" Little Big Horn differently. This new view challenged old ideas so that Little Big Horn became less massacre and more battle, less triumphant march of civilization westward, and more conflict of cultures. The information had been there all along, but its *meaning* changed dramati-

Downs (1993), Gardner (1991)

Attention to vocabulary building is important in enriching students' historical schema.

Temple, Nathan, Temple, & Burris (1993)

Developing baseline data is crucial to supporting student inquiry.

Newmann et al. (1995)

History is always "in progress."

Appleby et al. (1994), Novick (1988), Todorov (1982)

Linenthal (1994), Welch (1994)

Reinterpretations often challenge old assumptions and stereotypes.

Holt (1990a)

Facts may not change; what they mean often does.

53

cally. Much the same thing has happened with the history of the first encounters between Native Americans and Europeans, as well as between Black South Africans and Europeans.

As you can see, challenging the "known" is not just cognitively sound instruction, it is also an authentic disciplinary model for *doing* history. As we have already noted, children's schemas develop through generating questions and testing hypotheses. The same is true of historians; without challenges to existing schema there would be nothing for them to do. If the story of Little Big Horn were finished in 1876, there would be no need for rethinking how the site is interpreted, or for current historians to attempt to reconcile conflicting accounts to create a richer, more authentic interpretation. But the story is *not* finished, nor can it ever be; even if there were not conflicting accounts of *what happened*, historians would continue to reinterpret *why* it happened. Sometimes this interpretive restructuring involves minor tinkering—enriching but not significantly altering current schema. Other times, it generates major restructuring of schema, as when we stop telling the story of Columbus "discovering" a new world, and start talking about culture contact, exchange, and conflict. Children's and historians' mental models of the past are constantly restructured, not just by learning more historical information, but by regularly reflecting on what that information means, on what other points of view are possible, and on what light new historical knowledge throws on current events.

Levstik & Pappas (1993), Linenthal (1995), C. Young (1994)

Levstik & Barton (1996)

Mental models of the past are constantly restructured.

Both LeeAnn Fitzpatrick and Walt Keet wanted their students to reflect on how point of view influences historical interpretation and leads to controversy. Each approached the problem in different ways. LeeAnn decided that one way to help her students understand the controversy surrounding Columbus Day was to introduce them to different versions of the Columbus story. LeeAnn selected three picture books and she, a teacher aide, and student teacher divided the class so that each of the three groups listened to a different book about Columbus. In the class discussion that followed, the students recorded information on a comparison chart. As you can see by reading Table 6.1, there were several places where the books did not agree, or where one book gave information that another did not.

Walt was working with older students, so he began by presenting them with the African National Congress (ANC) and Nationalist positions, and then asking them to go backward in time to uncover the roots of dissension. In order to better help his students recognize the powerful emotions and perspectives behind the historic events, he used a graphic organizer (Fig. 6.1). This symbolic representation of perspectives helped students think about what points of view needed to be researched in order to

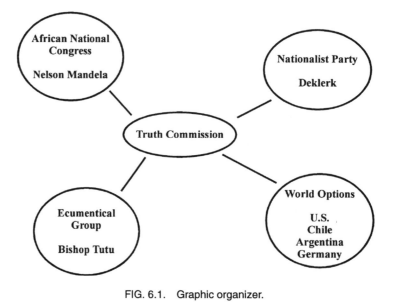

FIG. 6.1. Graphic organizer.

Table 6.1

Book Comparisons

Book Title and Author	Why did Columbus go on the Ocean Voyage?	What did People Think the World was Like?	What happened to the People who Already Lived in America?	What did Columbus Accomplish?
Where do You Think You're Going, Christopher Columbus? by Jean Fritz	Short route to the Indies (Japan & China)	Agreed that the earth was "round like a ball"	Traded beads and bells for gold and parrots.	Proved the sea was big.
	Wanted gold	Disagreed about how big the earth was.	Indians were friendly	Did not find Japan or China
	Wanted to make people Christians	Thought that there was gold, jewels, and spices in the Indies	Took 6 back to Spain on first trip	Did not know he was lost.
			Took 500 to sell as slaves	Found some gold
			Killed Indians for gold	Famous in Spain
				Named islands
Christopher Columbus by Ann McGovern	Wanted to reach "the east" by going west	Most people thought the earth was flat.	Traded glass beads	He was a hero in Spain
	Wanted gold for Spain	A few people thought the earth was round	Indians were "gentle and friendly"	He did not know he was lost
			Took 10 back to Spain on first trip	He did not want to find a new world
The Columbus Story by Alice Dalgliesh	Wanted gold for Spain	Far away was the "Sea of Darkness"	Indians thought Columbus came from heaven	He said all the land belonged to Spain
			Traded bells, beads, and caps for gold	He crossed the sea first
			Indians were "gentle and friendly"	
			Took "some" Indians back to Spain	

understand the dilemma faced by the new coalition government. It also served as a way of organizing inquiry groups. One group was assigned to each of the South African perspectives represented on the graph. A slightly larger group was assigned to provide a world perspective, with pairs of students given the task of investigating how the United States, Chile, and Argentina handled the issues of human rights violations and the national memory of these events. The class had already studied the aftermath of World War II and the Nuremberg Trials, so they had some historical precedent on which to base their current study. Chile and Argentina's history provided more recent examples of countries faced with major political changes following massive human rights violations, while a U.S. comparison encouraged students to think about what their own country faced in the aftermath of Civil War and in the midst of ongoing concerns over civil rights.

Selecting, Collecting and Organizing Data

Freeman & Person (1992), Hyde & Bizar (1989) Pappas et al. (1995), Wells (1994)

Both LeeAnn and Walt provided a variety of resources for their students to use, either in the classroom or in the school library. Each assumed different degrees of independence for student work. Both selected appropriate ways of helping students be successful as researchers, given the age and experience of their students. LeeAnn's first problem was that none of her students had previously been involved in disciplined inquiry. A number of her students were not yet independent readers. She decided not to focus on the selection of resources at this point; rather, she organized activities that would help the children select information from sources she selected, then organize that information, and communicate it in ways that would be usable by their peers. In addition, her use of an integrated curriculum model led her to look for ways of incorporating other content areas such as mathematics into her instruction. She divided the class into five groups, based in part on what tasks seemed within reach for each group:

Group 1: A Global Perspective. LeeAnn provided a large blank map of the world, globes, and flat maps. Students referred to the comparison charts they had already developed, used the globes and flat maps to answer the following four questions, then transferred information to the blank map. Their map was then hung up in the classroom as a reference for further discussion. Questions included locating the following on a world map:

1. The countries the kings lived in who turned Columbus down when he asked for financial assistance (England, France, Portugal).
2. The country that gave Columbus the money to finance the voyage (Spain).
3. The countries that Columbus wanted to travel to (India, China, the East Indies, and Japan).
4. The route Columbus followed to get to the Americas.

Group 2: Life in a Small Place. LeeAnn provided a large cross-section drawing of a ship, string, rulers, and the like. After measuring the size of Columbus' ship and cutting string to the appropriate length (90 feet), the children used books, illustrations, and the comparison chart they had worked on earlier to identify cargo (food, firewood, water, wine, clothes, ropes, sails). They then drew the cargo that they thought Columbus would need on the cross section of the ship (see Fig. 6.2). Later, LeeAnn marked out an outline of the ship on the playground, so the children could try to fit into the ship. Children were asked to think about what it was like living on the ships, with so many people, in such a small space, for such a long time.

Group 3: Seeds of Change. The task for this group was to find out what kinds of new plants were found in the Americas with which Europeans were unfamiliar. Again, LeeAnn provided appropriate books, along with a chart where the children categorized the plants as fruits, vegetables, and nonedible plants. Children drew pictures of the plants in each category, and then labeled their illustrations (see Fig. 6.3).

Group 4: Counting the Days. Groups 4 and 5 had some of the youngest children, for whom the concept of *time* needed considerable support and visual reinforcement. The task for Group

Comparative world history helps develop historical perspective.

Organize historical inquiry so that all students can be challenged as well as successful.

4 was to make a timeline showing how long Columbus' voyage lasted. The group took calendars from August until October, cut them apart, and put them on a time line, marked off the number of weeks, and then counted the days of the trip.

Group 5: How Long is a Century? This group also developed a visual representation of time, but their task was to make a time line showing how many hundreds of years separated 1492 and the present. They marked time in 100-year increments by first grouping unifix cubes in 10s, then placing markers after 19 groups of 10 to indicate a 100-year period. As the time

FIG. 6.2.

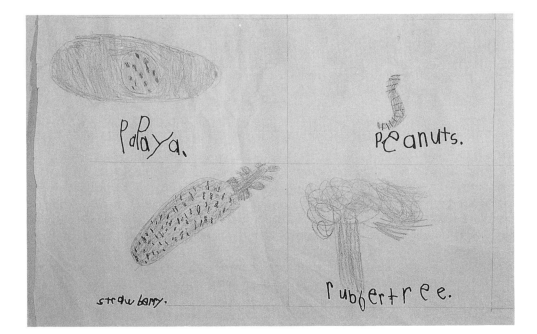

FIG. 6.3.   A world of New Plants

line grew, it snaked down the hall and provided an impressive visualization of just how long a span of time separated the children from Columbus.

Students need specific help in researching controversial topics.

Carlisle (1995), Dickinson (1993), McGinnis (n.d.), Shemilt (1987)

Walt's problem was somewhat different. His students had some experience with "looking it up"—selecting sources, notetaking, citing sources appropriately and the like—but less with researching a controversial topic. In particular, they had difficulty with moving beyond simply reporting opinion—"What do you mean, where's the support? Its just his opinion!"—to trying to uncover the cultural and historical roots of opinions. Walt decided to try several techniques for helping students to think about these historic sources of current perspectives:

Pappas et al. (1995)

Source Packets. Because he wanted students to learn to use some sources that were new to them—demographic data, newspapers, magazines, cartoons, videotapes—Walt put together sets of primary and secondary source material and background information on South Africa, Chile, and Argentina. Each packet contained demographic charts (age, ethnicity, education, etc.), photocopies of newspaper and magazine articles, photographs, and novels. He was able to obtain videotapes of some events in South Africa, footage of Juan and Evita Peron in Argentina, and photographs of the aftermath of the collapse of Chilean democracy. For each item, he attached a short set of guide questions that helped students use and critique the source.

Atwell (1987)

Journals help organize research.

Double Entry Journals. As each group began using the source packets to gather data on the point of view they were researching, Walt asked them to keep a double entry journal. At the top of each entry, students listed the source for the information. In the first column, they listed a position or argument, along with supporting data. Opposite that position, in the second column, students made notes on what they thought the counter arguments might be. So, for instance, the student citing deKlerk's position that a truth commission would lead to revenge and a possible coup, noted in the first column that some people were already calling for public trials of the notorious state police, and that military leaders had threatened to overturn the coalition government if that happened. In the second column, he speculated that Mandela and the ANC might not be able to maintain their standing with people who had been victims of the state police if past atrocities were swept under the carpet. Using this technique, Walt hoped to help the students think about what support they would need to make their position more clear and/or compelling. "After all," he reminded his students, "people organized governments, arrested and executed other people, went into exile, and sacrificed their lives for these beliefs."

Journals help students support positions.

Boner (1995), Cuthbertson (1995)

Charting Key People and Events. Walt also asked students to record significant names in the graphic organizer categories as a way of keeping track of people representing the different perspectives. Other students could then note where they might look for opposing viewpoints. A class time line also helped students organize information chronologically, and made it easier to think about cause and effect relationships.

In order to help students connect individual pieces of information to the larger framework of South African history, Walt also provided regular whole group experiences. He invited a guest speaker to talk about the new coalition government. He also required that each student select and read one novel set in South Africa (see literature list), conducted small group discussions of the novels, and had students read background material on the colonization of South Africa, the Boer War, and the origins of apartheid. During one class, he provided political and resource maps of South Africa and led a discussion of regional differences in the country. Students were expected to draw on their research as they participated in the discussions.

It is crucial to conduct research in class rather than as homework.

It is important to note that while some assignments in each class were done outside of class—conducting surveys or reading books—most of the research was conducted in class. This is an equity issue as much as it is an opportunity to teach students specific research skills. Conducting research in class means that students with fewer resources to draw on at home are not at a disadvantage. In addition, it does not place the instructional burden for teaching students *how* to research on the home. Finally, conducting research in the classroom allows the teacher to help students think about appropriate forms for communicating what they are learning with different audiences.

Reporting Out: Who's the Audience?

As communities of inquiry such as those developing in Walt's and LeeAnn's classrooms grow, they need to develop strategies for sharing and assessing work. Students who have done substantial inquiry require more than a final grade to bring their study to closure; they need an opportunity to make public sense out of what they have learned. "Going public" means students organize what they have learned during their investigations in order to present their findings to others. You will recognize the importance of this part of inquiry when you think about how much you learn when you teach a subject, as opposed to when you were simply studying it for a test. As you will recall from Tina's experience in chapter 4, students often have difficulty sorting out what is important about their studies and then organizing that information for particular audiences. Such "presentational talk" takes practice and substantial support from the teacher. Because LeeAnn's students had little experience in presentational talk, she incorporated a number of small in-class presentations where students were able to use the different graphic organizers their groups had used. Thus, two groups referred to charts, the map provided a focus for a third group, and the time lines were used by the last two groups. After each group explained what they had learned, LeeAnn opened the discussion up for questions and comments from peers. In a follow-up discussion, she also helped students further synthesize the results of their studies across groups. "Now that we have seen all the group projects," she said, "let's go back to our comparison chart and see if we still have conflicting information." In discussion, then, students noted where information from different sources agreed or disagreed. They found that some sources still claimed that Columbus' voyage proved the earth was round; other sources differed on whether Queen Isabella really sold her jewelry to finance Columbus' voyage, and not all the sources mentioned taking Native Americans back to Europe.

With plenty of discussion and debate as foregrounding, LeeAnn then drew the students back to their first questions: Was Christopher Columbus famous, and if he was, why was he famous? "Now each of you will have a chance to be a historian and answer the questions we've asked," she told them, asking them, too, if they remembered how historians told people about the past. Students gave several suggestions—books, movies, speeches—and finally decided to write books about Columbus. "Remember that historians can have different ideas about the past, but they have to use the facts," LeeAnn explained. "Historians also think about who might read their books, and explain things so their readers will understand them. Who might read our books?" Students decided that, since their parents and friends had helped them do the original survey, they might be interested in reading what the students had learned. The class decided to share their books with parents at a special "Christopher Columbus Presentation" at the end of October. With an audience in mind, a written genre—biography—selected, and the results of their study displayed throughout the classroom, the students were ready to write. During writers' workshop, a time set aside each day for student writing, editing, and publishing, those children who were independent writers began biographies of Christopher Columbus that would answer the question, "Was Columbus a hero?" Other students dictated their stories to an adult. Over about a 2-week period, children wrote, conferenced with an adult or peer, edited, illustrated, and then published their books. As editor-in-chief, LeeAnn made one suggestion about medium (mechanics) and one about message (content) components of each child's story prior to publication. At the Columbus presentation, children shared their biographies, presented their projects, and discussed what they had learned, including:

"Books on the same subject can give you different information."

Presentational talk takes practice.

Short & Armstrong (1993)

Questions can refocus inquiry.

Historians have to use facts.

Students can select appropriate historical genres.

Atwell (1987), Flack (1992), Graves (1983), Jorgensen (1993)

Pappas et al. (1995)

"Different maps can use different colors to tell you things. Oceans are usually blue, but could be brown, and Italy can be yellow or pink."

"We learned where France, Portugal, Spain, England, Italy, India, China, and Japan are. Also Africa, the Atlantic Ocean, the Pacific Ocean, Indian Ocean, and the Mediterranean Sea. And the United States and the Caribbean Islands."

"You need to take many of the same supplies on an ocean voyage today as you did 500 years ago."

"We learned that living today is more convenient compared to Columbus."

"Different countries grow different kinds of foods."

"It is easier to count to 500 if you count by 10s until you get to 100."

"Columbus did not treat the Indians fairly, so why was he considered a hero and named 'Admiral of the Ocean Sea?' He was famous."

Not every inquiry requires an outside audience in quite the way that LeeAnn arranged for her class. In Walt's case, his students tended to prefer peer audiences, and he wanted to focus on how individuals can take action on public issues. In addition, his state's assessment system required performance assessment, and Walt knew students needed individual, assessable products for their social studies portfolios. As a result, he organized "reporting out" at three different levels:

Roundtable Negotiations. Walt held a class training session on consensus building as students completed their research into the different positions regarding a South African "truth commission." He then selected one student arbitrator, and one student representing each of the different points of view on the issue for each roundtable. Arbitrators were to keep negotiations on track and serve as time keepers. Once all students had been assigned to a roundtable, they were given the remainder of the class period to lay out the major arguments for each position. During the next class session, negotiations began. Students were to see if they could reach some consensus in their groups regarding the establishment and functioning of a truth commission. As a homework assignment, students were asked to write a brief statement outlining their understanding of their group's results. What points of agreement were there? Of disagreement? In the next class, positions were again diagrammed on the board, and areas of agreement and disagreement discussed.

Letter Writing. Following the roundtable negotiations, students were asked to consider what action they could take as a result of their inquiry. Now that they had opinions, what purpose did those opinions serve? At first there was dead silence in the room. Finally, one student suggested writing to "Congress or someone" to offer suggestions. Walt began a list of places where their opinions might be registered: letters to the local paper, to news magazines, to Congressional delegates, Nelson Mandela, and Desmond Tutu. Each roundtable group selected one of these options, and wrote a letter offering their opinions and suggestions, along with supporting data.

Position Papers. Finally, Walt asked students to step back from their studies, and reflect on how their own ideas had changed from the beginning of the study. He asked them to look over their research notes and dialogue journals, and to think about what their study of South Africa told them about the kind of history people needed to learn. After a brief discussion, Walt passed out two articles, one criticizing school history for dwelling on problems such as the Ku Klux Klan, the other complaining that school history too often ignored problems in the past. "Now it's your turn to take a stand on this issue in your own country," he explained. "Use what you have learned about South Africa to help you respond to the critics in these two articles. What should American students know about the problems in our past?" In the criteria for this task, Walt emphasized that the quality of support for each position was the basis for assessment rather than the particular position a student might take.

Notice that both LeeAnn and Walt shuttle between the local and the global, trying to make connections between what happens in other parts of the world and what happens in children's historical backyard. LeeAnn asks children to consider whether we should celebrate Columbus Day; Walt asks them if what they think is good for

Assessment can match both state requirements and an inquiry perspective.

McGinnis (n.d.)

National Council for the Social Studies (1994)

Encourage students to use what they have learned in authentic ways.

Newmann et al. (1995)

South Africa is equally appropriate in the United States. There are many other ways of connecting children to more distant times and places that also relate the unfamiliar to the familiar. One way is through inviting international guests or travelers to the classroom. First graders in Ruby Yessin's class, for instance, studied Scotland and England because their teacher arranged for an adult who was traveling to both countries to send postcards to the class, and then to visit the class after the trip. The guest brought artifacts representing both current and historical England and Scotland: coins, a brass rubbing kit, a police officer's hat, directions for building a Viking settlement. Children enjoyed trying out the artifacts, figuring out the money, and discussing the symbology used in brass rubbings. In addition, they became fascinated with illustrated written resources, discussing the age of some of the buildings pictured in these materials:

Levstik (1994)

Darren: Some of those are real new, they just make them look like real castles.

Guest: Well, we do that in this country, don't we. The one you're looking at is pretty new. It's only 150 years old.

Catrina: 150 years! That's old!

Mitchell: The Vikings are older than that.

Teacher: How long ago were the Vikings? Does anyone remember?
No one can recall. They think it was "long, long ago, back when they had those ships."

This conversation led to more interest in Vikings, as students tried writing in Viking script, and constructing models of a Viking village. They also spent the larger part of an hour asking about details in a set of slides of a Viking excavation in York. They calculated how long ago the village was lived in, and talked about how the Vikings were European explorers like Columbus. They discussed the way in which Vikings used animal skins, antlers, and so forth. One child even turned in all his work with his name in Norse.

By starting with a person they knew (the guest) and artifacts from the places they had seen in postcards, the students' interest was captured. As they formed and reformed temporary interest groups, they sought out more information, and were especially attentive to the information slides and books could provide. The guest helped establish a personal connection between students and the places they were studying so that England and Scotland became knowable places—it was possible for someone with whom they were familiar to go there; perhaps it was possible for them as well.

Interest groups are generally temporary configurations.

Walt Keet, you will recall, also made use of an international guest. He invited a South African university student to discuss the results of the roundtable negotiations with his class. Once again, the guest's presence made South Africa more real, and further personalized the issues under study in the classroom. The guest, after all, had seen first hand the transition from apartheid to a more inclusive democracy, and also knew enough about the United States to help students see some of the differences and similarities. This is one of the advantages of developing a more global perspective in history. Studying other countries is, of course, interesting in its own right, but it also allows us to look with new eyes at our own culture.

Wilson (1983)

This approach is not without its problems. Encouraging cross-cultural inquiry challenges traditional interpretations and brings enduring myths into question. Other teachers may object to this approach. New interpretations may be thought to threaten national pride. Some parents, too, may find it disconcerting to learn from their 5-year-olds that Columbus did not discover America, or that Europeans did not treat Native Americans well, while others may not want explicit comparisons made between U.S. racial problems and those in other parts of the world. Teachers cannot ignore these potential problems, but you can plan ahead so that you respond intelli-

K. Young (1994)

gently to challenges. Present controversial issues in as balanced a way as possible, emphasizing what is supportable given the available evidence, and what is representative of current scholarship. Journals such as *Social Education, Social Studies and the Young Learner,* and *The Social Studies* provide help in making some of these judgments. In addition, documents such as the National Council for the Social Studies (NCSS) *Curriculum Standards for Social Studies: Expectations of Excellence* and the National History Standards provide support for the approaches described in this book, as well as help in deciding what constitutes a supportable interpretation. Kraus International Publications also produces a guide for Kindergarten through 12th grade social studies curriculum, *Social Studies: Curriculum Resource Handbook,* that provides further help in deciding on and defending the introduction of multiple perspectives in social studies (including history).

Finally, if you are presenting history as a process of interpretation, rather than as a single version of the "truth," you should be able to explain the grounds for that approach to concerned colleagues or parents. It often helps to explain that you are trying to help students develop supportable interpretations rather than requiring that they hold any single explanation to be the end product of historical thinking.

Most of the teachers with whom we work have found that when their students are excited and interested in historical study, most colleagues and parents are pleased and supportive. These teachers more often report that their most significant problem in challenging historical myths is the persistence of those myths in the larger culture. It is hard to challenge the myths surrounding Pocahontas, for instance, when they are enshrined in a popular animated film and reproduced in toys and commercial messages. The same is true for the persistence of the myth that Columbus proved the earth was round (that the earth was round was, of course, a piece of information known to just about all educated people of the period).

THE PERSISTENCE OF HISTORICAL MYTHS

Christopher Columbus discovered America Oct. 12, 1492. The pirates attacked him. His ship sank, but he had to leave others behind because there wasn't enough room on the other ships. The ship that sunk was called the Santa Maria. It was the best ship on the sea. Columbus survived and got on. He survived. All of Christopher's friends thought the world was flat. Christopher Columbus did not think so. His voyage proved he was right. It made him a hero.

—Steve, age 5 (dictated story)

In looking back on her first attempt at disciplined inquiry, LeeAnn noted that there were several aspects of her students' study that had surprised her. First of all, she was pleased with the level of the children's enthusiasm and the ways in which the different age groups in her class worked together on the project. "By working in small groups the children had to learn to work together. They had to locate their information by looking at pictures. The older children read what they could and shared their information with the nonreaders, so their project could be completed and understood. This developed a sense of pride and accomplishment by all children when the project was completed." But there were also problems. First, the project took more time than LeeAnn had anticipated. Her team teachers had moved on to other topics before her class had completed its study of Christopher Columbus. Second, it was very difficult for children who had been absent for more than a day or two to reenter the study. One child had been taken out of school for more than a week to go on a trip with his parents. While LeeAnn explained what the children would be working on, and the boy's parents agreed to help him learn about Columbus, he was not part of the class experience, and his final book showed his lack of engagement—there were only two lines of story, and they did not deal with the question of fame. Other parents were

---

Plan ahead to respond to concerns about controversial issues.

Kraus (1992), National Council for the Social Studies (1994), National History Standards Project (1994a, 1994b)

Know the grounds for your own curriculum choices.

When students are fully engaged and enthusiastic about their studies, parents often are, too.

In-depth inquiry takes time.

Blyth (1989), Newmann et al. (1995), Pappas et al. (1995)

quite excited about their children's work, and several commented that this was their child's best written effort of the year.

LeeAnn was also interested in the issues the children dwelt on in their books. Almost all the children noted that Columbus traded "fake jewels" for "real gold." More than half of them noted that Columbus took Indians back to Spain. On the other hand, LeeAnn was puzzled at the persistence of myths that she thought the class had clearly rejected in discussion. Despite having worked on developing comparison charts that pointed out discrepancies in accounts, several children, including Steve, wrote about Columbus "discovering" America and proving the earth was round.

Myths can persist despite in-depth inquiry.

Pappas et al. (1995)

The fact that some historical misconceptions persist really isn't surprising. As we mentioned earlier, school isn't the only place where children come in contact with history, and especially with historical figures who have become cultural icons. Think about all the images of Columbus that appear just before Columbus Day. There are Columbus Day sales, advertisements on local television that emphasize "discovery," and some that spoof Columbus' proving the world was round. In addition, some of the stories the children had read presented the myths as facts. Despite discussion to the contrary, some children focused on the more public parts of the story and missed the distinctions the teacher was trying to help them grapple with. While it would be nice if all students "got it" every time we taught, we know that isn't going to happen. Sometimes the myths persist because they are more appealing. As 6-year-old Jake wrote, "Columbus waze the bravest. The uthers thoet there were sea monsters and big waves but Columbus woz the bravist … Columbus was famous." There is something compelling in the story of braving sea monsters and proving others wrong. It is also a beginning point. These are, after all, 5- and 6-year-olds. They will meet Columbus again. It is important to remember that the development of historical thinking takes time and experience. While one experience with disciplined inquiry is certainly better than none, it is likely to take multiple experiences to counter prevailing myths. If students continue to encounter history as inquiry, they may alter their schema to account for different views of history. If, on the other hand, history is continually presented through myths and legends, early history schema may well remain intact.

CHILDREN'S AND ADOLESCENT LITERATURE

Different Perspectives on Columbus

Adler, D. (1991). *A Picture Book of Christopher Columbus*. Holiday House.
Ceserani, G. P. (1979) *Christopher Columbus*. Random.
Conrad, P. (1991). *Pedro's Journal*. Caroline House.
Fritz, J. (1980) *Where Do You Think You're Going Christopher Columbus?* G. P. Putnam's.
Jacobs, F. (1992) *The Tainos: The People Who Welcomed Columbus*. Putnam.
Levinson, N. (1990). *Christopher Columbus: Voyager to the Unknown*. Dutton, Lodestar.
Maestro, B., and Maestro, G. *The Discovery of the Americas*. Lothrop.
Meltzer, M. (1990). *Christopher Columbus and the World Around Him*. Watts.
Pelta, K. *Discovering Christopher Columbus: How History is Invented*. Lerner.
Roop, P., & Roop., C. (Eds.). (1990). *I, Columbus—My Journal*. Walker.
Weil, L. (1983) *I, Christopher Columbus*. Atheneum.
Yolen, J. (1992) *Encounter*. Harcourt.

Books on South Africa

Angelou, M. (1994). *My Painted House, My Friendly Chicken, and Me*.
Clarkson, *Beyond the Barricades: Popular Resistance in South Africa*. Aperture.
Biko, S. (1979). *I Write What I Like*. HarperCollins.
Gordon, S. (1990). *The Middle of Somewhere: A Story of South Africa*. Orchard.
Gordon, S.(1987). *Waiting for the Rain: A Novel of South Africa*. Orchard.
Harris, S. (1988). *South Africa: Timeline*. Dryad.
Mathabane, M. (1986). *"Kaffir Boy" The True Story of a Black Youth's Coming of Age in Apartheid South Africa*. Macmillan.

Meisel, J. D. (1994). *South Africa at the Crossroads.* Millbrook.

Naidoo, B. (1986). *Journey to Jo'burg: A South African Story.* Harper.

Naidoo, B. (1989). *Chain of Fire.* Lippincott.

Rochman, H. (Ed.). (1988). *Somehow Tenderness Survives: Stories of Southern Africa.* HarperCollins.

Sacks, M. (1990). *Beyond Safe Boundaries.* Dutton/Lodestar.

Stock, C. (1990). *Armien's Fishing Trip.* Morrow.

Williams, M.(1993). *Into the Valley.* Philomel.

Chapter 7
Creating a History Museum

After her fourth graders had completed family history projects, Amy Leigh introduced them to their next investigation—creating displays on how life has changed in the last 100 years. On the first day of the unit, she showed them an object she said was a common tool about a 100 years ago. Most students quickly identified it as a handheld drill, and several volunteered to demonstrate how it was used. After discussing how it differed from modern drills, the class gathered on the floor in front of Amy while she read *I Go with my Family to Grandma's*—which she explained was also set almost 100 years ago. Amy asked students to point out anything they found in the book that would be different today, and she kept track of their observations on a sheet of chart paper on the wall. After discussing the book, students worked in pairs with historical photographs to make further observations about change over the last century, and at the end of they day reported on these to their classmates and added new items to the chart.

Over the next several days, students examined physical artifacts, such as old watches, purses, tools, clothes, and appliances that Amy brought in to class. Guided by *Artifact Think Sheets*, they recorded ways these differed from similar objects today. After everyone had worked through all the objects, the class met together again to summarize what they had found and to develop a list of general categories of change—technology, clothes, transportation, and so on. Each student then chose two or three categories to find out more about. After several days of exploration with library resources—trade books, CD–ROMs, and encyclopedias—students chose partners and picked a single topic to investigate in more depth. Each group developed a set of specific questions they wanted to answer, and collected information using not only print and electronic resources but artifacts, interviews, and photographs. During the research phase of the project, Amy worked with each group to help them locate information and use it to prepare reports and displays. After collecting their information, students created exhibits for a history museum in their classroom. They explained their exhibits for other classes who toured their museum and for parents and grandparents during a final performance.

One of the most common suggestions for teaching social studies (at any level) is to have students "do research." Yet as we have noted, simply sending students off on their own to engage in that vague activity rarely results in anything positive or productive. Younger children are unlikely to have any idea what they are supposed to do, while older ones will do what nearly all of us did when we were in school—go to the library and copy something out of an encyclopedia. Obviously neither of those strategies helps students learn either about the past or about conducting inquiry. The students in Amy's classroom, on the other hand, learned both: they not only investigated how things have changed over time, but also learned to ask questions, collect information, draw conclusions, and present their findings.

Sometimes assignments are difficult, and students dislike doing them; other times, students enjoy themselves, but the activities are too easy for them really to learn very much. But teachers know they're on to something when students enjoy doing an assignment that does not come easily. The History Museum project in Amy's classroom is a perfect example of such an assignment: students immensely enjoyed it, *yet none of it came easily.* They spent approximately 1 month working on the activities just described, and nearly every minute of that time involved painstaking efforts by Amy to help students use resources to find information, reach conclusions based on their observations, and transform notes into reports and presentations. Having little or no

Teachers help students learn how to conduct inquiry.

previous experience with the process, students encountered numerous obstacles along the way; as a result, Amy could not *tell* them to do research, she had to *teach* them to. In this chapter, we show how she met the challenge of teaching students to ask and answer historical questions.

IMAGINATIVE ENTRY

Family histories lead to further historical investigations.

Getting students interested in the topic of change over time was the easiest part of Amy's job. Like Tina's students in chapter 5, Amy's students had completed family history projects in which they asked their grandparents how life had been different for them when they were children. As a result, the topic of change over time was fresh in their minds, and they could call on these experiences for specific examples to compare with the information they encountered at school. Moreover, changes in material culture are one of the historical topics students know the most about; in our interviews with children from kindergarten through sixth grade, for example, we have found that even the youngest know that clothes and transportation were different in the past, while older children have an even more complete inventory of generally accurate information about change over time. And during the project just described, students frequently pointed out having learned about different aspects of the topic outside of school—seeing an old shaving mug and brush in a local barbershop, for example, or having seen pictures of sod houses in a book. As we noted in chapter 3, instruction must begin with what students already know; thus Amy began with the details of everyday life—drills, shaving mugs, purses, and so on—rather than abstract topics like politics, economics, or society. (She did, however, eventually get to these topics; see, for example, chapter 11.)

Barton & Levstik (1996), Levstik & Barton (1996)

Instruction builds on students' experiences.

Visual images help students learn about the past.

Levinson (1992), Schroeder (1989), Cook (1965)

The visual aspect of history is also critical in helping students understand what the past was like—particularly any time period before they were born. Amy thus began the unit (as well as several other lessons throughout the unit) with books like *I Go with My Family to Grandma's*, *Ragtime Tumpie*, and *When Great-Grandmother was a Little Girl*. In most cases, she was concerned not with the language or thematic content of the books—*I Go with my Family to Grandma's* is written for young primary students and has only the most basic plot, for example—but with the information the pictures provided on historical changes. Of course, illustrations provide only indirect evidence of life in the past, and Amy called students' attention to aspects of the pictures that were vague or ambiguous, and asked how they differed from photographs.

Students can critically analyze visual images.

We cannot underestimate the importance of using visual images (particularly photographs) with children. The photographs were a very popular part of this unit, as students examined them with great interest and enthusiasm, and frequently called their friends over to look at particularly unusual or surprising details. They had no difficulty using the photos to develop a list of differences between 100 years ago and today, and they eagerly shared their findings with the rest of the class. (Amy used a set of photographs from Scholastic Book Service's *The American Experience* series, but similar sets are available through other publishers of social studies materials or on interactive videodisks. The advantage of using printed photos is that students can handle them, and several groups of students can use different pictures at the same time; the primary advantage of laser disks, on the other hand, is that they can store many thousands of pictures on a single disk, and each picture can easily be accessed with a barcode reader.)

Students respond enthusiastically to using pictures in history.

Just as important as photographs were the physical artifacts Amy brought in. The very sight of the old drill in the first lesson was exciting for students, and all of them made sure they touched it and played with it before the day was over. While working on their Artifact Think Sheets (Fig. 7.1), students constantly played with the objects—rubbing a shaving cream brush on their skin, flipping the handle of a cherry pitter back and forth, fidgeting with an old camera to see how it worked, using a cuff maker to create creases in paper (again and again and again). Because school tasks

Students enjoy physically manipulating historical artifacts.

often rely exclusively on written language, students' preoccupation with physical play can strike an observer as being "off task"; outside of school, though, no parent would expect students to sit still for hours on end. We agree with Dewey that children's behavior at school frequently appears in need of "management" precisely because they have so little chance to engage in their natural impulse toward activity. By encouraging them to handle and use the objects, Amy built on her students' inclinations rather than attempting to suppress them, and as a result they stayed interested in the objects for several days and developed clear ideas about how they could have been used. Of course, many teachers find themselves evaluated (implicitly or explicitly) on how quiet and physically inactive their students are, and they may need to be ready to explain why playing with a cuff-maker is more appropriate for an 8-year-old than writing quietly at all times. Fortunately, Amy's principal, Dan Kelly, encouraged—even expected—the kinds of hands–on lessons found in her classroom; he even walked in on the class one day during this project and joked, "Hey, there can't be any learning going on here—they're having too much fun!"

Dewey (1956)

Administrators can support and encourage active inquiry.

Amy's introduction to the History Museum project, then, demonstrated several principles that are fundamental to developing students' interest. First, she related the topic to what they already knew, both by focusing on aspects of everyday life and by connecting the topic to their previous family history projects. Rather than being an isolated, "cookie-cutter" plan, it flowed naturally from students' background knowledge and from the issues they had already begun to investigate during the year. Second, Amy made sure that students had a variety of means of entry into the topic, rather than relying solely on oral and written language; literature, photographs, and physical artifacts gave students a much more concrete understanding of life in the past, and helped stimulate their interest in the topic. Perhaps most importantly, this project had a significant element of authenticity. Outside of school, people really do take an interest in how things have changed over time: people save artifacts and photographs, and they tell their children and grandchildren how things were different in the past. Understanding historical change is a basic part of each person's life, and that understanding is often passed down through families. Students' excitement about extending these projects beyond school indicates just how much Amy had tapped into the meaning and purpose history has in our society: for several weeks, students rummaged through their homes and attics (and their grandparents') looking for their own artifacts to bring in and add to the "visual timeline" in the class. Their interest even motivated one girl to work with her parents to make a videotaped tour of the Victorian home she lived in, and another to help her grandmother photograph and catalogue the family's heirlooms. Even Amy's own grandparents were excited about explaining how to use the artifacts she brought in for students. When a project stimulates this kind of intergenerational communication, it clearly has a purpose beyond simply pleasing the teacher or getting a grade.

Historical inquiry stems from students' interests and experiences

Teachers provide a variety of means of entry to historical topics.

History is important to people in their everyday lives.

Authentic projects involve learning beyond school boundaries.

There are many artifacts from the past displayed throughout the room. Please write a paragraph for each of 5 artifacts. Your paragraphs should answer all of these questions:

---

a. Make up a name for this artifact that tells its purpose. You may write more than just the name if you'd like to better explain its function.

b. Explain what parts of the object gave you clues for its purpose.

c. Tell when you think the object was used (1800–1849, 1850–1899, 1900–1949, or 1950–NOW)

d. Name the object we now use instead of this artifact.

For each artifact you write about, please write the number of the artifact next to the paragraph you write. You only need 1 artifact think sheet completed per group.

FIG. 7.1. Artifact think sheet.

TURNING INTEREST INTO RESEARCHABLE QUESTIONS

On KWL charts, students record what they know, what they want to know, and what they have learned. *Ogle (1986)*

The first year Amy taught this unit, she proceeded directly from her introductory lesson to having students develop a list of questions they wanted to answer. At first glance, it seems that students who already know something about a topic and are interested and enthusiastic about learning more should have no problem sitting down and deciding what they want to learn. In fact, however, that task was tremendously difficult. Amy had students develop KWL charts on the topics they had chosen, and most encountered a roadblock when they got to the "want to know" section. Many simply stopped working, and apparently had no idea what to write. Others seemed to consider it a convenient time to sharpen their pencil collections or rearrange their desks, or they devoted their energy to making the physical layout of their charts as attractive as possible. Even with Amy's help and encouragement, most students weren't sure what it was that they wanted to know, and those who wrote anything at all confined themselves to very simple questions about dates—such as "When was the car invented?" "When did people stop wearing hoop shirts?" or "When did milk stop coming in bottles?" It seemed that most students didn't really understand the purpose of the questions; they were just eager to get to the library and start copying something down.

Students are not used to generating questions

When it became clear that students weren't getting much out of this question-developing activity, Amy called them back together as a whole class to give them more direction. She wrote the words *Where, What, Why, Who,* and *How* on the board, and told students they needed to come up with two questions beginning with each word; she then went on to model how to do that with the topic *schools*, a subject they had discussed in class but that no students had chosen to investigate in their projects. This was a kind of ad hoc solution to the problem, and it gave students enough structure to begin their research. It was clear, though, that students still failed fully to understand the role of questions in conducting research. Some, for example, tried to copy Amy's questions onto their own KWL charts by simply changing a few key words; when that didn't work, they protested that it couldn't be done, and were shocked when Amy explained that the questions would be different for each topic. Others didn't understand why they would come up with questions *before* doing the research, while one students asked incredulously, "Are we going to answer these questions *ourselves?*" With little prior experience in developing their own questions to investigate, the activity made little sense to students.

Teacher intervention helps students develop more meaningful questions.

The next year, Amy was much readier to help with this aspect of their investigation. As you can see in the description at the beginning of this chapter, she did not jump directly from sparking students' interest to expecting them to develop specific questions. Instead, she engaged them in examining artifacts for several days, and in the course of making their observations students found a number of things they wondered about—"How did they keep from getting the clothes dirty when they used this kind of iron?" "How did they keep it hot?" "Did everybody use this, or just rich people?" The experience of observing and discussing the artifacts gave students the chance to come up with specific questions they wanted to know more about, and to do so in a natural context. In addition, Amy gave students several days to explore library resources *before* asking them to specify either their topic or a list of questions. Although she had them narrow their interests to two or three (so their energy wouldn't be completely unfocused), she wanted them to have a chance just to play around with the available resources to find out what they wanted to ask. This turned out to be an enormously popular activity, as students excitedly scurried around the library, talking with Amy and each other about what they were learning. They were often very surprised at the differences they found; one group investigating changes in medicine, for example, was fascinated to find out that hospitals were not as sanitary in the past as they are now. They told anyone who would listen, "Did you know that 100 years ago, if you were in the hospital, you might wake up and see a *rat* in your room?! Today you'd probably wake up and just see a spider—*if* you're lucky."

Observation and discussion of historical artifacts leads to specific questions.

This time, there was no shortage of questions students wanted to investigate. When using science or math materials, students require exploration time before working with them in a more systematic or teacher-directed way—otherwise they'll still want to play with the objects when they're supposed to be using them for a more specific purpose. Similarly, students need time to explore at the beginning of historical investigations. By giving them several days to examine historical artifacts, and then several more days to explore library resources, Amy afforded students a much better chance than she had the year before to recognize what it was that they wanted to know. Once she asked them to come up with a list of questions they wanted to investigate, they didn't become stuck the way they had previously. And even during this exploration time, students were learning a great deal about history—not only information about the past, but also the process of making observations and drawing conclusions from historical sources.

That is not to say, however, that the process of developing questions required no further help from Amy. As they moved from exploration to specific questions, Amy called students together to find out what they wanted to learn in their research. As students suggested questions to investigate, Amy helped them rephrase them in such a way that they focused more clearly on "big ideas" (a concept she referred back to often) about changes over time. She asked for a sample question, for example, from students who were investigating the topic *houses*; they suggested, "What did they walk on, dirt, wooden floors, carpets?"—a question that by itself would have a fairly simple answer and would probably focus on only one time period. Amy responded, "So, 'How have floor coverings changed over the last 100 years?'"—a question that included what students wanted to know but considerably broadened it as well. After several similar examples, one member of a pair of students who had chosen *railroads* as their topic suggested, "What happened to James Watt?" (James Watt developed the steam engine.) Amy asked if he considered that a big question, and his partner said, "No, it would be, 'Why didn't trains run on electricity?' or 'Why did they stop making electric trains?'" Amy broadened it even further by suggesting, "How has the power used changed?" and pointed out that the information they wanted to include about James Watt would be part of their answer to that question.

People often think of education in terms of exclusive opposites: either students do what the teacher tells them, for example, or they do whatever they want. As discussed in chapter 2, we find both of those methods intellectually indefensible: purely from a cognitive standpoint, students are unlikely to learn anything very important from either method. The assistance Amy provided students in developing their questions, on the other hand, provides a clear example of *scaffolding*: she neither told them what to do nor uncritically accepted their first efforts. She knew that their projects had to grow out of their own interests and concerns, and she gave them several days to develop their ideas about what they wanted to do. But she also recognized that not all questions are equally significant: she knew that students would learn more from some questions than others, so she helped them rephrase their inquiries to address what they wanted to know within the context of bigger issues of change over time. In short, she helped them learn more than they would have solely on their own.

FINDING THE ANSWERS TO QUESTIONS

For all its pitfalls, helping students develop questions was a simple matter compared to helping them find the answers to those questions. One of the first challenges Amy faced was helping students locate the information that would be useful to them. At the simplest level, this just meant reviewing the kinds of sources they could use. Students immediately recognized encyclopedias as a major source of information, but Amy also emphasized that they could use trade books, CD-ROMs, and resources outside of school—relatives, other people in the community, and even videos. A more important task was helping students understand *how* to locate information in such resources. Many of them, for example, returned from their first foray into the library complaining, "There is *nothing* on it!" or "The encyclopedia doesn't have *anything* about how transportation has changed over time." The reason for students' frustration was quickly apparent: nearly all of them expected to find books or encyclopedia entries entitled *How transportation has changed over time* or *How floor coverings have changed over time*. When they found there weren't any, they concluded that no information existed on their topics.

Although students in the primary grades often are assigned dittos or workbook pages on "Using Reference Sources"—and assessed on that ability on standardized tests—such exercises are often poorly designed: students are shown a side view of a set of encyclopedias (or a sample table of contents from an almanac), and asked to identify the volume (or page numbers) where they would look to find information on *horses* or *volcanoes* or *frogs*. Unfortunately, such questions have almost no connection to the way people actually use encyclopedias or books; they certainly provide no assistance in helping students investigate how things have changed over time. As a result, much of Amy's effort was devoted to teaching them how *really* to use reference works.

In part, this meant working with the whole class and with groups of students to develop lists of words and phrases they might use in finding information. Knowing that one group was investigating *entertainment*, for example, Amy brought in a book called *What Did You do When You Were a Kid? Pastimes from the Past*. But students looked at the index and table of contents and—not finding the word *entertainment* in either—concluded the book had no relevant information. Somewhat surprised, Amy explained that the whole book was about entertainment—that pastimes are entertainment, and students would be able to find information on their topic by looking up other specific kinds of entertainment (movies, television, music, dance) rather than only looking for the word *entertainment* itself. Similarly, one group looked up *medicine* in the encyclopedia and found only information on present-day medicine. Amy suggested they look at the list of "related entries" at the end of that section; they saw that there was a separate entry under *medical care, history of*, and word spread like wildfire through the class that historical information could be found under similar headings. With each group, Amy had to provide assistance in developing possible alternatives to the main words they were looking for—helping the transportation group come up with *automobiles, railroads, ships, airplanes*, the fashion group come up with *clothing, jewelry, hairstyles*, and so on.

Once students had found relevant books or encyclopedia entries, Amy also had to help them use them efficiently. Most students started reading at the beginning and continued through a source word for word until they got bored (which was usually quickly). Amy thus had to show students how to look at section headings and tables of contents to find which parts of a source would be most likely to address their questions, and how to skim through those parts to find if they were indeed relevant. Although whole-class instruction on this skill seemed to make that idea clear to students in a general way, she still had to work extensively with individuals and pairs in order for them to be able to apply it to their own work. Particularly during the early stages of their research, Amy spent most of her time directing students' attention to this process of evaluating the usefulness of sources—looking together with a student at a source, for example, and asking questions like, "*Early hospitals*—does that sound like it would have information on how medicine has changed over time?" and "If you want to know if this has anything on railroads, what words are you going to look for when you skim through it?" Without this kind of explicit help in reading reference works, it is unlikely students would ever have gone very far with their research.

Interestingly, encyclopedias ultimately provided students with only minimal information. In the early stages of their research, many focused almost exclusively on encyclopedias, but most soon found that other works provided information in a more accessible form. In the end, most relied on juvenile trade books more heavily than anything else, and the kind of books they found most useful were very similar in form.

Students are not used to using reference sources to answer questions.

Students brainstorm words and phrases to use in locating information.

Sturner (1973)

Students learn to read selectively for information.

Students rejected any work that contained several pages of uninterrupted text (such as *Prairie Visions* or *Children of the Wild West*); no matter how much information a book might have contained, most students simply would not read through it to find what they needed to know. Nearly all students instead relied on books that contained profuse illustrations on each page and short captions to accompany them; the most commonly used such books were those in the *Eyewitness* series—such as *Car, Sports,* and *Costume*—although there are other series with similar formats. (See the book list at the end of this chapter.) The advantage of such books clearly lay both in their visual appeal and in the ease with which students could find the information they needed. As one girl remarked, "They get to the point better."

Conrad (1991), Freedman (1983)

Hammond (1988), Row-land–Warne (1992), Sutton (1990)

The most useful reference sources have rich visual information and short explanatory text.

People—relatives and other people in the community—also provided an important source of information. Some students decided from the beginning that they would interview people for their projects; one girl investigating changes in homes, for example, planned to talk to the interior designer who lived next door to her, and a boy whose project was on transportation knew the captain of a local steamboat. They had already interviewed relatives for their family history projects, and Amy reviewed with them how to plan out their questions for interviews. Because some of their questions were very specific, she also had to help them plan what they would do when people didn't know. One group, for example, planned to call a local bank to ask questions about old money; Amy asked them what they would do when the answer was, "I don't know." Most students, on the other hand, had not initially considered humans to be an important source of information on their topics (despite their family history projects!), but once they began planning their centers, they developed a renewed sense of interest in them. Most of them wanted to display objects—old clothes, appliances, money, and so on—and when they started collecting these from people, they learned new information that became important parts of their papers and presentations.

People serve as an important source of historical information.

REACHING CONCLUSIONS

A basic principal of conducting historical inquiry is that conclusions are based on evidence. Indeed, that simple proposition forms the intellectual foundation of the entire field of social studies—not to mention other disciplines—and even of democratic citizenship generally. In order for students to understand what it means to *know* something, they have to understand that knowledge is fundamentally different from either faith or simple blind opinion. History is not made up out of thin air, nor is it based on what we wish to believe or what has been revealed to us—it is based on evidence. Although different conclusions can in most cases be drawn from the same evidence, conclusions that are based on no evidence whatsoever have no place in history, social studies, or public debate. Basing conclusions on evidence, however, came no more easily for Amy's students than asking questions or collecting data.

Conclusions should be based on evidence.

One of the first challenges Amy faced was confronting students' belief that somewhere, in a single place, lay the answer to each of their questions, and their conviction that if they could only track down that source they could copy the answer and begin working on their displays. In this, Amy's students no doubt demonstrated the same understanding held by millions of schoolchildren who have developed their perspective from experiences answering questions at the end of textbook chapters. We all know that most such questions can be answered by finding the sentences in the chapter that provide the single and direct answer to them; in fact, most of us probably realized at some point that we could easily find the answers without every having read the chapter in the first place. Outside the topsy-turvy world of textbook information, though, few questions have such simple and direct answers. Significant historical questions—like those in Fig. 1.1 and those students developed in this project—require the synthesis of a number of pieces of information. The idea of collecting information from several different places and putting them together in their

Most important questions have no simple or direct answers.

own way, however, was not what students initially expected they would be doing, and it was some time before they realized that they would never stumble on simple answers to their questions, but that they would have to create those answers from the information they did find. (The influence of textbook assignments was also reflected in students' surprise when they found out they didn't have to answer their questions in any particular order.)

One way Amy addressed this problem was by having students keep a Venn diagram on their topic throughout their research. She began by demonstrating how to do this with the topic *schools:* she drew a diagram on the chalkboard, labeled one side "100 years ago" and the other "today," and asked students what kind of information might go in each space. As they conducted their research, students recorded new information on their own diagrams. These proved useful when they moved into creating displays and writing their reports; they had collected information from various sources, and the Venn diagrams allowed them to view the information together in one place. (One drawback to using Venn diagrams, on the other hand, was that they called attention only to the differences between two periods of time, rather than the actual process of change over the course of the last century.)

Because they weren't used to synthesizing information from different sources, Amy modeled how the diagrams could help them: using her diagram on *schools* again, she asked what conclusions they could reach—100 years ago children sat in desks at schools, and now we sit at tables; 100 years ago students dressed up for school, and now we dress casually; and so on. Following class discussion, she worked with each group to help them use their own Venn diagrams in this way, and she particularly focused on how they would express those changes over time—composing compound sentences and using words like *then, now, century,* and so on.

Perhaps the most surprising challenge Amy faced in helping students reach conclusions was getting them to see the connection between the research and their displays and reports. Students frequently came to Amy after 10 or 15 minutes of work and said, "We're finished." Because they weren't used to collecting the kind of information that would help them draw conclusions, they had little idea when they had enough and when they didn't. One group investigating *work,* for example, told Amy they had done all the research they needed to do. She looked over their list of questions and found that one of them was, "How has the way they make shoes changed?" In answer, they had written down the word "shoemaker," and they were now confident that they did not need to collect any further information on the topic. Amy asked if that told them what they needed to know to make their display or write their paper; they could tell by the tone of her voice that she didn't think it was enough, but they weren't sure what else was needed. She called their attention to the scoring guidelines for the project, particularly the section dealing with "use of details," and asked whether the word "shoemaker" gave them any details they would be able to use in their reports or presentation. They saw that it didn't, and Amy then gave them a way out of their dilemma—"Is this your research," she asked, "or just your brainstorming? I think this is just your brainstorming, and that you still need to do more research to find out the details that you'll use." Although they were still somewhat disappointed that they weren't ready to start working on their center yet, they at least saw that they needed more information to complete the assignment.

Similarly, when students finished their research and moved into the next phase of their projects, nearly all of them ignored the notes they had taken. They simply began working on their reports without making any reference to what they had learned while doing research. Students in a different group investigating changes in work, for example, discussed the topic among themselves and then wrote, "People who had good jobs would make a dollar a day, and people who didn't have good jobs would make like a penny a day"—a statement that was completely unconnected to what they had found; they just made it up in the course of their discussion. Nearly every group of students repeated the same process: they wrote about how things changed "because it was neater" or "because people just liked it better," making no reference

Venn diagrams provide a way of organizing information on similarities and differences.

Teachers model how to draw conclusions from evidence.

Students need help seeing how their information relates to their original questions.

Explicit scoring guidelines help students monitor their own achievement.

to what they had themselves discovered about changes. Again, Amy had to model for students how to use notes to draw conclusions and how to organize those in a report.

Our emphasis on the pitfalls Amy's class encountered may give the impression that this was a somewhat tedious or unexciting project, but nothing could be further from the truth. Students consistently stayed on task and made steady progress toward completing their work, and they were always ready to share with visitors and each other what they were finding out. The "feel" of the classroom was consistently open and relaxed, despite the many obstacles students faced in learning about the purpose and nature of inquiry. One reason students felt comfortable with this process was the emphasis Amy placed on making them responsible for their own learning. At the beginning of the project she distributed precise scoring guidelines, and she expected students to learn how to achieve the standards she had established. When their performance fell short—when for example, a student thought he had completed his research after having written the word "shoemaker"—Amy responded not by criticizing students or giving them bad grades, but by showing them how to improve their work so that it more closely matched the scoring guidelines. Throughout the project, she made it clear that they were in charge of their learning, and she was there to help them—thus each day she asked students at what stage of their project they were, what they were going to do next, and what their alternatives might be if they couldn't do the work they had planned. As we emphasized in chapter 2, students need to internalize the standards for achievement so that they know what they are trying to accomplish (and why), and Amy was largely successful in helping students make progress in that kind of metacognitive awareness. Near the end of the project, for example, she was reviewing paragraph structure with students, and asked what they should do if they found they didn't have enough details to support the main idea of a paragraph. "Do more research," students agreed—a concept that would have been completely alien to them just 2 weeks earlier.

Perhaps the most important reason students stayed interested and involved in the project, however, was that they knew their activities built toward their final performance—displays for their History Museum. These displays were clearly students' favorite part of their investigations, and they devoted careful attention to creating them—making sure they were visually appealing, easily understood, and full of interesting artifacts. And because they would be explaining their exhibits to other classes and to their parents and grandparents, they knew they had to understand their topics well enough to make these presentations and answer questions. Although teachers often ask students to *imagine* that they are writing or speaking for a particular audience (usually with mixed success), Amy's students really were preparing for an audience; rather than imagining that someone didn't know anything about their topic, they were preparing their explanations for primary students who really didn't know anything about them. The authenticity of their expectations led them to plan presentations in which they took clear account of their audience with hands-on demonstrations and questions like, "Do you know what these were used for?"

DEVELOPING AN UNDERSTANDING
OF TIME AND CHRONOLOGY

Traditional history instruction is sometimes stereotyped as the incessant memorizing of dates. By this point in the book, we hope it's clear that our way of thinking about the topic is very different. Yet it's hard to deny that understanding time is an integral part of understanding history. In some important ways, the relationship between time and history is similar to the relationship between spelling and writing. Spelling can hardly be considered as important to writing as purpose, voice, or organization, and few teachers would spend as much time on spelling as on meaning-centered components of composition; yet they also know that students' writing will be far more effective if they eventually learn how to spell. Similarly, the importance of time pales

Marginal notes:

Teachers model the use of notes to draw conclusions and organize reports.

Students take responsibility for their own learning.

Teachers help students take responsibility for planning and carrying out research.

Authentic activities and audiences help students maintain interest.

Learning history does not mean memorizing dates.

in comparison to issues like historical evidence, interpretation, agency, and significance, yet students' historical understanding will be more complete if they know when things happened. Just as spelling is a small but important part of writing, time is a small but important part of history.

One drawback to teaching students about time, however, is the temptation to confuse different aspects of the topic. Understanding historical time includes at least two separate components: being able to *order* moments in time (sometimes known as *chronology*), and being able to *match* moments in time to specific dates. Although these may at first seem simiilar, children actually are much more adept at the first. Our own research indicates that even children in kindergarten recognize that a picture of a covered wagon refers to a time longer ago than a picture with cars in it. Those in the primary grades can make even more complicated distinctions, and as they get older they become increasingly skilled at ordering historical pictures on the basis of clues in technology, fashion, and social roles. Children's chronological knowledge—their understanding of the order in which aspects of social and material life have changed—represents a very impressive area of prior knowledge that teachers can make use of.

But despite their knowledge of chronology, children's use of dates and other conventional markers of time—"the Depression," "the Colonial Era," and so on—is much less developed. Primary children know what dates sound like and usually know what the current year is, but they almost never associate periods in history with any particular years; they can put historical pictures in order, that is, but they don't match them with dates. By fourth grade, many children have begun to use some specific dates, most notably "the 1950s" and "the 1960s" (which generally refer interchangeably to the period ranging from poodle skirts to bell bottoms) and "the 1800s" (meaning a broad sweep of time including pioneers, the Civil War, and the Old West). By fifth and sixth grade, some (but not all) students can identify pictures from this century to within a decade, and match pictures from the 1700s and 1800s with the appropriate century; occasionally students at this age use terms like *the Victorian era*. These designations continue to be based mainly on clues in material and social life; even older students rarely know the dates of events such as wars or political developments.

Equating dates with an understanding of time, then, seriously underestimates students' abilities. Because younger children have so little knowledge of specific dates, and because even older ones do not readily identify the dates associated with events usually considered important in school, it's tempting to conclude that they don't understand time; such observations are sometimes used as justification for omitting history from the primary curriculum. In fact, however, most children have an extensive understanding of historical time—they just haven't learned specific dates yet. There are two important implications of these aspects of children's thinking.

First, dates and conventional time phrases (like "the Colonial Era") are unlikely to call forth any specific associations on the part of most students before fifth grade (nor for many after that point, either). Saying that something happened in "the 18th century" or "1920" or even "about 30 years" ago *doesn't mean anything* to most children, because those expressions don't match anything they can visualize. Early in the school year, for example, Amy happened to ask students if they thought there were televisions in 1980; most thought there were. She then asked if they thought televisions existed in 1970; the class was evenly split. Finally, she asked if there were any in 1960, and students were unanimous that nothing so modern could have been around so long ago. When students' knowledge of dates is as undeveloped as that, teachers cannot expect using dates will help students know when something happened.

Instead of assuming that learning a date helps students know when something happened, teachers have to approach dates as concepts to be developed: they have to help students associate their visual images of history with the dates that correspond to them. Although Amy's students didn't think there were televisions in 1960, they could easily place a photograph from the 1960s between those from the 1950s and the 1970s; one of her goals, then, was for students to learn to use dates that went with their images of different time periods. In part, this involved constantly calling students' attention to the dates associated with the topics they were studying and asking them when they thought various developments took place (see, for example, the Artifact Think Sheet in Fig. 7.1). Even more important was the use of a "visual timeline" on the wall of the classroom.

Timelines can be found in any history text and on the walls of many classrooms; we believe, however, that most timelines do little to develop students' understanding, because they provide no connection with prior knowledge. Timelines typically connect one thing students don't know much about—dates—with something else they don't know much about—wars and politics. The negative associations most people have with memorizing dates probably derive from just this shortcoming: neither the date nor the event that went with it had any meaning. In order for a timeline to be effective, it must build on students' prior knowledge—their visual understanding of changes in social and material life. In Amy's room, for example, two walls were taken up with a visual timeline; this consisted of signs marking the decades from 1895 to the present, with pictures placed at the appropriate points on the wall. As students brought in their own artifacts and photographs throughout the year, they added these to the timeline as well. Soon after she put up the timeline (and before she had even explained it to students), a striking phenomenon took place: whenever she mentioned a date, in any context, students' heads would swing toward the timeline—they were using it to *find out what the date meant*, to see for themselves how people dressed and what kind of machines they had in 1910 or 1940 or whatever. It was as though students were saying to themselves, "Oh, *that's* when 1940 was!" This visual timeline served precisely the purpose we're advocating here: it helped students match dates to what they already knew. Such timelines should be as indispensable to elementary classrooms as world maps or reading corners. If students are constantly exposed to the connection between dates and visual images, they will begin to develop an understanding of dates that will allow them to make sense of a statement like "World War II ended in 1945"—a statement that teachers may erroneously assume makes sense to students in the same way it does to them.

Students' prior knowledge of historical time has a second important implication: one of the principal purposes of instruction should be to help students further differentiate their categories of historical time—to break down broad periods like "close to now," "long ago," and "*really* long ago" into more finely detailed distinctions. Because students already have a basic understanding of some aspects of social and material life, these make a perfect starting point for instruction; the "History of Me" projects in this chapter are a clear example of one such attempt to use what students already know to develop a more complete and nuanced understanding of change over time. Developing students' understanding of time means, in part, helping them to distinguish between the antebellum period, the Civil War, and the Old West instead of lumping them all together into one broad category of "the 1800s."

One goal of such instruction should be to address a particularly common aspect of children's chronological thinking, their assumption of linear historical development. Children tend to assume, that is, that historical developments proceeded in a strict sequence—first one thing happened, then that period in history was over, and everything changed. They think, for example, that settlers came before cities, immigrants came before the first president, and so on; they fail to recognize that there were cities in some parts of the country at the same time people were settling on the frontier in other places, or that immigrants continued to arrive for hundreds of years after the American colonies were first settled by Europeans. (Even most adults probably think of the Dark Ages as a time characterized largely by ignorance and provincialism—ignoring the fact that there were flourishing centers of commerce and education outside of Europe at the same time.) Timelines (and the instruction that accompanies them) should be *comparative*, helping students to see what life was like for a variety of people at a given time. When students look at a date on a timeline of American history, they

75

should see more than a single image; they should see pictures drawn from several geographic regions and from the experiences of a variety of racial and ethnic groups, of women and men, and of working people as well as the wealthy. Helping students not only differentiate but also *diversify* their knowledge of historical time is a crucial but often overlooked purpose of instruction.

Instruction helps students make distinctions within their broad categories of historical time.

EXTENSIONS

An obvious way of extending these History Museum projects is by varying the time period covered. Amy chose to have students investigate the last 100 years primarily because she thought that would be the longest period of time for which students' families might provide information. Many families keep artifacts and tell stories that date back to the time of children's great-grandparents. Because elementary children are so often confused over what life was like before they were born, however, a teacher could just as easily plan the unit around changes over the last 50 years or even less. A primary teacher we know sets aside time for "History Show and Tell": each day a student brings in "something old" and describes what he or she has learned about it. The age of the items they bring in varies widely—from a 19th-century embroidery sampler to a 5-year-old softball. Although this activity is not as extensive or systematic as the History Museum, it also develops students' understanding of historical time: by discussing the objects and placing them on a semipermanent "artifact timeline" in the classroom, students enhance their understanding of life at various times in the past. (One of the first things students realize is that "looking old"—like the beat-up softball—is not a very direct indication of age.) Just as Amy's students did, students in this classroom develop an understanding of change over time and cease to think of the past as an undifferentiated period "long ago."

The time period covered can vary according to students' experiences and curricular requirements.

In "History Show and Tell," students bring in and describe historical artifacts of varying ages.

Students in the middle grades frequently study world history (or ancient civilizations specifically), and developing displays on change over time clearly fits well with such topics. If students fail to distinguish fully some period of time in American history, their distinctions in world history are even vaguer: one fourth grader described the entire pre-Colonial era as the time "back when God was around and everything." This impression is no doubt reinforced by coursework that races through the people and events of textbooks without ever really familiarizing students with the way people lived at different times in history. By investigating changes in daily life in the ancient world, medieval times, or the early modern era, students can develop much more sophisticated understandings of the civilizations that they too frequently rush through. This kind of project also lends itself to comparative timelines, in which students compare the changing ways of life in civilizations in China, Mali, Zimbabwe, Central America, Europe, and so on.

The study of world history benefits from a focus on everyday life.

Students in the middle grades can also devote more explicit attention to two aspects of historical change that were largely ignored by Amy's students. Most of the presentations in her class focused on aspects of material culture. Students occasionally touched on issues such as social relations—the *work* group, for example, included discussion of child labor, and the *fashion* group talked about changing expectations in women's appearance—but the main focus was always on physical changes as represented in photographs and artifacts. (This is not surprising, for as we have pointed out, elementary students tend to know more about these than any other aspect of change over time.) Students in the middle grades, though, could be given a different set of topics to choose from; instead of investigating changes in material culture, they could examine the way social relations have changed over time—topics could include changing attitudes toward women, minorities, childhood, the poor, war, family structure, religion, labor, law, or the environment. Just as in Amy's class, these topics would involve students in asking questions, collecting information from people as well as printed sources, drawing conclusions, and making decisions about forms of presentation.

Students in the middle grades can focus on changing social relations.

Middle-grade students could also focus attention on another aspect of change largely ignored in the History Museum projects—the *reasons* for change. Students in Amy's class almost never devoted any attention to explaining *why* technology, fashion, work, or anything else had changed over time; whenever she pressed them for explanations, they either seemed to regard the changes as self-evident improvements ("They just figured it out") or were entirely baffled as to why the changes took place ("They just got tired of doing it that way, I guess"). If students have a teacher like Amy in fourth or fifth grade, however, and develop an understanding of the nature of change over time, their experiences in later grades can focus on helping them understand how those changes come about—particularly the way they are related to broader changes in culture, economy, or society.

Students can focus on the reasons for historical changes.

CONCLUSIONS

The projects described in this chapter represent several significant elements of the historical methods and instructional principles laid out in chapters 1 and 2. First, investigating changes in everyday life builds on the historical topic students usually know the most about: even young children have already learned about changes in technology, fashion, and social roles from their relatives, the media, and popular culture generally. Investigating those topics further allows students to add depth and nuance to their understanding while dealing with familiar and comfortable content. Second, such projects engage students in genuine historical inquiry. Although young children who are still developing their reading skills will have trouble using some kinds of written primary sources—particularly from more remote time periods—analyzing photographs and artifacts allows them to use important historical materials in an authentic way. The questions students develop, meanwhile, are not contrived but derive naturally from their investigations and lead them to use a variety of other sources. Finally, directing such projects toward authentic audiences motivates students to develop the in-depth understanding that presentations or displays require.

As this chapter has made clear, of course, such authentic, disciplined inquiry is not easy; teachers must guide and support students at every step of the process—stimulating their interest, helping them develop questions, modeling procedures for collecting information, and so on. Yet the fact that teachers and students are so willing to stick with such projects attests to their potential for engaging students in meaningful historical learning.

CHILDREN'S AND ADOLESCENT LITERATURE

Aliki. (1983) *A Medieval Feast.* Crowell.

Bender, L. (1991). *Invention.* Knopf.

Bisel, S. C. (1990). *The Secrets of Vesuvius.* Scholastic.

Brooks, F. (1990). *Clothes and Fashion.* EDC Publishing.

Brooks, F., & Bond, S. 1989. *Food and Eating.* EDC Publishing.

Cahn, R., & Cahn, W. (1972). *No Time for School, No Time for Play: The Story of Child Labor in America.* Julian Messner.

Clare, J. D. (1992) *Living History: Pyramids of Ancient Egypt.* Harcourt, Brace, Jovanovich.

Cobb, V. (1989). *Brush, Comb, Scrub: Inventions to Keep You Clean.* Harper Trophy.

Cobb, V. (1989). *Snap, Button, Zip: Inventions to Keep Your Clothes On.* Harper Trophy.

Conrad, P. (1991). *Prairie Visions: The Life and Times of Solomon Butcher.* HarperCollins.

Cook, L. W. (1965). *When Great-Grandmother was a Little Girl.* New York: Holt, Rinehart, & Winston.

Edom, H. (1989). *Home and Houses Long Ago.* Usborne.

Edom, H. (1990). *Travel and Transport.* Usborne.

Fisher, L. E. (1967). *The Schoolmasters.* Franklin Watts.

Fix, P. (1994). *Not So Very Long go: Life in a Small Country Village.* Dutton.

Freedman, R. (1983). *Children of the Wild West.* Houghton Mifflin.

Freedman, R. (1994). *Kids at Work: Lewis Hine and the Crusade Against Child Labor.* Clarion Books.

Fradon, D. (1993). *The King's Fool: A Book About Medieval and Renaissance Fools.* Dutton Children's Books.

Giblin, J. C. (1987). *From Hand to Mouth: Or, How We Invented Knives, Forks, Spoons, and Chopsticks and the Table Manners to Go with Them.* HarperCollins.

Giblin, J. C. (1988). *Let There be Light: A Book about Windows.* HarperCollins.

Gumby, L. (1992). *Early Farm Life.* Crabtree.

Hamilton, V. (1983). *The Bells of Christmas.* Harcourt, Brace, and Jovanovich.

Hammond, T. (1988). *Sports.* Knopf.

Hart, G. (1990). *Ancient Egypt.* Knopf.

Hart, R. (1970). *English Life in the Eighteenth Century.* G. P. Putnam.

Hart, R. (1971). *English Life in the Nineteenth Century.* G. P. Putnam.

Hart, R. (1971). *English Life in the Seventeenth Century.* G. P. Putnam.

Hart, R. (1971). *English Life in Tudor Times.* G. P. Putnam.

Hart, R. (1973). *English Life in Chaucer's Day.* G. P. Putnam.

Hernández, X. (1992). *San Rafael: A Central American City Through the Ages.* Houghton Mifflin.

James, S. J. (1990). *Ancient Rome.* Alfred A. Knopf.

Kalman, B. (1991-1992). *Early Settler Life* series. Crabtree.

Kalman, B. (1992-1994). *Historic Communities* series. Crabtree.

Katz, W. L. (1978). *An Album of the Great Depression.* Franklin Watts.

Kentley, E. (1990). *Boat.* Alfred A. Knopf.

Kurjian, J. (1993). *In My Own Backyard.* Charlesbridge.

Lasker, J. (1979). *Merry Ever After: The Story of Two Medieval Weddings.* Viking Press.

Lessem, D. (1994). *The Iceman.* Crown.

Levinson, R. (1992). *I Go with My Family to Grandma's.* Dutton.

Loeper, J J. (1984). *Going to School in 1876.* Atheneum.

Moser, B. (1993). *Fly! A Brief History of Flight Illustrated.* HarperCollins.

Nahum, A. (1990). *Flying Machines.* Knopf.

Parker, S. (1995). *53 1/2 Things That Changed the World and Some that Didn't.* Millbrook.

Perl, L. (1986). *Blue Monday and Friday the Thirteenth.* Clarion.

Perl, L. (1990). *From Top Hats to Baseball Caps, from Bustles to Blue Jeans: Why We Dress the Way We Do.* Clarion.

Platt, R. (1992). *Film.* Knopf.

Rowland–Warne, L. (1992). *Costume.* Knopf.

Sanchea, S. (1982). *The Luttrell Village: Country Life in the Middle Ages.* Crowell.

Schroeder, A. (1989). *Ragtime Tumpie.* Little, Brown.

Sturner, F. (1973). *What Did You do When You Were a Kid? Pastimes from the past.* St. Martin's Press.

Sutton, R. (1990). *Car.* Knopf.

Tanner, G., & Wood T. (1992). *At School.* London: A & C Black.

Tanner, G., & Wood, T. (1992). *Washing.* A & C Black.

Unstead, R. J. (1979). *See Inside a Castle.* Warwich Press.

Weaver, R., & Dale, R. (1992). *Machines in the Home.* Oxford University Press.

Chapter 8

Historical Inquiry in an Integrated Social Studies Setting

It is 10 a.m. on a surprisingly pleasant January day. A bank of windows along one wall lets in the sunshine; when several children complain that the room is too warm, Dehea Smith opens a window and a breeze moves through the room. The 21 children in Dehea's third-grade classroom are working at a variety of tasks. One group of three works with a set of geography materials, two children work at the computer, typing in their newsletter entry about the stage design they are working on for the school television news program. Others work on a "Museum of the World" display that will organize some of the artifacts that the class has collected over the first semester of the year. Others are completing their "Morning Goals"—usually work in math or literature. The classroom is small and crowded. Children sit in groups of three, either at desks turned to face each other, or at two round tables in the middle of the room. These are new groups, and the children have hung signs above each set of desks or table with their group name on it: Radical Red Rovers, Chkemy, Brown-eyed Tigers, and so forth. Earlier in the year students had trouble working cooperatively. Over the first semester, Dehea assigned partners, occasionally moving into larger groups for some tasks. They have been working in groups of three since the new semester began. As the children finish up their work, Dehea passes out booklets entitled "Government is for Kids, Too!"

Dehea Smith:	We've studied things far away, either in time or location—or both! Can you think of anything we've studied that was far away in location?
Several voices:	The rainforest!
Dehea Smith:	Yes, rainforests are far away from here. What about something we've studied that was far away in time?
Lily:	Native Americans in the old days.
Dehea Smith:	Right. It's interesting to study things that are far away from us, but it is also important to know something about things a little closer to home. There's also something else that will be different about this study. When we studied the Rainforest, I picked many things that we were going to study. And when we studied Native Americans, Ms. Armstrong [student teacher] made a lot of the decisions about what questions we would investigate. But this time, you are going to make most of those decisions.
Kayla:	So, we're kinda like the teacher?
Dehea Smith:	Well, you will certainly be doing some of the things that teachers often do.
Justin:	Alright!
Marshall:	We get to decide on the questions?

Dehea Smith:	That's right. But in order to know what questions we want to answer, it's good to find out what we already know. I'm curious to know what you already know about Lexington. For instance, how many of you have ever been to a place that's bigger than Lexington? [General discussion of places that are bigger]. Can you think of a place smaller than Lexington?
Rena:	Nicholasville.
Dehea Smith:	How many have been there?
Justin:	I've been there, but I don't know if it's smaller. Seems like it, but I don't know for sure. [more discussion about how you can tell if a place is big or small]
Dehea Smith:	Hmm. How many of you have walked around downtown? Not just driven through. Really walked around. [About 11 hands go up—although the school is close to downtown, most of the children are bussed in from other parts of the city]. Well, let's brainstorm about what we already know. While I'm getting some paper, just look through—survey—the booklet I just gave you.
Tad:	Should we write any questions down?
Dehea Smith:	Ah—good idea! Write down questions.
Amelia:	Can we use our research folders?
Dehea Smith:	Another good idea. Use your research folders. [She places a large pad of chart paper on the board, and waits a few minutes for students to look through the booklets. She walks through the room, monitoring progress until it seems that most of the students have at least glanced through the booklet and written down a question or two]. OK, close your books. [Students turn their chairs to face the charts where Dehea waits to take dictation]. What are some of the places you knew about downtown?

The children start dictating a list of places: sports arena, theater, opera house, library, museums, hotels, park, banks, big buildings. Dehea looks over the list and notes that she thinks many of these places have something in common. She asks the students to take a couple of minutes to write what they think these downtown places have in common. As they work, she moves between groups, glancing over students' shoulders, commenting that "several people have seen different things," "keep thinking along those lines!" or "This is exciting! It tells me you're ready to learn what's *behind* all of this." Next, she collects their ideas, explaining that "if somebody says what you have on your list, check it off." Children mention that all except banks and buildings have something to do with entertainment, are popular with kids, involve action or fun. "Yes," Dehea agrees, "they solicit children to come. They invite you to come. But there are many other places downtown, too. We've got to decide on some questions to help us learn about these places, too." She tells the students that she will use *quick writing* (a term previously introduced to identify a form of notetaking) as they dictate their questions. The first questions involve size and number: How many windows are there? What's the tallest building? The oldest building? But soon children move on: "Why do we need a mayor?" "Why are there taxes?" Dehea also intervenes to ask questions. "I was wondering, too, what *are* taxes?" or, after someone asks how big downtown is, she asks, "Why *is there* a downtown?" She then asks students to take 5 minutes and write down all the questions they can think of, sharing their work with their partner. Next, children categorize their questions, with Dehea transcribing comments, and asking them for key words to describe each category: government, history, structures, entertainment, people, geography, urban planning, and employment. Anna mentions that some of these categories overlap, and Dehea agrees.

While critics have sometimes argued that schools should teach separate disciplines such as history rather than integrated fields such as social studies, there are sound cognitive and disciplinary reasons for teaching history in the larger context of social studies. First of all, disciplinary boundaries are increasingly permeable. Instead of being neatly defined as *historians* or *anthropologists* or *political scientists* or the like, modern scholars more often tend to identify themselves with the problems or issues they address. Because so many of these issues cross traditional disciplinary boundaries, an integrated social studies approach is often a more authentic context for historical study. As we noted in the first chapter, such contexts support students' sense-making in history. More authentic contexts provide examples of history-in-action rather than of history separated from action; students can see how historical thinking grows from and contributes to problem solving in the real world.

An integrated social studies approach can provide authentic contexts for studying history.

National Council for the Social Studies (1994)

This chapter focuses on doing disciplined, reflective inquiry in the context of an integrated social studies unit. We begin with a common third-grade social studies topic, "communities," that often becomes little more than the "community helpers" we all remember from our elementary years. We visited the fire station, learned about doctors and dentists, police officers and the safety patrol, but rarely went much beyond that. Dehea Smith, the teacher in the vignette that opened this chapter, also decided to focus on the concept of community, but in a more substantive way that will involve students in a long-term set of inquiries into their community. Dehea also has to align her curriculum with state and local mandates. Her state's newly developed "academic expectations" define social studies as an integration of concepts and principles from a number of disciplines for the following purposes:

Disciplined, reflective inquiry occurs in integrated social studies contexts.

Kentucky's Six Learning Goals (1994)

Kentucky Council on School Performance Standards (1991)

- Democratic understanding, civic values and social participation
- Knowledge and cultural understanding (including diversity of U.S. culture, and cultures of the world)
- Self-knowledge

To meet these goals, instruction and assessment are supposed to focus on democratic principles, the structure and function of political, social, and economic systems, human and geographic interactions, cultural diversity, and historical perspective. While this may seem overwhelming, if you go back to the vignette, you will see that on the very first day Dehea's class inquiry touches on almost all of these aspects of social studies. This is especially apparent in the way in which her students organize their initial questions into broader categories. After lengthy discussion and debate, students select labels such as *government, history, structures, geography, employment.* They argue that buildings, for instance, can be categorized as structures, but they also function as places of employment and entertainment, of government and historical interest. As Dehea puts the category headings on separate sheets of chart paper, she suggests that the students provide *key words* to help them remember what they have decided goes into each category. These key words also provide a good deal of information about how students understand each category at this point in their study, and give Dehea some idea of where to place greater instructional emphasis. The *history* category, for instance, began with only a few questions focusing on finding the oldest building or street. There were no questions about the significance of these things, the sources of current problems, or even more generally how the city had changed over time. On the other hand, there were a number of government and urban planning questions—"What are taxes?" "Why do we need a mayor?" "Who decides on how a city looks?"—that lent themselves to historical as well as current treatment.

Teachers can coordinate local, state, and national standards.

Key words help students classify and organize data.

ALL QUESTIONS ARE NOT CREATED EQUAL: MOVING BEYOND THE SUPERFICIAL

If Dehea had stopped with the initial set of questions, the students could probably have completed their study in short order. Many of these first questions were superficial. As often happens in classrooms, one type of response can start a domino effect; when Julie asked "How many windows are downtown," Martin chimed in with "Well, then, how many *bricks* are downtown?" As did Amy in chapter 7, Dehea reminded her students that good questions often start with "how," or "why," and this

Initial questions are often superficial; developing good questions takes time and patience.

Blyth (1989)

helped some, with one student asking "Why do we need a mayor," after another suggested "Who is the mayor?" This type of approximation seems to be a common response as children struggle to frame substantial questions. Another response typical of this stage of question development is the personalization of questions—"Why do *we* need a mayor" rather than "Why does *a community* need a mayor?" Of course a study of students' own community is more likely to elicit such statements of ownership as opposed to, say, a unit on rainforests.

As we have already noted, question generation is hard intellectual work, and Dehea was not satisfied with how things were going. "We spent all that time gathering facts on the last project, that they are just in that mode," she concluded. She had promised that on this project they could ask their own questions, but she did not want the study limited to mere fact gathering. Instead, she had planned on emphasizing continuity and change in the city, how conflicts were resolved, and how even third graders could participate in their urban community. She decided to try another question-generating technique. First, she gave students a homework assignment: interview people at home, and ask them to suggest good questions to ask if someone wanted to learn about Lexington. Students were to decide which of these questions matched categories they had already developed, and to identify any new categories they would need.

"Facts" are not enough for disciplined inquiry.

Short & Armstrong (1993)

A social studies approach emphasizes participation. (See, for instance *National Council for the Social Studies, 1994*)

The next day, Dehea took each of the pieces of chart paper headed with the category labels and descriptions that had already been developed, put one at each work center around the room, divided the class into groups, and assigned each group to a different category. Their task was to edit the list of questions already generated, emphasizing *how* and *why* questions. Next, she told the students to rotate through the centers, adding to the charts all the new questions generated by their homework interviews. Again, they were to check for duplications, and not write questions that were already listed. In the end, they created one new category: *miscellaneous*. As their work period ended, the students recorded the number of questions in each category, estimated the total, and then confirmed their estimation by adding category totals. They had generated 204 questions.

Students edit their own questions, emphasizing *how* and *why* questions.

J. Dickinson (1993)

When students generate this volume of questions, they can easily become bogged down in trivia rather than engaged in substantial inquiry. There are several techniques for narrowing the scope of investigation to a more manageable size, including having children collapse several questions into one, or letting students decide on a set of "most important" questions (see chapter 7 for other ideas). Dehea chose not to limit the number of questions; instead, she noted that some of the questions could be easily answered, and suggested that students take the rest of that day's research time to see how many questions they could answer using the sources already in the room. She also reminded them to plan their record keeping: "Think about how you want to keep track of your answers first, then share your ideas with your partners." This kind of metacognition—thinking about thinking—was a classroom constant. Dehea set aside time for full class review of work plans, for individuals to consider how they could best organize their thinking, for students to share their thinking and planning with a peer, and, as you will see later in this chapter, for the development of metaphors to support children's visualization of tasks. After students had planned their work, they began sorting through the questions. Dehea made suggestions for sources they might use: phone books to find out what kinds of restaurants were downtown, maps to locate major geographic landmarks, the *Lexington Answer Book* to find out where the courthouse was located. As the research period drew to a close, one group had answered all but two of the questions on its list, and most of the others had made substantial progress, too. "This is good information," Dehea told them. "Now, let's see what kinds of questions we have left." In the next few minutes, the class decided that they could eliminate some categories, concentrating more of their efforts on just a few. They also noted that each category contained several different types of questions:

Hyde & Bizar (1989)

Metaphors help students visualize tasks.

"*Lexington Answer Book,*" (*n.d.*)

Categorizing questions helps focus research.

- questions that required a trip to the school library
- questions that required both library research and sources from outside the school
- questions that were "ridiculous"

"Ridiculous" questions included finding out how many bricks or windows there were downtown. "That would take forever to do!" Jason exclaimed. "It's just ridiculous!" Once they had named the category, the students decided that they might answer some of these questions "just for fun," but they were not going to put much effort into them. They also edited a couple of "ridiculous" questions, made them more manageable, and moved them into the history and structures categories. The questions about windows and bricks, for instance, changed from *how many* windows or bricks to *what different styles* of windows and buildings could be found in Lexington. The history group decided that they would see if window styles changed over time; the structures group thought they would see if the uses of buildings influenced their styles.

With time, students can identify nonproductive questions.

In a relatively short time, then, these third graders had honed their questions to a manageable and substantive list. They were able to quickly dispose of some that seemed initially interesting, but had little significance, and focus on others that they decided were more important. It took time and patience to get to this point, but in the end, most of the students had a surer sense of what they were investigating and how their questions fit the larger theme of community. Given the opportunity and sufficient scaffolding, these students were able to distinguish between superficial and substantive questions. Dehea supported their efforts by allowing them time to work with the questions, to sift and categorize them, debate and discuss their merits, do some initial investigation, and, finally, hammer out their own working definitions of categories. By their next research period, student inquiry was more focused, the theme of change over time began to emerge as a significant issue, and it was time to think about field trips and guest speakers.

Students may need help thinking about what questions have historical significance. (See, for instance, Jorgensen, 1993)

Taking time for question development in the beginning of a study saves time later.

FLEXIBILITY IS ESSENTIAL:
BUILDING ON STUDENT DISCOVERIES

As Suling and Jason study maps of Lexington and the surrounding county, trying to locate water sources that might have enticed people to the area, they find two exciting pieces of information. First, they discover that the site of the first White settlement in the area was probably a spring close to their school. "Wow!" Suling exclaims. "That's a trip we need to take!" The librarian helps Jason find an old picture of the spring in a picture history book of Lexington, and Suling and Jason decide that they could make a copy of this "before" picture, and then take "after" pictures if they visit the spring. Their second discovery is that a creek runs underneath part of the downtown area. Why would people want to bury a creek? Where did it come out? Who could they ask about this? They list their new questions in their research notebooks and go in search of their teacher.

As students conduct their inquiries and make discoveries, they need as many opportunities as possible to pursue sources. Since teachers cannot anticipate all the directions a study will take, flexibility and planning are essential. Before Dehea began the community study, for instance, she made a list of contact people for possible field trips and guest speakers. Obviously, schools do not have unlimited access either to field trips or outside experts. Choices must be made, and made far enough in advance to assure access at the necessary time. Dehea called several of her contacts before the unit started so that she knew what arrangements would need to be made. She also decided that the class would use public transportation for any field trips. This accomplished two things. First, transportation was a significant part of the community. It was also part of a community controversy over budget cuts that might eliminate bus routes and services for handicapped passengers. Second, the bus company required only 1 day's notice to pick up a whole class, whereas school buses had to be scheduled at the beginning of each school year. Dehea, then, was prepared for several

Flexibility and preplanning facilitate student inquiry.

K. Young (1994)

possibilities. She felt strongly, however, that planning should be joint work. She wanted her students to be intentional in their thinking. "After all," she explained, "that's the only way they'll learn to do this on their own." One day, she noticed that some of the students seemed anxious to stop researching and pick a construction project—"Let's build a model of Lexington!" Dehea stopped the class and suggested they needed a "metaphor to help us think about our work."

Dehea began by drawing a metaphor on the board: a field of questions, and beneath the soil, information; a researcher digging for information, piling that information into a knapsack, bringing it back to a "house of knowledge" where it was organized and used to answer questions. "Which part are we working on now?" she asked. The students agreed that they were digging, just beginning to fill their knapsacks. "Do you have enough in your knapsacks to really fill a house of knowledge?" she asked. Again, most of the students agreed that they needed more information before they were ready to build anything. Dehea told them to draw the metaphor in their research notebooks to remind them of their task. At each stage of work, then, she referred students back to this metaphor. Developing the metaphor helped students visualize the multistep task of reflective inquiry.

At one point, Dehea asked her students to stop and decide how best to allocate their remaining time and resources. "Make a list of sources you will need," she told them. "If we need to talk to people or visit downtown we have to plan way ahead of time, and we'll have to make one trip answer a lot of questions. This will take a lot of planning and phone calling." As a group, then, the class made the plans listed in Table 8.1 (and recorded in each students' research notebook).

While a field trip to McConnell Springs, the site of the first White settlement, would have been nice, the city bus did not go there. Instead, the students decided to ask a representative of the "Save Our Spring" group to come to the class, show slides of the spring, talk about its history and explain some of the problems encountered in trying to turn the area into a natural and historical park site. Although no speaker was available, the group sent a box full of materials for the students to use. In many ways, this was more productive in terms of Dehea's goals because the unsorted resources in the box made it necessary for students to develop their own interpretations.

Dehea wanted her students to understand some of the ways in which conflict shaped their community. The conflict over what responsibility the local government had in preserving both history and the natural environment seemed one possibility. In addition, several students had decided that they were interested in crime- and weather-related problems in the community—topics that Dehea had not anticipated. In investigating whether crime had increased in Lexington, for instance, one group

Table 8.1

Class Constructed Work Plan for Part of Community Study

March 3: Bus trip downtown

Purpose:

1. Research in Kentucky Collection at the library (collection of newspapers, maps, photographs, and the like related to state and local history)

2. Walking tour of downtown. Take pictures of structures and historic places

April 13: Bus trip to city council work session

Purpose:

1. See how city government works

2. Find out what kind of problems the city council has to solve

3. Tour government buildings

Visit from the mayor (to be scheduled)

Visitor from McConnell Springs (to be scheduled)

came upon an article reporting a public hanging in the city. The article included a gallows speech by the convicted murderer, pleading for other young men to avoid "strong drink and weapons." A second group, curious about why Lexington had few tornadoes or hurricanes, wrote to the regional weather service and discovered, among other things, that their city was on the eastern edge of "tornado alley," but that flooding was a much more common problem historically and currently. A major current conflict involved updating storm sewers, which did not seem particularly interesting until two students found a picture of a 1932 flood that inundated the downtown area. While there had been heavy rainfall that day, the flooding was largely due to inadequate storm sewers. Both groups added new questions to ask the mayor.

MAINTAINING FOCUS

Dehea reminds the students to take out their research notebooks, and there are a couple of moans.

"If you whine," she says, "there are consequences!"

"Oh, goody," Cheyenne says. "Research!"

There is general laughter as the students retrieve their notebooks. Dehea has noticed some falling off of interest in some of the groups, especially after a week of frequent interruptions. Momentum seems to be lost, and she wants to refocus the class on their research tasks.

"We're going to go back in the past this morning," she tells them. You will need to take notes. Head your notes *The Quest for McConnell Springs*." Several heads go up in surprise. McConnell Springs is part of their study.

"I know where that is," Jason exclaims.

Dehea smiles, relieved that their interest seems to be reviving. "Now, lets refresh our memories. How do we take notes? Chad, how do you like to take notes?

"Don't write down everything they say."

"Just use phrases."

"Use abbreviations."

Dehea interjects a warning to write enough to "trigger your memory," and other students add that pictures can give clues.

"Don't concentrate on just one fact," Kelly adds.

Dehea turns on the video. "If you need me to stop, we can watch it again. Everybody ready? Let me get my notebook, so I can take notes, too."

The video is brief—a 7-minute reenactment of the discovery and settlement of McConnell Springs. At its conclusion, Dehea asks the students to share their notes.

"Too short!" Karla cries. "I only got two notes."

"Want to see it again?" Dehea asks. The students ask for a replay, and Dehea reminds them to pay attention to the pictures. "Most of my notes came from the pictures!"

After the video has played through a second time, the class begins to discuss what they have learned. This time they have many more notes to share, and Dehea asks them if they could tell from the video what time of year it was. Initially, several of the students are convinced that it must have been fall. They also seem to think that the McConnell brothers are just visiting, not settling here. "Hmm," Dehea murmurs. "We'll need to discuss this!"

In the ensuing discussion all children participate. If a child is silent too long, Dehea asks for her ideas, and enforces the rules about not interrupting someone when they are trying to formulate an opinion. Finally, Kelly says, "I don't think they're coming back 'cuz they're claiming land. They'd come in the spring, so they could clear the land and get their house built before the cold weather."

"Yeah," Jason agrees. "You can't count on luck. You have to be prepared."

Suling adds that "they need time to settle in."

At this point, Dehea introduces a contour map of the area around McConnell Springs along with several overlay maps that show how the area grew and changed, shifting eastward along the Town Branch, the creek that now runs under the city. The children lean forward to see the map, tracing the creeks flow and exclaiming when buildings they recognize from their trip downtown appear on the map.

Because research takes time, and work in classrooms is frequently interrupted, sustaining inquiry can be a problem. Dehea, for instance, lost 1 week to spring break, another to statewide testing, several days to the science fair, schoolwide assemblies, and similar events. Sometimes it seemed that each time students became deeply involved there was another interruption. Some of these interruptions were necessary, even interesting, breaks in routine, but their effect was also to extend the community study to the point that students sometimes lost interest. Dehea found that regular whole-group presentations and discussions helped rekindle interest and kept students on task. She focused each of these whole-group experiences around a different aspect of the class study. In the excerpt just presented, she focused on the process of notetaking, but also on the interaction between the early settlers and their environment. Similarly, a discussion of the role of government preceded an interview with the mayor.

Perhaps one of the most striking aspects of these discussions was the time Dehea took to allow students to build interpretations based on the data they had been accumulating and the information presented in each of these whole-group experiences. It would have been much quicker, for instance, to simply tell the students that the first White settlers came in the spring. Instead, she engaged in a lengthy (30-minute) analysis of evidence that could support student assumptions about season, solicited conclusions—"I think it's early spring"—supporting evidence—"because they are dressed warmly, but there's no snow, and some leaves are on the trees"—and interpretations—"if you get there in the spring you have time to build up food for winter."

Note, too, that Dehea worked along with the children, modeling the processes she wanted them to learn, and then sharing her work as they did theirs. As the video played, for instance, she stood to the side, clipboard in hand, visibly taking notes. As students shared what they had written down, she would say, "Oh, yes. I wrote that down, too," or "Oh, I missed that. I think I'll add that to my notes, too." At other times, she would write notes to the class on the board—"Does anyone have a book with a picture of an old-fashioned radio?"—and students would respond by writing their name next to her question. By the end of the project, then, the blackboard became a center of communication where teacher and students could write notes without interrupting another group's work.

At the end of a research session, Dehea ran through the notes on the board, making sure inquiries were answered, notes made or materials returned; then she erased the board. Other teachers use a large sheet of colored paper as a more permanent communications center. In either case, however, having such a system helps keep students focused on their own tasks with relatively few interruptions and gives the teacher a running record of current issues within and between groups.

NOW, WHAT DOES IT MEAN?

Interviewer: Hello, I'm Kelly James, here today with William, the famous criminal. Before we go on to your life, lets find out some things about general life in the 1800s. What were some of the places you saw or heard of as a child?

William: On Main Street there was a business called Gibney and Cassell. It was run by Gibney and William H. Cassell.

Interviewer: Yes, after a long time, it became Parcell's Department store. That was torn down in the late 1970s.

William: It was? (acts surprised)

Interviewer: Yes. It was made into an office/hotel building.

William: One place I REALLY remember was the fourth Fayette County courthouse. I had my trial there. The courthouse was built in 1883 and 1884. It was designed by Thomas W. Boyd.

Frequent interruptions can defuse student interest.

Pappas et al. (1995)

Building interpretations based on historical data takes time, especially with younger students.

Jorgensen (1993), Lindquist (1995

Lindquist (1995)

Interviewer:	That building was burned down in 1897. Lots of valuable oil paintings and a valuable sculpture by Joel T. Hart were lost in that fire. At this time Lexington was pretty busy. Let's hear some about your life, William.
William:	When I was 9 years old and I had to leave my parents was when I began my criminal life. I had to steal just to stay alive!
Interviewer:	No wonder you did such an awful thing!
William:	Before I was hung, I made a speech. The speech was a warning for young men to stay away from guns and alcohol. That's how my life got messed up.
Interviewer:	Since childhood was a bad experience for you, how do you feel it affected your adulthood?
William:	I felt like I didn't have a future so it didn't matter what I did.

At some point researchers must draw at least tentative conclusions about their work. Dehea's third graders decided that they wanted to share what they had found with their parents through a series of skits. Each group was charged with writing a short script that "shows some of the most interesting things you have learned about Lexington." This turned out to be the most challenging aspect of the research. The students had accumulated lots of "facts" and had found answers to most of their questions, but deciding which pieces of information went together, and whether any of it would be interesting or important to anyone else was difficult. As it turned out, however, what the students were most intimidated by was writing a script. This was somewhat surprising as they had written scripts for a puppet show about the rainforest earlier in the year, and frequently wrote other types of stories and reports. As one of the boys explained, however, "we didn't all write the script for the puppet show. Some people worked on scenery, and some people gathered information and like that. I have no experience with this." His partner agreed, saying that she had never even been in a play, and had no idea of what to put in the script.

At the end of 1 week of work, most of the children were still struggling. They knew what story they wanted to tell, but they tended to tell it in outline, leaving out all the information they had so painstakingly accumulated. The partners who had found out about the 1832 flood drafted a half page script that involved waking up, shouting "Flood!" and swimming for their lives. While this was certainly lively, it was short on historical information, the current connection that had captured their initial interest, and accuracy—the flood was only 3 feet deep; its major danger was typhoid rather than drowning. Similarly, the first draft of the group investigating crime in Lexington consisted of an interview with the criminal, William, in which he explained that the "happiest time [in his life] was when I was hung." While William had actually said this in his gallows speech, the students' script provided no context for the statement. Two other groups wrote more substantial first drafts involving the founding of Lexington and city government.

Dehea looked over the students' drafts and suggested that they edit their scripts to make sure that each line included important information about their topic. "Oh," Cheyenne said. "We need facts in each line." This notion of anchoring each line of script in facts seemed to make a lot of sense to the students. As you can see from the script at the opening of this section—a third draft—the interview with the murderer took on a whole new dimension, introducing the audience to "general life in the 1880s" and then more specific information "about your life, William."

The pair who worked on the flood struggled for some time, finally working with a classroom volunteer to construct the outline and dictate the introduction in Fig. 8.1. At this point, the partners took over the writing on their own, explaining why flooding was a more frequent problem than tornadoes, describing what Lexington looked like in 1832, mentioning the deaths due to typhoid fever, and ending with one of the characters going down to city hall to demand better storm sewers.

Because their grasp of dates was still shaky, another group became frustrated with figuring out the sequence of events. They needed to find out if their main character

Students need to develop a broad repertoire of ways to share what they have learned.

Cope & Kalante (1990), Jorgensen (1993), Lindquist (1995), Newkirk 1989), K. Young (1994)

First drafts are often only outlines of information.

Sometimes students need to be reminded to include the information they have uncovered in their writing.

Barton & Levstik (1996), Thornton & Vukelich (1988)

```
Geography:      Flood p. 207

                Town Branch                                    Main things

                Weather Letter

                Size of city                                   Side things

                Where was flood

Skit:           Flood

                Debate about sewers

                How changed Lexington

Needed:         Fake water

                Story: Someone in the flood

                Radio reporter telling people about the flood

                Script: (Main idea) What reporter sees.
                        Emergency!  Flood Warning!
```

Still stymied by the thought of what to write, students found it helful to dictate the following introduction for their script

```
Narrator:

Where: Here we are in downtown Lexington

What it looks like: There used to be a beautiful creek here called Town Branch. Now, the creek is hidden underground. It
    runs underground through downtown Lexington under what will one day be Rupp Arena [Show map of Town Branch]

Why are we here: We are here to tell a story about the Town Branch creek and how Lexington finally got strom sewers.
    Travel back with us to the morning of August 2, 1932. We are in the home of Robert E. Mackenzie and his mother Alice
    Mackenzie, on Main Street in downtown Lexington.
```

FIG. 8.1. Outline for script on the 1932 flood in Lexington, Kentucky.

would have been alive in order to witness some of the events they were putting in their script. With some urging, they constructed a timeline to which they could refer when deciding what things could go in their script. Other groups found that they had not taken careful enough notes to add the details they needed for their scripts. This was particularly apparent when they were deciding on scenery. If a character was supposed to open a door, they wanted to know what the door might look like; if a character was supposed to be in a cabin, they needed to know what furniture and tools were inside. Because it was an authentic assessment, putting together a presentation made it very clear to the students which aspects of their research they really understood, where they had holes in their data, and what pieces of information made convincing arguments for a particular perspective.

Timelines help students visualize the sequence of events.

Authentic assessments help students determine what they need to know.

TIME FOR REFLECTION

Third-grader, Laine, has been interviewing her classmates all week. She has a list of questions on a piece of looseleaf paper attached to her clipboard.

"Are you ready to be interviewed?" she asks Jason and Suling.

"OK."

"Which of your questions took the most time to answer?"

Laine's interview goes on for some time. She is compiling the responses to use for an article about the research project on Lexington. As she interviews each group, the students pause to decide what things were hard, or most interesting, or told them the most about Lexington. "Writing the script was hardest," Jason says. "And I'd never memorized lines before." For others, visiting the mayor and the trip downtown were most memorable. Alana describes how difficult it was for her to work with her partner.

Self-reflection can be built into inquiry projects in different ways.

"We kept having different opinions about everything!" she says, although their final project is quite ambitious, and involves taking Chelsea Clinton on an imaginary tour of Lexington. Taylor notes that he will make sure he writes down the important dates connected to events "so I can keep track of things better. I had this guy remembering things that happened before he was even born!" Finally, Stuart explains that he learned that "some things changed" but a lot of problems "just seem to be here all along."

CONCLUSIONS

Dehea could have narrowed the focus of her community study to a more traditionally historical approach—the not uncommon "pioneers" unit. Instead, her work reflects a commitment to some of the principles outlined in the NCSS Standards document:

- Teaching and learning integrate across the curriculum. Besides the integration of social studies disciplines such as history, geography, and political science, the students regularly drew on math and language arts, and, especially in the reporting out phase, on the arts. As they reflected on their experiences as researchers, these third graders noted that many of their categories overlapped. "It was hard sometimes to decide if something was history, or like government, or maybe structures," commented one girl. Along with scholars from the various disciplines that comprise the social studies, they discovered that in-depth study of authentic issues frequently cuts across disciplinary boundaries and that it is often difficult to mark the place where one discipline begins and another leaves off.

  National Council for the Social Studies (1994)

- Students learn connected networks of knowledge, skills, beliefs, and attitudes that they will find useful both in and outside of school. In addition to learning to access information from print sources, students learned to use interviews, the built environment, and different types of maps. They gained experience in forming connected networks of knowledge and skills in putting together their presentations, as well as in reflecting on the process of inquiry.

  "Knowing" involves networks of knowledge, skills, beliefs, and attitudes.

- Teachers model seriousness of purpose and a thoughtful approach to inquiry and use instructional strategies designed to elicit and support similar qualities from students. Throughout the unit, Dehea modeled the practices she wanted students to learn and use. She also made sure that there were multiple opportunities for students to put these skills into action. Notetaking, for instance, was not an exercise to be used at some future date. It was learned in a context where it was needed.

  Newmann et al. (1995).

  "Skills" are learned in context and through teacher modeling.

- Teachers show interest in and respect for students' thinking, but demand well-reasoned arguments rather than opinions voiced without adequate thought or commitment. A constant refrain throughout the community study was the emphasis on giving "facts and reasons to support your opinions." In addition, students were taught ways to agree and disagree that nurtured discussion rather than attacked individuals.

  Students need to learn to discuss, agree, disagree, and support their ideas.

Clearly, history was a primary focus of the class' study. In fact, all but one of the group presentations were historical. Unlike studies of one period, however, this study shuttled between past and present. Sometimes this presented problems for children whose time sense was tenuous, but we think the benefits are considerable. First of all, students recognized the continuities in their community as well as the changes. They discovered that certain problems—flooding, for instance—persist over time. They also were able to make comparisons between current and historic issues such as crime and punishment. This helped put currently controversial issues into historical context. The constant comparison between past and present also encouraged students to determine historical significance at least in part on the basis of an event's impact on later times. Finally, we think the connections made between controversial issues, both historic and contemporary, and civic action are more likely to encourage students to see themselves and others as having historical agency—the power to make history. The next chapter deals more explicitly both with issues of conflict and consensus and historical agency in the history classroom.

Historical study does not have to be organized chronologicaly over the school year.

Historic study puts current issues in historical context.

Connecting historic and current issues can help students develop a sense of agency.

CHILDREN'S LITERATURE FOR COMMUNITY STUDY

Art and Architecture

Gaughenbaugh, M., & Camburn, H. (1994). *Old House, New House: A Child's Exploration of American Architectural Styles.* Preservation.

Manning, M. (1994). *A Ruined House.* Candlewick.

Community Issues

Anderson, J. (1993). *Earth Keepers.* Gulliver Green.

Grossman, P. (1994). *Saturday Market.* Lothrop.

Nichelason, M. G. (1994). *Homeless or Hopeless?* Lerner.

Showers, P. (1993). *Where Does the Garbage Go?* HaperCollins.

Communities Through Time

Ayoub, A., Binous, J., Gragueb, A., Mtimet, A., & Slim, H. (1994). *Umm El Madayan: An Islamic City Through the Ages.* Houghton.

Dorris, M. (1994). *Guests.* Hyperion.

Fix, P. (1994). *Not So Very Long Ago: Life in a Small Country Village.* Dutton.

Hall, D. (1993). *The Farm Summer 1942.* Dial.

Levine, A. A. (1994). *Pearl Moscowitz's Last Stand.* Tambourine.

Polacco, P. (1994). *Pink and Say.* Philomel.

Provensen, A., & Provensen, M. (1994). *Town and Country.* Browndeer.

Ray, M. L. (1994). *Shaker Boy.* Browndeer.

Sigerman, H. (1994). *Laborers for Liberty: American Women, 1865-1890.* Oxford.

Sneve, V. D. H. (1994). *The Seminoles.* Holiday.

Wilson, K. (1993). *Earthquake!: San Francisco, 1906.* Steck-Vaughn.

Wilson, L. (1994). *Daily Life in a Victorian house.* Preservation.

People in Communities Around the World

Ancona, G. (1993). *Pablo Remembers: The Fiesta of the Day of the Dead.* Lothrop.

Binch, C. (1994). *Gregory Cool.* Dial.

Calmenson, S. (1994). *Hotter than a Hot Dog!* Little, Brown.

Chin, S. A. (1993). *Dragon Parade.* Illustrations by Mou-Sien Tseng. Steck-Vaughn.

Graff, N. P. (1993). *Where the River Runs: A Portrait of a Refugee Family.* Little, Brown.

Griffin, P. R. (1994). *The Brick House Burglars.* McElderry.

Jakobsen, K. (1994). *My New York.* Little, Brown.

Jenness, A. (1994). *Come Home with Me: A Multicultural Treasure Hunt.* New.

Keller, H. (1993). *Grandfather's Dream.* Greenwillow.

Kendall, R. (1994). *Russian Girl: Life in an Old Russian Town.* Scholastic.

Krull, K. (1994). *City within a City: How Kids Live in New York's Chinatown.* Lodestar, (see also *The Other Side: How Kids Live in a California Latino Neighborhood*).

Levinson, R. (1988). *Our Home is the Sea.* Dutton.

Morris, A. (1990). *When Will the Fighting Stop? A Child's View of Jerusalem.* Atheneum.

Patrick, D. L. (1994). *The Car Washing Street.* Tambourine.

Thiebaut, E. (1985). *My Village in Morocco: Mokhtar of the Atlas Mountains.* Silver Burdett.

Wright, D. K. (1994). *A Multicultural Portrait of Life in the Cities.* Cavendish.

Chapter 9

Fiction, Nonfiction, and Historical Thinking

As she comes in the door, Jennifer announces that there was team practice in answering social studies questions today. Each child made up a series of questions about the American Revolution, and these were used as part of a five-team contest. Jennifer's team tied for first place. "But this unit wasn't so good. All we did was learn about a few battles and fill in charts. I want to know a whole lot more!" She is particularly annoyed because so much of what she is learning in class either contradicts what she has read on her own, or gives only part of the story.

"The text was talking about George Washington and how good he was to his soldiers. There was a part about Martha Washington knitting warm socks for the men, but in one of the books I read it said Washington had deserters at Valley Forge shot. Why wasn't that in the textbook? They just want you to think he was perfect."

This is not Jennifer's first encounter with the disjuncture between historical narratives and history texts. Earlier in the year she announced during a small group discussion that she thought Puritans were "cruel and stupid." Shocked, her classmate, William called the teacher over and asked, "Do you know what Jennifer thinks!!"

"No," Mrs. Bainbridge answered.

"She thinks the Puritans were stupid!" William sputtered.

"Oh?" Mrs. Bainbridge smiled. "That's interesting. What made you decide that, Jennifer?"

Jennifer, having read two novels dealing with witchcraft in the early settlement and colonial periods, explained that Puritans had to be evil if they used religion as an excuse to torture and kill people. "They made their religion as bad as what they were trying to escape. It's wrong because you aren't the person to decide that . . . just because someone doesn't agree with you doesn't mean you have to kill them. And even if you were a person who didn't believe you would have to just act like you did, or you'd be in big trouble. They accused innocent people, and even if they were witches, they shouldn't have killed them. These people are supposed to believe in God, you know. Real religious. And God doesn't go around killing people."

Jennifer went on to argue that the textbook told "nothing interesting about the Puritans. They just said that the Puritans were very religious people who wanted to make religion more pure, and they didn't say anything about them, what they did bad . . . just that they were very organized people."

As we said earlier, historical stories are powerful cultural forces. They present historical interpretations in a memorable format; they also have a significant impact on children's historical thinking. It is pretty commonplace to hear advocates of history education claim that story, with its emphasis on human response to historical events, is the beginning of historical understanding. Moreover, a number of people argue that teaching history is largely a matter of presenting "a story well told." Clearly, narrative is a more powerful influence on Jennifer's historical thinking than her textbook. In fact, she judges the historical interpretation in her text and in her classwork against the narrative history she reads independently. That she, or anyone else, should do this is not surprising. Stories are, after all, generally more compelling reading than textbooks. For centuries, historians have used narrative, and narrative devices, to order and assign cause and effect to events in the past. Yet Jennifer's experience

Barber (1992), Blos (1993), Levstik (1993)

Egan (1983, 1989), Egan & Nadaner (1988)

History is more than a story well told.

Levstik (1995)

Tunnell & Ammon (1993)

indicates that the relationship between narrative, history and historical understanding is more complex than appreciation of a story well told.

To begin with, defining what is meant by *narrative* is a challenge. Of course narratives are created and understood within a particular sociocultural context, so that definitions of narrative vary over time and between places and individuals. Generally, however, historical narratives are assumed to share certain elements with fictional stories and such nonfictional accounts as biographies, autobiographies, and traditional histories. They linguistically represent past experience, either real or imagined. Events in these narratives are expected to be connected, to have some point or conclusion. This may seem simple enough, but there is still quite a bit of difference between the grand narratives that present the rise and fall of empires and the narratives of individual agency Jennifer and others find so appealing or even the more narrative textbooks now being published. And, because all narratives are created within a particular sociocultural context no historical narrative (or any other genre, for that matter) can possibly tell readers "the way it really was." Instead, narratives shape and interpret lives and events from the past, embedding them in a particular culture and often making direct parallels to the present. Consider, for example, how narrative shapes the events surrounding the destruction of Hiroshima in World War II. Perhaps you are familiar with Eleanor Coerr's book *Sadako* (You may have read an earlier version, *Sadako and the Thousand Paper Cranes*). Coerr does not simply lay out a chain of events and let readers make what interpretation they may. Instead, she carefully anchors her story in the details of one child's life and death in order to make a point about the present. The story has a clear moral—"This is our cry, this is our prayer: Peace in the world"—that resonates in the present as it gives meaning to the past. Compare this to Jennifer's experience with her history textbook: "The social studies book doesn't give you a lot of detail. You don't imagine yourself there because they're not doing it as if it were a person." For Jennifer, as for many children with whom we have worked, a narrative acts "as if it were a person" by particularizing and personalizing history. As Coerr explains, "If you tell people that 200,000 died as a result of the bombing of Hiroshima, it doesn't have as much impact as the story of one little girl."

Neither a history textbook nor "battles and filling in charts" have this sense of personal agency. Listen to the depersonalized and lawlike voice so often used in textbooks: "*Whenever*, within a feudal system, towns and trade begin to grow, . . . *then* feudalism gives way to capitalism." This kind of language not only depersonalizes the transition from feudalism to capitalism, it deproblematizes it as well. History, once again, is presented as the result of inexorable forces seemingly beyond human control. Compare that lawlike tone to the voice of Karen Cushman's *Catherine, Called Birdy*, describing a medieval manor during the same period:

> Today is quarter-rent day. My greedy father is near muzzle-witted with glee from the geese, silver pennies, and wagonloads of manure our tenants pay him. He guzzles ale and slaps his belly, laughing as he gathers in the rents. I like to sit near the table . . . and listen to the villagers complain about my father as they pay. I have gotten all my good insults and best swear words that way.

In this passage, the narrative voice is distinctly personal. Cushman touched on universal qualities—greed and gluttony, injustice, resentment, the need for dignity, and the capacity for fear and joy—as well as the economics of a medieval manor, but locates them within a framework of human intentions. As *Catherine, Called Birdy* progresses, for instance, you discover that Catherine's father treats her with much the same greedy muzzle-wittedness as he does his tenants: he wants to marry her off like a "cheese sold to the highest bidder." He thinks a merchant would be a good choice, because the newly developing towns are better off financially than small manors. Birdy, on the other hand, sets out to foil his attempts to arrange her life for financial advantage. This small human drama contains many of the elements of the transition from feudalism to capitalism, but the narrative description of a greedy father swilling

For further discussion of this issue, see also Bruner (1986), Geertz (1983), Kermode (1980), Rabinowitz (1987), Traugott & Pratt (1980), Toolan (1988), White (1980).

All narratives are created within a sociocultural framework.

Coerr (1994)

Narratives often make connections between past and present moral and ethical dilemmas.
Levstik (1989)

Coerr (1993) flyleaf

Bruner (1986), Saul (1994)

Megill (1989, p. 633)

Depersonalized language can also deproblematize history.
Cushman (1994, p. 7)

Cushman (1994, p. 5)

ale while his tenants suffer, and selling his daughter to the highest bidder makes more intuitive sense than the distanced and lawlike explanations of the text (and it is much funnier!).

Of course not all historical narratives are either fictional or particularly personal. Increasingly, informational books for children present history in lively narrative (and non-narrative) form. Russell Freedman's books on immigrant children, children of the old west, and the like are certainly narrative—they tell a story (or stories) about American history—but they do not focus on a particular set of characters in the way that a biography or historical fiction might. Instead, Freedman weaves his story around the lives of people the reader may only meet for a moment. Milton Meltzer also writes nonfiction narrative history with a passion that captures readers' attention. He supports his narratives with personal accounts, as when he describes the work of children at Thomas Jefferson's Monticello nail factory. The factory was worked, he reported, by a dozen young slaves, ages 10 to 16. "They labored for twelve hours a day, six days a week . . . When several of the boys in his sweatshop ran off to freedom, Jefferson had them hunted down relentlessly and flogged when caught" (p. 23). Although this is not the story of a single child, or even a single family, it certainly "tells it as if it were a person." In other words, Meltzer's and Freedman's work moves beyond exposition—laying out the facts in order—to storytelling a tale "of common humanity . . . to help young readers understand the world as it is, and to realize that we need not accept that world as it is given to us." Such narratives can help young readers see that although the turn of historical events is not inevitable, economic, political, and social forces can sometimes overwhelm individual choice.

Part of the appeal of such narratives, as we have said, is that they have a moral. This is probably because the most readily available schema students have to bring to bear in understanding history are "human behavior" schema, where morality, or at least fairness, is often a central concern. In addition to being readily available, too, these schema are among the most fully developed, especially in young children. Moreover, they are particularly appropriate in understanding historical fiction, biography, and autobiography, based as they are on the particulars of human, and often child, behavior. Unfortunately, they are not equally useful in interpreting historical textbooks in which individual human intentions and motivations are often replaced by political and economic analyses. As a result, students may find it more difficult to identify and recall these more analytical historical accounts without considerable assistance.

Because children have more readily available schema for interpreting some types of historical narrative, however, does not mean either that these are the only texts they should read or that children are naturally critical readers of narratives. In fact, narrative is not the only history genre available to students, and the very accessibility of narratives may work against critical reading—if the narrative is intuitively right its underlying historical interpretation is unlikely to elicit criticism. In addition, the ethical and moral context of the narratives we have described adds enormous weight to an author's historical perspective. Readers of books such as *Sadako* or *Catherine, Called Birdy* may find out how particular people lived their daily lives, and that more than one point of view existed, but they are invited to sympathize with or at least understand the protagonist's point of view. When Jennifer read *Sarah Bishop* and *The Witch of Blackbird Pond* she clearly identified with Sarah and Kit, the main characters in each book. While she recognized that another view of the events was possible, she was still convinced that such a view "would be an awful story . . . They'd probably try and make it seem that the witches [Sarah and Kit are accused of witchcraft] were awful."

In other words, to the extent that young readers believe a story, they also read it as "telling what really happened." As Jennifer explains, "Even if it weren't all true, it could have been true, and it could have happened like that." This can make it very hard to dislodge narrative interpretations, especially if no equally compelling case is made for alternative perspectives.

Narrative often has a distinctly personal voice that makes intuitive sense to young readers.

Person & Cullinan (1992), Saul (1994)

Freedman (1980, 1983)

Well-written nonfictional narratives have voice and passion.

Meltzer (1994)

Meltzer (1994a, p. 21)

Historical events are influenced by more than individual choice.

Bardige (1988)

Human behavior schema are among the most fully developed in elementary and middle school children.

Barton (1995), Carretero, Jacott, Limón, Manjón, & León (1994) Levstik & Pappas (1987)

Children are not naturally critical of historical narratives.

The moral context of narratives adds weight to their historical perspective.

Coerr (1993), Cushman (1994)

O'Dell (1980), Speare (1958)

Levstik (1989)

It can be very difficult to dislodge interpretations drawn from well-written narratives.

Collier & Collier (1974), Forbes (1943), Fritz (1967), Turner (1992)

Too often textbooks underestimate children's ability to handle complexity.

An outline of events is rarely memorable or persuasive to students.

Degenhardt & McKay (1988)

Narrative can support informed and disciplined imaginative entry into history.

Teachers can honor children's search for truth while helping them to become more analytical in their response to history.

Bardige (1988)

As she read different novels, Jennifer encountered a variety of historical perspectives on the American Revolution. In the Collier brothers' novel, *My Brother Sam Is Dead*, British and Loyalist sympathizers and the American Rebels commit atrocities, and there is little to chose between them. In Jean Fritz's *Early Thunder*, good and evil exist in both Loyalist and Rebel camps, and people of conscience chose where they think the most good must lie. Esther Forbes' *Johnny Tremain* presents a clear argument for the Rebel cause, and *Katie's Trunk* shows the Rebels as disgruntled marauders. It was clear to Jennifer that the textbook version was inadequate. The textbook, she declared, just said that "Americans were right but it doesn't tell you exactly why they were right, or why the British fought." She expected—and wanted—history to be interpretive, and to involve moral issues. She wasn't interested in neutrality so much as she wanted to understand why the two sides fought. You may think that the textbook does precisely that. It outlines the events leading up to rebellion and military conflict: taxation without representation, British control of the colonial economy, ideas about "unalienable rights." But these reasons, potent as they may be to historians, are not fully explanatory for students. From Jennifer's perspective, such explanations are neither persuasive nor memorable precisely because they ignore the human behavior schema we have already discussed.

Jennifer was angered by what she perceived as the single perspective taken by her textbook—Americans (Rebels) were right. In her reading, she had already encountered other perspectives, and expected a more complete story. She wanted to be engaged by history, rather than distanced from it. Unfortunately, expository texts that emphasize greater and greater degrees of abstraction while trying to maintain a neutral or "objective" stance often distance students from history. Well-written, historically sound narratives (fiction as well as nonfiction), on the other hand, can support *informed and disciplined* imaginative entry into events—and help students to make better sense out of expository texts. This is not sugar coating the bitter pill of academic history, or turning history into one big storytelling session. Dealing explicitly with students' ethical sensitivities is, we think, more likely to make history a compelling part of the curriculum. This requires, however, a delicate balance between honoring children's search for historical truth and developing their recognition that other people in other times saw the world differently, not just from us, but from each other. Students do tend to value the "truthfulness" of historical narratives, and use narrative interpretations as the standard against which other information is measured. What we are suggesting, then, is that a variety of good literature, combined with careful teacher facilitation, can help students see and understand the complexities that multiple historical perspectives suggest without sacrificing their ethical sensitivities and impulses.

SELECTING GOOD NARRATIVE HISTORY

Obviously, any piece of historical narrative is not as good as any other. In fact, if you read much historical fiction from the first half of the 20th century you might well wonder whether historical narratives have any relation to "what really happened." Geoffrey Trease, an author of historical fiction, listed just a few of the restrictions that applied to children's historical fiction in the 1950s: no liquor, no supernatural phenomenon, no undermining of authority, no parents with serious weaknesses, no realistic working-class speech (including even the mildest cursing), and no budding love affairs. In addition, texts sprinkled with "prithees," and "methinks," and the like, too often are historical caricatures rather than historically real. The historical realism of the type that garnered *Catherine, Called Birdy* a Newbery Honor award for children's fiction in 1994 is a relative newcomer to children's literature. Unfortunately, the problems with historical fiction are not confined to the past. Some more recent fiction is also blatantly inaccurate, cursed with tunnel vision, and mired in romanticism. In Robert Newton Peck's *A Day No Pigs Would Die*, for instance, Peck creates a Shaker community that violates almost every tenet of the Shaker faith. Where historical

Trease (1983)

Historical realism in children's literature is a relative newcomer to the field.

Cushman (1994)

Peck (1972)

Shakers were celibate, Peck's Shakers marry and bear children. Where historical Shakers lived in separatist communities away from "the world's people," Peck's Shakers live in the world. In other books, historical events are rearranged, or facts omitted to avoid controversy. A biography of Andrew Jackson, for instance, may barely mention the forced evacuation of the Cherokee, while books on Columbus often ignore the impact of exploration on the inhabitants of the "New World."

The teachers throughout this book rely heavily on historical fiction as well as informational books. Initially, most of them felt intimidated by the task of selecting historically accurate, well-written literature. They weren't all history majors, and didn't always know the latest scholarship. Over the years, however, they developed selection criteria that worked for them. The following guidelines represent the kinds of considerations these teachers have found useful:

- Does the book tell a good story? Scholarship is not enough to carry historical fiction. If the narrative does not hold up, even the best-documented history will not matter. Ask yourself if the book you are considering tells a story that is interesting in its own right, blending fact and fiction so that the historical background is subordinate, but essential, to the story. In Margaree King Mitchell's *Uncle Jed's Barbershop*, living in the segregated South of the 1920s is the backdrop for a story of commitment to family, as well as dreams deferred and realized. Yet the backdrop is integral to the story. Segregation and economic collapse are the stage on which the story is played out:

  Huck, Hepler, & Hickman (1987)
  A book must be both good literature and good history
  Mitchell (1993)

  Even though I was unconscious, the doctors wouldn't look at me until they had finished with all the white patients. . . .
  My daddy didn't have that kind of money. And the doctors wouldn't do the operation until they had the money.

- Is the story accurate and authentic in its historical detail, including the setting and the known events of history? Again, this attention to accuracy and authenticity must not detract from the story. Instead, the historical details should make the story ring true, not just in the description and use of material culture, but in the values and spirit of the time. As Cushman notes, the differences between past and present run deeper than what people in the past ate, where (or when) they bathed, or who decided to marry whom. Historical people lived "in a place we can never go, made up of what they value, how they think, and what they believe is true and important and possible."

  Children's fiction deserves the same attention to historical accuracy as non-fiction.
  Cushman (1994, p. 165)

- Is the language authentic to the times? This is a challenging criteria. For one thing, the language of the past, even if it was English, is not the English spoken anywhere today. Instead of striving for complete authenticity, then, look for language that has the flavor of the times. Idioms, for instance, should be plausible, given both the historical period and the characters. One of the delights of *Catherine, Called Birdy* is Birdy's experimentation with cursing. Her brother tells her that the king no longer says "Deus!" or "Corpus Bones!" as "ordinary folk do." Instead, he uses "God's breath!" Her brother adopts "God's feet." Not to be outdone, Birdy tries a different oath each day. First she tries "God's face!", than "God's ears!", and finally settles on "God's Thumb!" "because thumbs are such important things and handy to use."

  Completely authentic language is rarely possible in children's historical fiction. Look for the "flavor" of the times.

- Is the historical interpretation sound? Overly romanticized, outdated interpretations may be useful for comparison's sake, but not for the core of literature to be used in class. Select several books representing the same topic from different perspectives, but make sure that each perspective is supportable, given what is currently known about the topic. Make sure characters act in accordance with these interpretations. In Robert Conley's *Nickajack* , the Cherokee nation has split into warring factions, some advocating resistance to the treaty that took away their homelands; others advocating cooperation and relocation. Conley based his story on recent scholarship about the period immediately following the "Trail of Tears." Its impact comes, at least in part, because of the inexorability of the central tragedy—the continuation of vengeance. In the last paragraph of the book, one character lies dying, and his wife sinks to her knees: "The murderer's face was firmly etched in her mind. She would never forget it. This was not the end."

  Avoid overly romanticized historical fiction.

  Conley (1992)
  .

  Conley (1992, p. 182)

Consider who the participants in an event might have been, and select literature to represent those perspectives.

Hudson (1989, 1990), Cornell (1993), Eisenber (1991), Holtze (1988), Wright (1995)

Well-written historical narratives speak *to* the present as well as *about* the past.

We tell new stories as we rethink the past.

Yep (1994)

- Whose voices are missing? Because literature is so powerful, it is important to select as many different, historically sound perspectives as possible. Think about who the participants in an event were, and how those participants might have told their story. Traditional stories of the Westward Movement, for instance, have often been told from the perspective of white male pioneers moving from East to West. More recently, however, literature focusing on women, and on Native American, African-American, and Spanish perspectives have begun to appear. Jan Hudson's *Sweetgrass* and *Dawn Rider*, Kate Cornell's *These Lands are Ours: Tecumseh's Fight for the Old Northwest*, Sollace Hotze's *A Circle Unbroken*, and Courtni C. Wright's *Wagon Train: A Family Goes West in 1865* are a small sample of some of the books now available that provide insight into the impact of culture clash in the American West.

- Does the book provide insight and understanding into current issues as well as those in the past? As we said in the first chapter, history is not just about who we—or other people—were, but about who we are and who we can become. Well-written historical narratives speak to each of these conditions. It is no accident that as we struggle to come to terms with our history, we rethink many aspects of the past, and come to tell new stories about ourselves. A recounting of the building of the transcontinental railroad, for instance, is no longer a simple and single story of Euro-Americans conquering the wilderness. Instead, it is also the story of Chinese and Irish immigrants, of displaced Native Americans, and of the fear and racism that accompanied expansion. Lawrence Yep's *Dragon's Gate*, then, is not just about a young boy's experiences working on the railroad, but about the struggle of many immigrants to survive in a new land.

Students need a variety of fiction and nonfiction.

Pappas (1991)

Levstik (1993)

When nonfiction receives the kind of attention usually accorded fiction students respond with enthusiasm.

Extensive and intensive use of fiction and nonfiction builds a "web of meaning" in the classroom.

"Finding out" is a valued activity in inquiry-oriented classrooms.

As we emphasize throughout the book, students of history need experience with multiple historical genres. Fiction is certainly one of those genres, but so is informational (or nonfiction) literature. Sometimes adults assume that students will invariably prefer fiction to nonfiction, but we have not found this to be the case. In classrooms where nonfiction is used in meaningful ways, students select it at least as often as they select fiction. Moreover, where inquiry is the basic approach to history, informational literature is an essential classroom resource.

Ruby Yessin, for instance, often starts the school day by reading and discussing nonfiction with her first-grade class. During these times, illustrations are discussed, facts checked, and questions raised about the authenticity of the information. A pop-up book of historical sailing vessels, for instance, fascinates her students, and sends them to other books on Columbus to see if they accurately represent the Niña, Pinta, and Santa Maria. In Ruby's class, a child may be called on to check with the librarian for further information, or to use one of the reference books in the classroom to answer questions raised in reading an informational book. Children keep these books at their desks and are allowed to read them during "free reading time." Several students are more likely to check out informational books from the library than fiction, too.

Many of these informational books are difficult for Ruby's students, but they read as much as they can and allow the teacher, their partners, or other adults to help them understand the rest. It is not unusual in the classroom for a visitor to be asked to read an informational book to a first grader intent on finding out about Shakers, Columbus, or China. Ruby explains that her extensive use of information literature is part of the "web of meaning" that she and the children are building. In her class "finding out" is so highly valued that there is plenty of incentive for making use of nonfiction. Fortunately, there is more and more high quality nonfiction available to support such use. Just as with fiction, however, careful selection is important. While Ruby does a lot of book selection on her own, she also relies on recommendations from the school librarian and her colleagues. In general, Ruby uses the following selection criteria:

- What are the author's qualifications? A quick check of the "About the Author" page in a book or on the book's jacket will generally let you know what qualifications an author possesses. Sometimes an author is not an expert on a topic, but has consulted with people who are, and acknowledges them in the book. Jerry Stanley, for instance, is a history professor who knew a good deal about the background for Japanese internment during World War II, but his book, *I Am an American: A True Story of Japanese Internment*, heavily relies on interviews with Shi Nomura and other former internees. As a result of these firsthand recollections, Stanley's book has a greater degree of authenticity and sensitivity than he could have provided on his own.

  Stanley (1994)

- How accurate and complete are the facts? It has been our experience that the most blatant errors in historical nonfiction have more to do with what is left out than with errors of fact. Books on Native Americans, for instance, too often deal only with life on the frontier, or lump all Native peoples into one amorphous group of *Indians*. Books on traditional heroes may present one sided portraits of such complex people as Abraham Lincoln or Martin Luther King. One way to guard against errors either of commission or omission is to invite students to compare different versions of historical people and events, noting where sources differ, and researching to find the most supportable facts. In addition, *Social Education* and *Hornbook* publish yearly reviews of children's literature by topic. While *Social Education* confines its review to books specifically related to social studies topics, *Hornbook* provides a more general guide with sections on social science, history, families, technology, and the like.

  Even when the facts are accurate, check to see if important information or perspectives are missing.

  Encourage students to critically review the books they use.

- Is the book up to date? Children in one primary classroom found a book in their collection that discussed the history of space travel, noting in its conclusion that one day man might walk on the moon. While the children, who all knew full well that people had been to the moon and back several times, found this book amusing, they are less likely to recognize similar errors on less familiar topics. They might not notice sweeping generalizations that identify an entire group of people as thrifty or prone to violence. Checking publication dates is a good place to start in ascertaining whether a book is relatively current. Examining illustrations for datedness and stereotypes also helps. Nevertheless, some books will slip through with mistakes or misrepresentations. Don't toss them out. In an era of budget cutbacks and limited resources, even weak books have their uses. Encourage students to bring a critical eye to bear on their reading of all sorts of fact and fiction.

  Students are less likely to spot errors in unfamiliar topics.

- Does the author distinguish between fact and supposition? One of the best examples of this is Jean Fritz' *The Double Life of Pocahontas*. Unlike books that tell a straightforward rescue story, Fritz acknowledges throughout the text that much of what we know about Pocahontas cannot be verified. In fact, she explains that there is very little evidence that Pocahontas saved John Smith's life at all. In similar fashion, Kathy Pelta's *Discovering Christopher Columbus: How History is Invented* systematically deconstructs the Columbus story, explaining how and why this story has changed over time, and what sources are known to exist. Some authors, including Russell Freedman, provide extensive endnotes that include sources, discussions of different interpretations, and other books students might want to read on the same topic. Be especially cautious about books that seem overly romanticized, too-good-to-be-true depiction's of the past. Too often this means an author has uncritically accepted tradition rather than critically analyzing sources in order to write good history.

  Fritz (1983)

  Pelta (1991)

  Freedman (1990, 1993, 1994)

  Check the author's notes for sources and additional information.

- How well is the book organized? Generally, an author's sense of purpose and prospective audience helps shape how a book is organized. A good deal of nonfiction will not be read cover to cover, or at least not in front to back order. Instead, readers of nonfiction often skip around, searching for a particular piece of information or explanation. Illustrations are very important in this search, and should complement and extend the information in the text. Captions should let readers know what they are seeing in clear and vivid language. Think about how readers might use this book, and check for a usable index and table of contents.

  Think about how readers will use the nonfiction you select

Saul (1994)

Meltzer (1994)

Look for works of nonfiction that not only have solid historical content, but are distinguished literature as well.

Kobrin (1988)

Selection of good books is not enough; organizing their use is crucial.

Cushman (1994), Fleischman (1992), Aliki (1983), Macaulay (1977), Sancha (1990), McKinley (1989)

Book sets help organize student reading.

Focusing student attention on the historical substance of literature requires careful teacher planning.

Keating (1994), Wells & Chang-Wells (1992), Atwell (1990)

Cushman (1994), Fleischmann (1992)

Good questions facilitate response group discussions.

- What literary distinction does the book have? A good piece of literature reveals the personal style of the author. As Milton Meltzer noted, if a writer is "indifferent, bored, stupid or mechanical" it will show in the work. The facts must be there, of course, but so must the author's voice and vision. The author shapes the facts, and in that shaping makes some facts more significant than others. Meltzer, for instance, could have simply described the tasks given to the young men working in Thomas Jefferson's nail factory and left out the personal cost of those tasks. Instead, his powerful authorial voice makes vivid the desperation of these young men: "The work was so repetitive, boring, mindless, and, of course, payless that they did as little as possible . . . several of the boys in his sweatshop ran off to freedom . . ." In a work of literary distinction , the author cares about the topic as, most likely, will the reader. For help in finding these kinds of books, you might want to subscribe to *The Kobrin Letter,* a periodical that reviews and recommends children's fiction literature. Beverly Kobrin's book, *Eyeopeners* also provides suggestions (as well as titles) for selecting fiction.

Selecting good books is, of course, just the beginning. Organizing their use is crucial to helping students appreciate the books they read as literature and as historical interpretations. One technique that several teachers find helps students move beyond an attachment to a single perspective is the use of book sets. A book set usually includes paired selections of fiction—Cushman's *Catherine, Called Birdy* and Fleischmann's The *Whipping Boy* for a medieval study—and several informational books at different levels of difficulty—perhaps Aliki's *Medieval Wedding*, Macaulay's *Castle*, and Sancha's *The Luttrell Village: Country Life in the Middle Ages*. In Abby Mott's classroom, she combines book sets that the students read with at least one "read-aloud" novel. For a medieval unit, for instance, she chose McKinley's *The Outlaws of Sherwood*, a retelling of the Robin Hood legend that reinterprets the roles played by Robin and Marian. Sometimes students only read one of the paired books and the selection that Abby reads aloud serves as contrast. In the medieval set, however, both books were relatively short, so she required that students read both.

Simply assigning reading, Abby discovered early on, is not always motivating. After a couple of years of trying different techniques, she settled on several things that seemed to engage her students in discussing historical perspective. First, she found that dialogue journals provided an important opportunity for students to discuss their personal responses to their readings. In the dialogue journals, Abby and her students carry on a written conversation about the books students read or hear. Sometimes Abby asks students to respond to a specific question such as "What do you think are the most important differences between your life and Birdy's?" This question might require little beyond having read *Catherine, Called Birdy* and thought about how an adolescent's life has changed over time (or not). In other cases, she asks questions such as "How accurate do you think Cushman's and Fleischmann's depictions of the Middle Ages are?" and "What sources helped you answer this question?" These require more attention to the construction of a historical interpretation, and encourage students to draw on the nonfiction sources in the book set.

Abby also found that peer discussion helped students move beyond their first impressions of a book. Since not all students necessarily read the same books at the same time, she arranges two types of response groups of three to five students each. The first is a discussion opportunity for students who *are* reading the same book. Abby may start the group with a couple of questions or a problem that will require their reference to the book they are reading and will focus on both the literary and historical aspects of the book. In one group, for example, she asks students to select three passages that show how Birdy changes over the course of the book. In another, students search for passages that capture the differences between life in the manor and in the village. A third group selects historical descriptions from Birdy that can be supported by evidence from one of the informational books. Notice that the groups are not duplicating each other. Instead, each group is organized so that it will have something specific to contribute to a follow-up discussion among response groups.

The second type of response group mixes students who have read different books. The tasks for such a group might involve creating a list of medieval rules for childrearing, a description of medieval wedding customs that have current counterparts, making a comparison chart of the roles of different levels of medieval society, or creating a story map that locates each of the places described in the books. In one class, a group discussing childrearing practices was appalled at the level of violence directed against children. They collected current information about child abuse, found other books on child labor, and ended up making a chart of requirements for a "child-friendly world." Abby then gave them a copy of the UN Declaration on the Rights of Children, and asked them to compare it to their own recommendations.

When students read different books, discussions focus on comparison and contrast, as well as supportable arguments.

As you can see, some of these activities were relatively short term—writing a dialogue journal entry—while others became in-depth studies—the child-rearing practices, for instance. Students had opportunities to share what they were thinking with their teacher and with small groups of their peers. In the small groups, most of that sharing happened in conversation. But not all students find this the most effective way to share what they know, and even in the most supportive environment, not all students participate equally in conversation. As we discuss in chapter 13, honoring students' different ways of knowing is as important in history as in any other cognitive domain.

Gardner & Boix-Massilla (1994)

Abby discovered early in her teaching career that creating opportunities for students to respond to their reading using a variety of media resulted in richer historical thinking. During their medieval study, her seventh graders presented a reader's theater production, *Rent Day*, based in part on Aliki's *Medieval Wedding* (where the lives of a noble and his tenants are juxtaposed), and drawing on *Catherine, Called Birdy*, *Luttrell Village*, and the students' research in other books. In *Rent Day*, different characters living on a medieval manor describe their feelings about their lives, the people with whom they live, and the practice of paying rent to the lord of the manor. Another group created a mural styled after the Bayeaux tapestry, except that instead of depicting the Norman conquest, their tapestry contrasted life on the feudal manor with life in the newly created merchant towns. With help from their music teacher, another group put on a concert of recorder music that might have been heard in a medieval castle. One of the more interesting presentations involved the sale of Papal indulgences. Several students had focused on Birdy's brother Edward, a monk working in a scriptorium, on her description of Jews forced to leave England, and on the religious activities at village fairs and in her home. In their research they discovered that monks and priests sometimes sold indulgences—Papal forgiveness for mortal and venial sins committed for a set period of time. The students' created illuminated "indulgences" for the characters in each book, including pictures of the torments of hell and the delights of heaven (authentic to illuminated manuscripts of the time) as well as descriptions of the sins each character needed to have forgiven (based on the students' analysis of the books they were reading).

Encourage a variety of ways of responding to history

Aliki (1983), Cushman (1994), Sancha (1990)

As students worked on these projects, questions arose that sent them back to their reading. Sometimes debates would reignite as new information came to light. By arranging opportunities to encounter and reencounter a topic, Abby provided a context for communal construction of meaning. Students adjusted their ideas, not just in response to the text, or to teacher comment, but on the basis of interactions with their peers. In addition, Abby encouraged reference to other sources of information. When a dispute over the accuracy of historical information arose, she arbitrated first by having students check each author's credentials, and then by sending students to the library to look for confirming or disconfirming information. In doing so, she directed them to other history genres—art, primary sources, textbooks.

Wells & Chang-Wells (1992)

Arbitrate rather than eliminate intellectual disputes.

Finally, Abby used literature as a springboard to more in-depth inquiry. Based on their reading, students selected other topics to investigate. They were very interested in childrearing, in general feudal practices, and the kinds of jobs people might do as adults, in addition to the usual fascination with knights, armor, King Arthur, and Robin Hood. These became individual and group projects that were presented at a medieval fair attended by parents and students from other grades. Notice that, while

Literature is not the end of historical study; it is one source among many.

children began with a personal response to narrative: "It made me frustrated for Birdy," or "I thought that she should just run away with Perkin!" they were also encouraged (indeed, required) to move beyond narrative. Their interest might be captured by a well written story, but their responses were educated by a wide variety of genres.

"I DID NOT PANIC": CREATING HISTORICAL NARRATIVES

April 6, 1862

"Boom!" The cannon thundered across the sky. That's what happened on this bloody day. Even now the gunboats' cannon flash across the sky. I can hear the cry of wounded but nobody dares help them. I've heard the tales about bloody battles but none could be as bad as this! Men were falling all around me but I did not panic! The situation is grim but we'll hang on although General Sherman was wrong before, he's pulling us through.

So we Yanks ain't licked yet!

—Hugh B. McKay
(historical character as interpreted by fifth-grade student)

Every piece of writing stands on the shoulders of all the literature that came before it. This is as true of your students' writing as it is of a published author's. Consider the sources for the student's creation of the diary entry for Huch McKay, an actual Civil War solider. The fifth grader who wrote this first heard *Thunder at Gettysburg*, and *The Drummer Boy of Shiloh*, and read actual diaries from the period. Relying largely on primary sources and historical narratives, he reconstructed the life of this Union soldier injured at the Battle of Shiloh. While he is also in a classroom that overflows with books, in which he expects to write in a variety of genres, he has had little prior experience with primary sources. Nevertheless, narrative devices including the use of dialect and first-person narration are familiar and comfortable literary tools for him. Writing is an important way in which he and his classmates construct their own historical interpretations. Students who have not been similarly immersed in literature may be less likely to produce as literate a narrative, but all students can benefit from the opportunity to create historical narratives.

Pamela Vachon's fifth-grade students eagerly anticipated their upcoming study of the Civil War. In previous years, the study had included a reenactment of the Battle of Shiloh. A storage closet contained a tempting collection of military paraphernalia, including hats and flags that Pamela's predecessor had acquired as he visited historic sites. Unfortunately, as far as Pamela was concerned, the main thing that the students seemed to anticipate was the romance of feather cockades, gold tassels, and cardboard bayonets. She was especially surprised at how many of the students wanted to be Confederates. They were, after all, in a Union state and in an area that had sent many men to fight for the Union. As it turned out, the appeal of the Confederacy had little to do with sympathy for the "lost cause." Instead, as Jacob, one of her students, explained, "the Confederate uniforms are better. Those big feathers are great!" While there was no way she could get out of reenacting the battle—it was a tradition started long before her entry into the school, and involved all the fifth grades in the district—Pamela decided that she could better prepare her students to understand the historical context and the costs of war.

Pamela's students loved historical fiction, especially when she read aloud to them; they were also used to vigorous discussions of literature. When she introduced Arthur C. Clark's *The Drummer Boy of Shiloh*, they settled in their seats expectantly. As she finished the story, and the students discussed their responses, Pamela called their attention to the list of questions they had previously developed for historical fiction:

- What would you need to know in order to write this story?
- Where would you find the necessary information?
- How does the author help you understand what the characters are feeling?`

Gauch (1974), Clarke (1974)

All children can benefit from writing their own historical narratives.

Writing their own history can help students understand the context surrounding historical events.

Read aloud to students of all ages.

Clarke (1974)

Students can generate discussion questions for different historical genres.

100

- What other options did the character have, given this time and setting?
- Could this story have been told from another point of view?
- In what ways might this story have been different if it had been set in our time and place?

With Clark's vivid images of Shiloh as introduction, Pamela asked students to carefully analyze a portrait displayed on the overhead. This was a picture of a man from a small town in Ohio, she explained. What clues could they find to the time when this person lived? Did they think this was a wealthy person, or poor? As the students made their observations, Pamela recorded them on sheets of chart paper. Next, she showed them a primary source—a surgeon's report on an injury. This document, she told them, was a piece of evidence to help them figure out the identify of the person in the picture. As a class, they discussed the document, listing new information, and new questions that were raised.

Over the course of the next several days, Pamela introduced a variety of other sources that she had collected and organized in folders:

- Public documents: military records, surgeons' reports, and pension applications available from the National Archives.
- Family records: obituaries, a county history that included Hugh's family, and photographs. The pictures were from a family collection. The rest of the materials were from the county library and local historical society. Some collections also have photographs.
- Newspapers: samples from Hugh's hometown paper included stories about secession, as well as farming news, recipes for sorghum and butter, advice, poetry, and local politics. Pamela's local library had old newspapers on microfilm; in some areas, these are kept in state and local historical societies or university libraries.
- Samples of personal writing: other people witnessed the events Hugh lived through. Several diaries and collections of letters were available in the state historical society's manuscript collection as well as in periodicals such as *Civil War Times Illustrated*.
- Other sources: maps, drawings, photographs and a timeline of events from April 1861 through April 1865 provided a graphic framework for the other primary sources. Pamela used material from textbooks and photocopied pictures from Civil War histories.

Each day's work was organized around a set of questions related to the sources with which students worked. For the obituary of Hugh's mother, for instance, students were asked how many siblings Hugh had, and what had happened to them by 1898. Pamela also moved between groups, helping them decipher antique penmanship or asking probing questions: Was this document sufficient evidence for a particular interpretation? What seemed to be the general feeling of the new soldiers as they marched South? Although each group worked with the same set of documents, their interpretations were often quite different, and discussions at the end of work sessions were lively. Pamela found that she needed to make rules for polite debate and discussion, and finally spent time establishing ground rules for "supportable interpretations:"

Students need clear rules for debate and discussion

- Evidence must be from a reliable source. Check publication date, author, possible bias.
- Interpretations should be true to the values and social rules of the time. Think about how people thought *then* not *now*.
- You cannot move historic events around just to suit your interpretation. You have to account for the facts.

Pamela reminded students that historians have similar arguments, and that agreement was not required, although supportable interpretations were. She also found that, although students enjoyed the "decoding" aspect of reading primary sources, some sources just produced frustration. In deciding how to handle this, her students suggested developing a "primary source key," showing common forms of script for a specific time period. Pamela also decided that next time she would transcribe some of the most difficult sources.

While some primary sources may need to be translated, most should be used "as is."

Fulwiler (1982), Harste & Short (1988)

After each day's work, Pamela asked students to write a letter or diary entry based on what they had learned about Hugh. Writing encouraged students to think about what they knew and could support. It also required organizing information in some meaningful way. In the sample given here, the student author included details about the battle obtained from reading diary entries from other soldiers. He also incorporated an assessment of General Sherman based on a letter from another soldier. Another student discovered that field hospitals were used at Shiloh, and incorporated that information into her story, along with details from the surgeon's report on Hugh's injury:

> Dear Diary,
>
> Today I got shot in the hand. My hand is almost completely destroyed. My middle finger is completely gone. I went to the field tent. The doctors did not do anything because there were other more important patients. I am not writing this diary entry, my best friend is. I am telling him what to write.

This type of writing certainly gives the teacher clues as to how well students understand source materials, but it also challenges children's notions of the romance of war. There was little in Hugh's story, or in any of the other sources, about feathers, sabers, and gold tassels. Instead, soldiers' letters and diaries describe rain and mud, terror, injury, and death. In one vivid diary entry, a young soldier described struggling to find a place to sleep with no shelter from the pouring rain and discovering in the morning that he had spent the night sleeping against a pile of amputated limbs discarded behind the field hospital. In response, a student wrote about April 7, 1862:

> Today is the worst day of my life. It seems as if all my friends are dead. . . . We are being picked off like grapes off a grapevine.

Although Pamela felt that her main purpose was achieved by having the students write diary entries or letters home, other teachers who have used primary sources find that the students benefit from the experience of writing a final, more comprehensive narrative. This takes time and access to all the sources that students have used throughout their project. One sixth-grade teacher has students write historical fiction based on the sources they have investigated. The characters do not have to be real, but the historical context must be authentic. This allows students to fill in the gaps in the historical record while remaining true to the period or situation.

Kiefer (1995)

Ahlberg & Ahlberg (1986)

While young children can make less use of some types of written primary sources, they are perfectly capable of using art, artifacts, and interviews to write and illustrate biographies based on living people. Children's picture books can often suggest different techniques to use in creating biographies. One first grader, for instance, created postcards to tell the story of her uncle, a soldier stationed in Germany. The idea for postcards came from another book her teacher had read, *The Jolly Postman*.

CONCLUSION

Takaki (1993)

I will tell you something about stories . . .
They aren't just entertainment.
Don't be fooled.

—Leslie Marmon Silko

It is important in the development of any mature historical understanding that learners see history as a human enterprise made up of interpretations, subject to revision, and expressed through a variety of genres. The structure of narrative encourages readers to recognize the human aspects of history, and, with some help, to develop a better sense of its interpretive and tentative aspects. In addition, narrative may help students maintain a balance between the abstractions of history as an intellectual exercise, and history as an ongoing, participatory drama. But narrative is only one piece of the puzzle, for history is more than narrative. It is also learning to sift evidence before it has been shaped and interpreted. It is putting one's own time and place into a broader perspective, and seeing oneself as making choices that are, cumulatively, historic.

Levstik (1995)

The task of the teacher is to help students judge the interpretations appearing in narrative, to make sense out of alternative points of view, and to make careful historical judgments. Questions of fact and interpretation raised in this context can be used to initiate historical inquiry, refer students to other sources, including the full array of narrative genres, and provide a forum for the presentation of student interpretations. This, we think, is a crucial and often overlooked component to thinking and learning in history. This type of mediation also helps guard against the uncritical acceptance of literary constructions of history. The power of narrative is not an unmitigated good. As we noted previously, a good story can mask bad history and blind students to other interpretations. Children are likely to believe bad history if the narrative is compelling and may ignore good history if the narrative is insipid. This should serve as a caution to those currently recommending teaching history as a (often single) story well told. There is no evidence that a history curriculum based primarily on narrative and storytelling is either good teaching or good history. As one of Jeannette Groth's students notes, different genres provide different historical insights. The text, she explains, "told exact dates, places, names and etc. Other sources provide more explanations of why something happened or why someone was famous. They give more details of actual reasoning and even feelings. For instance, I was *inside* on who wanted the states split up, and why." As you read through this book, you will notice that while teachers use narrative in both its fictional and nonfictional forms, they also provide many other ways for students to think and learn in history.

The teacher's task is to help students make sense out of the literary and historical aspects of different written genres.

Different genres provide different historical insights and serve different social and cultural purposes.

Albert (1995)

CHILDREN'S AND ADOLESCENT LITERATURE

Aliki, M. (1983). *Medieval wedding*. HarperCollins.

Clarke, A. C. (1974). Drummer boy of Shiloh. In D. Roselle (Ed.) *Transformations II: Understanding American History Through Science Fiction* (pp. 13-23). Fawcett.

Coerr, E. (1994). *Sadako*. Putnam.

Collier, J., & Collier, L. (1974). *My Brother Sam is Dead*. Four Winds.

Conley, R. J. (1992). *Nickajack*. Doubleday.

Cornell, K. (1993). *These Lands Are Ours: Tecumseh's Fight for the Old Northwest*. Steck-Vaughn.

Cushman, K. (1994). *Catherine Called Birdy*. Clarion.

Fleischmann, P. (1992). *Whipping Boy*. HarperCollins.

Forbes, E. (1943). *Johnny Tremain*. Houghton, Mifflin.

Freedman, R. (1980). *Immigrant Kids*. Dutton.

Freedman, R. (1983). *Children of the Wild West*. Clarion.

Freedman, R. (1990). *Franklin Delano Roosevelt*. Clarion.

Freedman, R. (1993). *Eleanor Roosevelt: A Life of Discovery*. Clarion.

Freedman, R. (1994). *Kids at Work: Lewis Hine and the Crusade Against Child Labor*. Calrion.

Fritz, J. (1983). *The Double Life of Pocahontas*. Putnam.

Gauch, P. L. (1974). *Thunder at Gettysburg*. Coward, McCann & Geohegan.

Holtz, S. (1988). *A Circle Unbroken*. Clarion.

Hudson, J. (1989). *Sweetgrass*. Philomel.

Hudson, J. (1990). *Dawn Rider*. Philomel.

Pelta, K. (1991). *Discovering Christopher Columbus: How History is Invented*. Lerner.

Meltzer, M. (1994). *Cheap Raw Material : How Our Youngest Workers are Exploited and Abused*. Viking.

Macaulay, D. (1977). *Castle*. Houghton, Mifflin.

Mitchell, M. K. (1993). *Uncle Jed's Barbershop*. Simon & Schuste.

McKinley, R. (1989). *The Outlaws of Sherwood*. Berkely Publishing Group

McKissack, P., & McKissack, F. (1994). *A Long Hard Journey: The Story of the Pullman Porter*. Walker.

O'Dell, S. (1980). *Sarah Bishop*. Houghton, Mifflin.

Sancha, S. (1990). *The Luttrell Village: Country Life in the Middle Ages*. Crowell.

Speare, E. G. (1958). *The Witch of Blackbird Pond*. Houghton, Mifflin.

Stanley, J. (1994). *I Am An American: The True Story of Japanese American Internment*. Crown.

Turner, A. (1992). *Katie's Trunk*. MacMillan.

Wright, C. C. (1995). *Wagon Train: A family Goes West in 1865*. Holiday House.

Yep, L. (1994). *Dragon's Gate*. HarperCollins.

Chapter 10

Putting Conflict in Context

Viktor Komac, an eighth-grade teacher from Ohio, attended a professional meeting at which the speaker mentioned that American children have few strategies for dealing with public conflicts. Having noticed that his own students had precisely this difficulty, he decided to begin the year by underlining the controversial nature of history and helping students develop skills in conflict management. He began by asking each student to bring in newspaper articles regarding current local, national, or world conflicts. He arranged a large bulletin board with four columns: *Conflict, Perspectives, Resolutions, Changes.* After students categorized the conflicts they had identified, Viktor asked them to read over the articles and see if they could identify at least two sides to each conflict. Next, students cut out letters to the editor, editorials, and articles representing these perspectives. Small groups formed around each of the conflicts. Their first task was to see if their textbook could provide any background information. The group investigating the conflict over altering an antidiscrimination law, for example, found a section of their textbook on the Civil Rights movement useful. Another group discussing funding cuts for the arts found information on the establishment of governmental agencies such as the National Endowment for the Arts (NEA) and the National Endowment for the Humanities (NEH) useful. For the most part, however, their textbooks had little or nothing on their topics. Instead, they had to rely on other sources, especially newspapers and periodicals.

Viktor knew that as his students tried to juggle different sources, they would need help in keeping track of their work. Over the last several years he had adapted several techniques to help students keep track of different perspectives on controversial issues. Figure 10.1 shows a discussion web used by a group studying the operation of a nearby nuclear power plant. In this instance, the plant had already been built, and the controversy was over its operation, not its construction. As a result, students could go back to old newspapers to find out how the decision to build the plant had been made, and what arguments were originally made against its construction. They could then compare current operation with the claims made for the plant in the past.

Viktor also asked each group to fill out two other forms to help students think about the historical significance of current conflicts. On a page headed, "What Caused This?" students first identified a conflict and then wrote their best research-based guesses on what they thought caused the conflict. Another page headed, "What Might This Mean?" asked students to explain what might be different tomorrow as a result of a current conflict. These two forms required that students infer both historical causes and possible current effects. Later, they compared these hypotheses against actual outcomes, where those were available. When it appeared that a conflict was resolved, they listed the solution and discussed compromises, whose perspective won out, and the like. In the *Changes* column on the bulletin board, they listed evidence that either the conflict or its resolution created change. What difference did it make, for instance, when a controversial art show was closed down, an antidiscrimination law altered, or a new union contract signed? Finally, Viktor asked the students to use both forms to help them look into the future. Each group developed a 10-minute presentation *as if they were historians* explaining the conflict to people 50 years into the future. In their presentation they were to explain the historical significance of the conflict they had studied from two perspectives: that of participants in the events, and that of a future historian. What did this conflict look like in its own time? What historical significance might it have later on in time?

We may long for consensus, but we live with conflict.

Many teachers are afraid to engage students in controversial topics such as this. They worry that their students will not be able to handle conflict, that parents and others will attack them if they try it, and that their task is to help students "get along." Not surprisingly, teachers who strive for harmony in often disharmonious environments

Pro	Con
Cheaper, cleaner, power	Danger of accidents
Provide new jobs	Jobs are hazardous
Safer than mining	Too close to schools and houses
Will have safety features	Lower value of homes
Saves natural resources	No safe way to get rid of waste

POSSIBLE OUTCOMES

With Nuclear Power	Without Nuclear Power
1. All the "pro" things happen	1. We continue to use current sources until they are all used up
2. Cincinnati becomes like Chernoble	2. Fuel costs keep rising because resources are scarce
3. Nuclear waste pollutes ground water	3. Scientists fund a safer power source, before resources run out
4. Other power companies go out of business or sell for less	

FIG. 10.1.   Conflict: Should the nuclear power plant be operated?

often long for consensus—some shared set of values— rather than conflict. In the 1940s and 1950s American historians of the "consensus" school also tried to focus on uncovering a broadly shared set of values that, they argued, overrode ethnic and class distinctions. Much like current critics of multicultural education, these historians searched for something that could unify a diverse society. They, too, worried that diversity would cause fragmentation and that emphasizing conflict rather than consensus could lead to cynicism and the failure of citizens to participate in civic life. Echoes of the same charges and counter charges continue to be heard in current debates over the place of history in the social studies curriculum. We, like Viktor and several other teachers in this book, argue a contrary position. Conflict is built into the fabric of our public and private lives. Democracy is rooted in a conflictual model. The U.S. Declaration of Independence lays out a rationale for the right of people to overthrow governments that violate their rights, and the Bill of Rights begins with a guarantee of freedom of speech, including disagreeable speech. Democracies worldwide have similar foundations. Democratic governments are generally based on conflicting ideas, dissent, debate, negotiation, and even litigation. When we vote, the majority wins—we don't wait for everyone to agree. We also limit majority rule with laws intended to protect minority rights and we use a court system to adjudicate disputes. In addition, our own lives force us daily to recognize the reality of conflict in the world—whether it be ethnic wars in Europe or Africa, calls for disunion in francophone Canada, disputes over prayer in schools in the United States, or disagreements about preserving green space. We live in a contentious world, yet research indicates that American students better understand the place of consensus than of conflict in our political system, are unsure of how conflict might be managed or resolved, or what happens when conflicts remain.

As you can see, to assume that conflict is something to avoid misunderstands and misrepresents both the foundations of democracy and the nature of much of the world. We suggest being more honest with students about both conflict and consensus. This requires shifting the focus of history instruction from an oversimplified emphasis on "progress"—every day in every way we are getting better and better—to more indepth study of how groups and individuals now and in other times exercise power publicly and privately, how society deals with competing claims between order and protest and how political and social meanings are transmitted to individuals and groups. This certainly means that the history curriculum is more complex, but not that it disintegrates. Instead, the focus shifts from *telling* a mainstream narrative to *studying* the relationships between groups of people, *recognizing* their differing conceptions of social reality, and *developing supportable interpretations* based on that study. This is a perspective that shares substantial common ground with the NCSS Curriculum Standards. The NCSS standards argue that students need "tools that will inform their decision-making processes," that "most issues, when framed from the perspective of

Bestor (1953), Hertzberg (1989), Lybarger (1990)

Cheney (1987), Hirsch (1987), Ravitch & Schlesinger (1990)

Engle (1970), Gordon (1990), Gutmann (1987), Parker (1991a), Novick (1988)

Conflict is fundamental to democracy.

Parker (1991a, 1991b, 1991c), Skeels (1989)

McGinnis (n.d.)

Holt (1990a), Kessler-Harris (1990)

National Council for the Social Studies (1994)

Gordan (1988), Gutman (1976), Sklar (1995), Takaki (1993), Thompson (1963)

Seixas (1994a, 1994b)

Holt (1990b)

Hahn & Tocci (1990), Kelly (1986)
National Council for the Social Studies (1994)

Most conflicts have more than two sides.

two or more differing points of view, allow for a broader, more reasoned discussion rather than an immediate debate of one view versus an opposite view." We agree, suggesting further that such an approach also supports important aspects of historical thinking, including understanding historical agency and perspective.

Agency refers to the power to act. As we have already mentioned, we are all participants in the ongoing drama of history. We are both the subjects of history and its agents. We make history by the collective activities of our lives, including our participation in both the enduring and ephemeral dilemmas of our times. Unfortunately, history instruction often loses exactly that sense of agency. To the extent that we make history seem both finished and inevitable, students have difficulty seeing themselves as having agency—the power to make history. Focusing disciplined, reflective inquiry on persistent issues and conflicts in history gives students practice, as the Social Studies Standards suggest, in discussing the arguments and evidence that surround such dilemmas, but it is also more likely to help students see themselves as having agency. Note, too, that the NCSS Standards argue for the importance of seeing issues from multiple perspectives. Part of developing a sense of one's own agency is recognizing that there are alternative positions and alternative actions that could be taken. Imagine trying to represent the current political climate in the United States to your grandchildren. What perspectives would you have to explain? If most conflicts had only two perspectives they might be easier to resolve, at least by voting, but there are obviously more than two ways of looking at such issues as a balanced budget amendment, term limits, or changes in affirmative action legislation. A wide range of options and opinions are available to citizens in responding to each of these issues. One of the challenges facing history teachers is dealing with complex issues so that students develop both civic competence and a sense of historical agency.

IT IS HAPPENING RIGHT NOW: STARTING WITH CURRENT EVENTS

Current conflicts encourage speculation about multiple causes and possible effects.

Investigating current, unresolved issues has a sense of immediacy often lacking in historical study. Because they are unresolved, current issues encourage students to speculate about how conflicts might turn out—and provide a framework for analyzing other historical conflicts. Students learn to think about the options available to participants in a specific time and place, the likelihood that any particular option might be chosen, and the possible outcomes that might result. They learn to look for the decision makers—who has power, and how is it exercised? What can people distant from the immediate crisis do? How have such people reacted in the past? If, on the other hand, students perceive history as finished, it can be hard to get them involved in rethinking historic controversies, much less in thinking about what those controversies might have to do with their own lives.

C. Bennett & Spalding (1992)

One option for teaching history, then, is to begin with controversies that are still unresolved. This was certainly Dehea Smith's (chapter 6) approach, and one of the reasons she preferred to teach history in an integrated social studies framework. She used current events to help students see how conflicts changed their community, and how groups and individuals influenced those changes. One current controversy—development of green space—was easily observed and lent itself to historic connections. Students could develop *before* and *after* illustrations to show shrinking green space, they could see how much construction altered their community, and they could debate whether development should be slowed, stopped, or left unfettered. In addition, the public librarian showed children how to access maps and photographs, newspaper articles, and blueprints showing how Lexington had coped with similar controversies in the past, and the local Trust for Historic Preservation provided boxes of primary and secondary materials, maps, photographs, children's literature, slides, and a videotape showing attempts to reclaim the site of the first town in the area. By the

Teachers can work with librarians and other history interest groups to help students access different types of sources.

time the students began debating their first question, they had already accumulated a good deal of information. Dehea gathered the class in a circle on the floor:

> "Make the circle wide enough so that everyone can see and be seen," Dehea reminds her students.
>
> "Oh, good, we get to argue!" announces one of the boys.
>
> "Yes, I think we probably need an argument here, but remember that this is a special kind of argument," Dehea says, and then reviews the rules for turn taking, polite forms of disagreement, and the need for full participation [all clearly listed on a bright pink poster tapped to the wall].
>
> For the next 25 minutes the students discuss and debate issues surrounding the original settlement of Lexington. Twice Dehea intervenes to remind students to sit back in the circle so that no one's view is blocked. She also asks several students to provide information based on their reading, has one student read a passage from an informational text, and replays relevant parts of a video. It is clear that the discussion could go on longer, but the bell signals lunch break.

Most of Dehea's third graders claimed to "love to argue" and Dehea had worked hard to help them to do so in constructive ways. They could disagree about ideas, she said, and various opinions were always sought because "it helps to think out different opinions before we start," but students could not attack people or make fun of their ideas. "If we did that, no one would speak up, and then we wouldn't have as many good ideas to work with," Dehea reminded one student who said an idea was "stupid." In general, though, students used a discussion model that gave them two discussion templates. The first template began with a child saying, "I agree/disagree with _____ because_____." Considerable emphasis was placed on being able to give a solid reason for agreement or disagreement. The second template allowed students to agree with part of someone's idea but disagree with or modify another part. Thus, a sentence might begin, "I agree with _____ about _____, but I disagree about_____ because _____." Using these templates allowed for quick reminders when students violated the rules for debate. Sitting in a circle also helped, as everyone could see and be seen, and Dehea could make sure that everyone participated.

Older students sometimes chafe at such formulaic debates and can be especially intractable if they have had little experience dealing formally with controversy. Viktor preferred emphasizing the historical significance of controversies. While students certainly engaged in debate, their work was most often organized around comparing how a conflict might look in its own time relative to what historical significance it might assume in the future. "It helps to get a little distance on 'hot' topics," Viktor explains. "I ask them, 'How would a historian explain this controversy, or, what would it look like to someone from another culture?' That makes them stop and think. Maybe not change their mind, but at least consider how it might look from another perspective."

Both Dehea's and Viktor's studies of local conflicts have the advantage of a wide variety of easily accessible resources, but students can also study more distant, although still current, conflicts. This often requires rethinking the kinds of sources that will be used for student inquiry. Billie Davis, a sixth-grade teacher responsible for helping her students make sense out of war in Bosnia, for instance, found that there were relatively few appropriate print resources for her students. Her sixth graders had little prior knowledge and some misconceptions about this part of the world, especially in relation to Bosnian Muslims. She decided to begin by introducing her students to Zlata, a child of about their age living in Sarajevo. *Zlata's Diary*, a book somewhat similar to *The Diary of Anne Frank*, puts a human face on a historic tragedy. Because her students were less familiar with some of the names and places in *Zlata* than with *Anne Frank*, Billie decided to read parts of the diary aloud to her students. Students read other passages silently, and then performed others as reader's theater. During reader's theater, students selected passages that they thought demonstrated particular aspects of Zlata's life or of the war and read them dramatically, sometimes using solo voices interspersed with choral reading. The multiple readings and attention to timing, emphasis and pronunciation required for these performances seemed to improve students' comprehension of the text. Nonetheless, some students still had

Constructive argument serves important functions in historical thinking.

Hahn & Tocci (1990), National Council for the Social Studies (1994)

Templates for argument and debate help students formulate constructive discussion.

Historical perspective helps students develop a broader view of current controversies.

The way sources are organized can have an impact on their effectiveness.

Filipovic (1994), Frank (1967)

Pappas et al. (1995)

difficulty picturing the geography of Zlata's homeland. Billie put a large map of the former Yugoslavia up on a bulletin board. As they read the diary, students located relevant places on the map. They also collected newspaper and magazine articles about the war, and matched them to locations on the map.

Zlata's Diary makes clear the frustrations of being a historical subject without feeling much agency. Before the war, Zlata took music lessons, went to school, loved MTV, and went skiing in the mountains around Sarajevo. Once the war starts, her world becomes a narrow, frightening place. The politicians she calls "the kids" lob shells onto her street, kill her friends, and make it necessary to spend nights in a rat-infested basement. Water and power are cut off; school is closed when the Serbs target schools for shelling. Most of Billie's students were easily caught up in the power of Zlata's story, unable to understand why someone did not stop the madness. Just as Amy's students began by thinking that people in the past were stupid, these sixth graders were convinced that only stupidity could explain the Serbs' behavior.

At first, students did not want to move beyond Zlata; they just wanted there to be a happy ending for her. "Those newspaper reporters should get her out of there!" one student declared. This response is, we think, an important component of historical thinking. Too often students are asked to leap past emotion to analysis. This can blunt student interest and cut off a healthy sense of outrage at injustice. Instead of dismissing her students' strong emotional response to the conflict that enmeshed Zlata, Billie provided an outlet for their feelings. Earlier in the year, she had introduced biographical poems. Now, she reminded her students of the format they had used, and asked them to write a poem about Zlata (see Fig. 10.2).

> Literature can make a strong connection between otherwise distant people.

> For further discussion of the bifurcation of emotion and reason in historical thinking see *Kerber (1993)* and *Bardige (1988)* and for discussion of historical empathy, see *Lee (1978)*, *Portal (1987, 1990)* and *Shemilt (1984)*.

> *Garfield (1991)*

Directions
Write your character's first name.
Write four adjectives that describe the person.
Son, daughter, or sibling of . . .
Lover of (name three things)
Who fears (name three items you fear)
Who would like to see (name three places)
Resident of (city, state)
Write your character's last name

S. Garfield (1991)

Biographical Poem Based on *Zlata's Diary*

Zlata
"Peace"
Loving, kind, hopeful, depressed
Lover of writing in her diary, peace, and letters
Who believed that there should always be
PEACE
Who wanted freedom, to stay with her family and
PEACE
Who used her pencil, her diary, and her brain power to write to Mimmy
Who gave love, Mimmy, and her words to the world
Who said, my childhood has been ripped away from me, stolen
Filipovic

FIG. 10.2. Biographical Poems

Afterward, the students shared their poems and Billie read portions of both *I Dream of Peace…*, a book of poetry by the children of Sarajevo and *I Never Saw Another Butterfly*, poems and artwork by children held at Terezin concentration camp during World War II.

Writing and sharing their own poems and hearing the poetry of other children generated further conversation and pushed the students to think beyond Zlata and her family. Now they were more ready to step back a bit from their first emotional response and study the historical and current manifestations of inter-ethnic and nationalist conflict: Why did these people start hating each other after such a long time? How had all these different people ended up in one country to begin with? Why couldn't the United Nations seem to stop the war? Could anyone help? It seemed that good people on both sides struggled to end the violence, but had no power—no agency—to stop what was happening to them. Why was that?

With these questions to guide them, the students were ready to make sense out of the background material their teacher had gathered. Unfortunately, most of the available resource material was a bit complex for sixth graders; there were interviews with leaders of different factions, magazine and newspaper articles, and videotapes of news coverage, but few books or articles written specifically for early adolescents. In addition, Billie's students were adamant about not wanting only to *study* about Bosnia. They wanted to *do* something about it. They wanted other people to know about Zlata. This can be a sensitive point in many studies. It is not always possible to do something in quite the immediate sense that middle school students desire. In this case, however, Billie suggested that students prepare a program for the schoolwide television show that was broadcast each morning. This received enthusiastic agreement from most of the students, and later from the principal. Billie was pleased because the news program could, in the long term, encourage a schoolwide response to the Bosnian crisis, and in the short term, provide additional focus for the kind of research that she believed should precede such action. As reporters on the broadcast, students had a role to play that required both "investigative reporting" and "background briefings." Billie developed "briefing" packets for her students. These contained a two-page overview of "the Case of Bosnia-Hercegovina" that she adapted from materials available through ERIC. She gave a list of additional resources to each reporter, varying the list so that different students would have expertise in different areas, and could be matched to appropriate print or visual materials. Billie also arranged for two visits from professors who specialize in Slavic Europe. Student reporters used the briefing packets to prepare questions for their guest experts.

The final television program, *The End of Childhood: Zlata's Sarajevo* combined interview data, excerpts from *Zlata's Diary*, students' own poetry, and a comparison with Anne Frank and the Nazi holocaust. At the end of the program, the students asked their school mates to contribute cards and letters to be sent to Sarajevo to let people there know they had not been forgotten. Not only did they create an interpretation of a historic event, they acted as historical agents, adding their voices to the international debate about the fate of Bosnia and its neighbors.

WHAT IF?: IT COULD HAVE BEEN DIFFERENT

Historical agency is an important concept because it is the aspect of historical thinking that helps students see themselves as historical actors. Just as the actions of people in the past produced history, so too do students' actions today and tomorrow make history. History is real and current. Unfortunately, textbooks too often make the outcomes of historical conflicts seem inevitable. Think about all the times you memorized the three causes of the Civil War, or the major events leading up to World War I. Taught this way, history seems inexorable, a train moving along a track of someone else's devising. Yet one of the fascinating aspects of history is how easily events could have gone otherwise. What if Lincoln had not gone to the theater, or

Children of Yugoslavia Staff (1994), Statni Zidovske Museum, Prague (1964)

Different genres provide outlets for different types of historical response.

Joliffe (1987)

National Council for the Social Studies (1994)

Cox (1993)

Gordon (1988), Gutman (1976), Sklar (1995), Takaki (1993), Thompson (1963)

Kennedy to Dallas? If African American parents had kept their children home, rather than let them face hatred and harassment in order to integrate schools? If Nelson Mandela had succumbed to his long imprisonment, or Slobodan Milosevic had worked for peaceful coexistence between Serbia and its neighbors?

As you might suspect by now, a train metaphor for history only works in retrospect. At any historic moment, all sorts of forces come into play. The economy takes a downturn, and anti-immigration fervor mounts, a terrorist attack threatens peace negotiations, the development of home computing, e-mail, and fax changes how workplaces are organized, and changes in attitudes toward smoking alter social and economic relations. And, just as students need to see how current conflicts can alter by the moment, they also need to recognize that historic conflicts could also have played out differently. Conflict may be inevitable in human interaction, but the outcomes are dependent on human agency. The Freedman's Bureau could have redistributed land in the American South instead of supporting a tenancy system in the wake of Civil War; President Daniel Arap Moi of Kenya could still decide to allow full, free elections rather than incite civil unrest in his country. People make choices, singly and collectively. Sometimes they take stands against overwhelming obstacles. Sometimes they succumb to the basest motivations. Often they are unsure where reasonable solutions to dilemmas lie. In the end, however, each of these choices makes history. Speculating about the outcomes of current conflicts certainly helps students see the potential impact of such decisions.

"What if . . . ?" activities are another way to help students think more carefully about the impact of conflicts, inventions, and events in the past. Look at the list in Fig.10.3, and think about the kind of background knowledge students might bring to each question, and the kind of research they would need to do in order to make better grounded speculations.

"What if . . . ?" activities can also make vivid the longevity of historical dilemmas. Jim Farrell's eighth graders discovered this as they participated in a simulated Constitutional Convention with an interesting twist. The class had already studied the convention, along with the debates and compromises made to make the Constitution acceptable to its constituents. "Now," Mr. Farrell asked his students, "consider what voices were left out of the original debates, and what difference those voices might have made. What if women or Native Peoples, African Americans or nonlandowners had been heard?" Groups of students were assigned different roles based on this discussion. Some represented the disenfranchised; others the original members of the convention. Rules were established (no filibustering allowed) and debate began.

Sometimes students found it hard to keep to the time period and use the arguments that might have been broached in 1787. For one thing, they discovered that some of these issues were very current. Gender turned out to be most volatile because it

Novick (1988)

Holt (1990a)

A variety of factors, including individual choices, influence historical outcomes.

Speculating about alternative outcomes helps students recognize that particular events are not inevitable.

Historical dilemmas are often longstanding

Contemporary issues challenge students to think differently about past and present.

What if . . . ?
- George Washington had been crowned king, as many wanted.
- The United Nations had not been created?
- The Equal Rights Amendment to the U.S. Constitution had passed?
- Television had never been invented?
- Constantine had not become a Christian?
- There had been no anit-apartheid boycott of South Africa?
- There was no First Amendment in the U.S. Constitution?
- Labor unions had never formed in the U.S.?
- The Moors had not been defeated by Isabella and Ferdinand of Spain?
- Europeans had not conquered the Americas?

FIG. 10.3. Speculating about alternative outcomes in history.

touched on problems students faced in the school every day. Did the Constitution need an Equal Rights Amendment? If there had been such a thing in 1787, how would life in the United States have altered? As the debate progressed, students were amazed at how differently they began to feel about the convention, about the way in which their textbook presented the major issues, compromises, and successes, and at how difficult these issues remained in their own lives. In fact, several students found the simulation disturbing and sometimes threatening. "There's no sense talking about the past" one student announced, after a heated debate on gender. "I don't like to pick sides. People just get mad all over again. We're all equal now. Let's be done with it." Another retorted that, "There's still problems in this school and in this class. Maybe it should come out so we can deal with it." Similar controversy swirled around issues of race and class, with frequent conversational shuttling between the 1780s and 1990s. One student declared that, since everyone was essentially alike, it did not matter who had been left out, and finally asked the teacher to "just tell us the information. Looking at all this controversial stuff is just confusing."

Avery, Bird, Johnstone, Sullivan, & Thalhammer (1992), Bunton (1992), Kelly (1986), Sadker & Sadker (1994)

The students' responses and their sometimes poignant discomfort are not unusual; rather, they are an indicator of how powerful historical study can be. Hard intellectual work, especially when it touches areas of current sensitivity, is not comfortable, but it can be compelling and memorable. As one student wrote about racism and sexism, "I always thought people back then just didn't know. They did, though. So do we, but we don't do anything about it either."

When history challenges our world view it can be discomforting—and compelling.

It would have been easy for Jim to back away from controversy and "just tell . . . the information." Had he done so his students would have lost an opportunity to grapple with issues of historical agency, not just in the past, but in their own lives. Certainly the class discussions did not cure current social problems, but some issues that had been taboo were now public and students had a language to use in describing and responding to them. In addition, pretending that such issues were not relevant, or that there could be a simple right answer to persistent dilemmas would misrepresent history and undermine Jim's instructional goals. Jim's goal had been to prepare students to look at persistent issues in American history; the students made those issues their own and at least some of them found a degree of personal agency in the process.

Parker (1991b), Wade (1994)

IT ISN'T FINISHED YET: YOU CAN MAKE A DIFFERENCE

As we have said, one feature of historical agency is that things in the past could have been otherwise; an equally important aspect is that history is not final—some things can be undone. Certainly the bloodshed in the former Yugoslavia is evidence that hatreds long suppressed can be revived. In other cases, laws once passed—separate but equal," or apartheid—can be revoked. And, perhaps more fundamentally, attitudes and beliefs—a "separate sphere" for women, or the appropriateness of child labor—can alter. Choices are rarely finished. In Jeanette Groth's eighth-grade American history class, the students study the Bill of Rights. As an assessment, Jeanette assigns them the task of proving that one of the first 10 amendments to the Constitution still has a direct impact on their lives. One group, assigned to the First Amendment, produced a video that began with a mock news report. As the "anchorperson" began delivering the news, there was an interruption. A message flashed across the screen: "The President has declared a national emergency. All First Amendment Rights are suspended!" The anchorperson looked up from her desk: "Well, that means we're off the air!" The screen went dark. Moments later, the video showed a series of vignettes of life without the First Amendment: people being told they had to go to church—and which church they had to attend—a protester being led off to jail, and so forth. In each case, as the victims objected, they were reminded that the First Amendment no longer applied. At the close of the video, the students stood in front of an American flag and slowly read the First Amendment. Their video was certainly powerful, and generated a good deal of discussion of possible limits on free expression that operated in their lives as well as in the United States as a whole.

Decisions made in the past can be changed in the present

McGinnis (1995), National Council for the Social Studies (1994), Parker, Mueller, & Wendling (1989)

Keller & Schillings (1987)

CONCLUSION

One of the functions of historical thinking is to help students make informed and reasoned decisions that promote personal and public good. When individuals begin to make such decisions, they are less likely to become the objects of manipulation, and more likely to shape their own lives in dignity and respect for others. On the other hand, individual decisions are not made in a vacuum. Some cultures and subcultures model violence as a primary means of solving conflicts, and reject mutual problem solving in favor of competitive one-upmanship. It is not always easy or comfortable to alter these patterns, but we think it is worth the effort. If, as we argued in chapter 1, history is fundamentally controversial, then we have an obligation to help our students recognize and respond intelligently to controversy. If, in addition, democracy is based on a conflictual model of decision making, and if many of our public conflicts have historic roots, it becomes even more important to help students better understand how those conflicts played out historically. Finally, if our sense of historical agency influences how we respond to conflict and consensus, then we have another powerful argument for encouraging our students, not just to analyze conflicts, but to take reasoned and deliberate action to shape the future.

History can support informed decision making for personal and public good.

National Council for the Social Studies (1994)

This chapter focused on two related aspects of historical thinking—recognizing the impact of conflict and consensus, and understanding historical agency. In Dehea's class, these aspects were dealt with in the context of a social studies thematic unit on *community* (see chapter 8 for more detail on this unit). In order to help her students understand the impact of conflict and consensus in their community, she explicitly related public conflict management to classroom protocols. Her emphasis on metacognition—establishing metaphors to describe tasks, modeling procedures, and than asking students to analyze them, thinking aloud with students as they outlined the parameters of a "good argument"—provided cognitive "touch stones" for students new to inquiry into controversial issues. Focusing on controversies in the local community where they could interview relevant people, write to local officials, and survey participants in decision making also served to initiate Dehea's students into the role of civic participant. Not only did they learn that other people have historic agency, they practiced being agents themselves. On the other hand, Jim Farrell's students began with a more distant problem, but found that some issues spread tentacles into the present. In their discomfort with the present manifestations of historic problems, some of the students rejected the role of historic agent; others embraced it. Like historic actors in the past, they made choices about how those issues would play out in their own lives. Jeanette Groth's students took the Bill of Rights and discovered that it was a living document that had a daily impact on their lives. In each of these classrooms, as well as in Viktor's and Billie's classes, disciplined, reflective inquiry helped students establish the significance of historic events, and the impact of individual and collective agency—social participation—on the ways conflicts are managed. While not every current or historic controversy requires such extensive treatment in the classroom, some issue or contention or question lies at the heart of all historic inquiry. With no controversies, no questions to be resolved, nor perspectives to be understood, history is a lifeless thing—able to tell us little about an increasingly interdependent, complex, and controversial world.

Historical agency influences how we respond to conflict and consensus.

Historical agency implies active civic participation.

CHILDREN'S AND ADOLESCENT LITERATURE

Nonfiction on Historical Controversies

Aaseng, N. (1994). *You Are the Supreme Court Justice.* Oliver. (Look for other titles in the "Great Decisions" series)
Altman, L. J. (1994). *The Pullman Strike of 1894: Turning Point for American Labor.* Millbrook. (Look for other titles in the "Spotlight on American History" series)
Ashabranner, B. (1994). *A New Frontier: The Peace Corps in Eastern Europe.* Cobblehill.
Children of Yugoslavia Staff. (1994). *I Dream of Peace.* HarperCollins.
Colman, P. (1994) *Mother Jones and the March of the Mill Children.* Millbrook.
Filipovic, Z. (1994). *Zlata's Diary.* Viking.

Frank, A. (1967). *Anne Frank: The Diary of a Young Girl*. Doubleday.

Frank, A. (1989). *The Diary of Anne Frank: The Critical Edition*. Netherlands State Institute for War Documentation & Doubleday.

Freedman, R. (1994). *Kids at Work: Lewis Hine and the Crusade Against Child Labor*. Clarion.

Fritz, J. 1983. *The Double Life of Pocahontas*. Putnam.

Gay, K. (1994). *The New Power of Women in Politics*. Enslow. (Look for other titles in the "Issues in Focus" series)

Howard, T. A. & Howard, S. 1992. *Kids Ending Hunger: What Can We Do?* Andrews & McMeel.

Knight, M. B. (1993). *Who Belongs Here?: An American Story*. Tilbury.

Meltzer, M. (1976). *Never to Forget: The Jews of the Holocaust*. Harpers.

Meltzer, M., & Cole, B. (1974). *The Eye of Conscience: Photographers and Social Change*. Fawcett. (With 100 photographs by noted phtographers, past and present).

O'Neill, L. A. (1994). *Little Rock: The Desegregation of Central High*. Millbrook. (Look for other books in the "Spotlight on American History" series)

Statni Zidovske Museum, Prague. (1964). *I Never Saw Another Butterfly*. McGraw-Hill. (See also, Bernstein, 1990). Chichester psalms: I never saw another butterfly: Musicmasters.

Sullivan, G. (1994). *The Day the Women Got the Vote: A Photo History of the Women's Rights Movement*. Scholastic

Weisbrot, R. (1994). *Marching toward Freedom, 1957-1965: From the Founding of the Southern Christian Leadership Conference to the Assassination of Malcolm X*. Chelsea. (Look for other books in the "Milestones in Black American History" series)

In my opinion, it could happen again

Chapter 11

How Attitudes and Beliefs Have Changed Over Time

Throughout the year, Amy Leigh draws her fourth grade students' attention to the way ideas, attitudes, values, and beliefs have changed over time. Near the beginning of the year, for example, the class investigates changes in names. After talking about their own first names, students collect information on names in their own, their parents', and their grandparents' generations—which names have become more or less common, how the length of names has changed, and how the reason for choosing names has changed. Students work in groups to record and analyze the data they collect, and make presentations to the rest of the class on their findings. Afterward, they visit a nearby cemetery to collect information on names further back in time, and examine 19th-century census records of Cherokees and enslaved Africans for information on naming patterns among those populations.

Later in the year, Amy begins a unit on how social relations have changed over time. The class reads and discusses several works of children's literature that focus on attitudes toward racial, religious, and gender differences—works like *Teammates*, *The Number on my Grandfather's Arm*, *The Bracelet*, and *Bloomers!*—and students respond through activities such as simulated journals and written dialogues. Throughout this unit, Amy's focus is on the way people treat those different than themselves, and the attitudes that underlie such treatment.

Later in the year, during a unit on life in Colonial America, students study the Salem witch trials. Amy begins by explaining how villagers' religious beliefs and their ideas about work and community influenced their attitudes toward each other. Over the next 2 weeks, students take on the roles of villagers and plan a simulated trial of a woman accused of witchcraft. Students have to plan their actions and statements based on the beliefs of people at the time; witnesses, for example, have to decide what evidence would have been convincing to people at the time, and jurors decide what evidence would have convinced people then—not people today.

Historical thinking involves understanding the perspectives of people in the past. *Lee (1978)*, *Portal (1987, 1990)*, *Shemilt (1984)*

Jordan (1968)

Jennings (1975)

Being able to take the perspective of people in the past is a requirement for meaningful historical understanding. In order to understand why people acted as they did, it's necessary to be familiar with the cultural context that shaped their thoughts. Without examining the ideas, attitudes, values, and beliefs of people in history, their actions have no meaning. The development of racial slavery in British North America, for example, can only be understood with reference to Englishmen's ideas about the differences between themselves and Africans; the conquest of Native Americans by reference to ideas about what constituted civilization. Although advocates of a purely "factual" approach to the teaching of history sometimes claim that getting into the minds of people in the past is impossible—and therefore has no place in schools—nothing could be further from the truth. Most historical interpretations take into account people's motivations, and historians are careful to distinguish between ideas that are based on contemporary attitudes and those that may have influenced people in the past. "Reading the present into the past"—explaining historic events by referring to contemporary standards—is a cardinal sin among historians; one cannot explain the actions of a medieval serf or lord, an 18th-century Japanese merchant, or a Texas farmwoman in 1890 by pretending that they're all middle-class European Americans of the late 20th century. Their world views, mentalities, and

Historians avoid attributing contemporary attitudes to people in the past.

114

ideologies were different than those of people today, and those differences have to be taken into account; otherwise, their actions may just seem stupid. Without understanding Salem villagers' attitudes toward God, the Devil, work, and community, for example, the practice of dunking someone in water to determine if he or she is a witch looks like a flaw in logic. Most of us agree that there are no witches, and that even if there were, dunking them in water wouldn't prove much; if we apply our standards to Salem villagers, they all appear to be mentally defective.

And in fact, children often think precisely that until they have studied the perspectives of people in the past in more depth. We have emphasized that students come to school already knowing some things about how material life has changed over time—they quickly recognize historic clothes and technology, for example, and can even put them in a relatively accurate chronology of development. But students' understanding of changes in ideas is much less sophisticated. They do know some things about the topic: they often recognize that people had different attitudes toward women and minorities in the past, and they may have learned that European settlers didn't consider Native Americans their equals. But they have rarely had the opportunity to see these attitudes as part of a coherent system of beliefs, one different than their own; instead, they tend to think of them as idiosyncratic and inexplicable mistakes, and generally conclude that people in the past weren't as smart as we are. By consistently asking students to think about *why* people did things differently in the past, however, Amy helps them develop a much more complex understanding of how ideas have changed over time.

Barton & Levstik (1996), Levstik & Barton (1996)

Many children know that attitudes toward race and gender were different in the past *(Barton, 1994a)*.

CHANGES IN NAMES

Students' belief that people in the past were stupid is often striking. While reading *Immigrant Kids*, for example, students in Tina Reynolds' class (chapter 5) began to discuss how people at the time washed their clothes; some thought they washed them in sinks because there were no washing machines, but one student was certain that there were indeed washing machines then—but that people were too stupid to use them! Clothing styles often inspire similar comments. Tina found, for example, that students sometimes asserted that people long ago knew they were dressing "old fashioned," and realized that someday people would start doing things the right way. And in doing their family history projects, several students brought in their parents' high school yearbooks from the 1970s—"Why did they dress so nerdy?" they all wanted to know. The tendency of people in the 1970s to wear such obviously unattractive clothes led several students to conclude that "they must not have known it was picture day." Having never systematically explored the way ideas change over time, students had no way of explaining polyester leisure suits other than outright ignorance.

Freedman (1980)

Children sometimes assume people in the past were not as intelligent as they are. *(Barton, 1994a)*

Without understanding that people in the past did not consider themselves stupid or old-fashioned, it's difficult to understand much about history. If students think that people would have used washing machines if someone had just shown them how, or would have dressed differently if they had known how bad they looked, then studying the past must appear as an exercise in futility; all it shows is that people back then needed to be shaken until they got some sense. Fortunately, Amy has found it easy to move students beyond their initial belief in historical stupidity, and to help them recognize that people in the past considered themselves "normal," not old-fashioned—that they saw things from a different perspective than we do. The "Names" project described here is the way Amy introduces students to this aspect of historical understanding.

The entire project is popular with students, and provides a good transition from their personal and family histories (similar to those described in chapters 4 and 5) to the "History Museum" projects in chapter 7. Students like to talk about their names, and they usually have a great deal to say about them. Amy began the unit by reading *Wilfred*

Gordon MacDonald Partridge, a book in which a boy makes friends with an elderly woman who also happens to have four names. In discussing the book, Amy asked students about their own names: Do any of you have four names? Do any of you have nicknames? Do you know how you got your name? Their response was passionate: they could barely stay in their seats, they were so excited about sharing what they knew about their names, whether they liked their names, and what they wished they had been named. For homework, students had to find three additional facts about their names—such as who they were named after, or what they would have been named if they were they opposite sex—and share these in class the next day. They then used this information as the basis for essays that became part of their writing portfolios.

Having developed their interest in the topic, Amy later moved on to the more specifically historical aspects of the project. She asked whether there were names people used in the past that were no longer common, and most students could easily think of several—Gladys, Mabel, Thelma, Nola, and so on. They also thought there were names that were common now—Tiffany, Amber, Crystal—that weren't used in the past, although they were less sure of their examples. Noting that most of their suggestions were women's names, Amy asked if they thought women's names had changed more over time than men's; although again they weren't sure, they thought they probably had. Finally, Amy asked whether they thought the reasons names were chosen were different in the past. Students were interested in the reasons for their own names, but most had no firm opinion on how those reasons may have been different in the past; a few suggested that more people were named after family members a long time ago.

Amy then introduced students to an assignment that allowed them to investigate these questions more systematically. She gave each student a data collection sheet (Fig. 11.1) on which they were to collect information on the names found in their generation, their parents', and their grandparents'. The next day, after giving students time to talk about what they had discovered, she divided them into groups and gave each group one of the following questions to answer:

- How have the reasons for men's names changed over time?
- How have the reasons for women's names changed over time?
- Are there some men's names that are found in only one generation, or in all generations?
- Are there some women's names that are found in only one generation, or in all generations?
- Have men's names gotten longer or shorter?
- Have women's names gotten longer or shorter?

Students can use mathematical procedures to draw historical conclusions.

Over the next week, students worked in groups to use their data sheets to answer these questions and design displays to communicate their findings.

The inquiry-oriented aspects of this project are obvious. But what does it have to do with taking the perspective of people in the past? This project did, in fact, go a long way toward helping students overcome their assumptions about the lack of intelligence long ago. As they were working on their projects, students very frequently commented on some of the more unusual names they found, particularly in their grandparents' generation: "*Opal,* I like that name," or "*Cleatus,* I *know* nobody's named that anymore!" Whenever such comments arose, Amy asked why they thought those names weren't used anymore. Students' initial responses sometimes reflected their previous idea that people didn't know any better: "You wouldn't want to have a really cute boy, and name him Oliver, or a really cute girl, and name her Pearl." (One student even suggested that people a long time ago didn't have enough education to be able to say all the letters of the alphabet, and thus couldn't pronounce all the names we can.) But almost as soon as a student made such a suggestion, another student would correct him or her by pointing out that the names didn't sound funny back then, that they sounded perfectly normal or even "high tone"—and other students quickly agreed.

Students learn that people in the past didn't consider themselves old-fashioned.

116

Your generation (you, siblings, cousins)	Parents' generation (parents, aunts, uncles)	Grandparents' generation (grandparents, great aunts/uncles)
Name: _____ Reason chosen: ____ liked the sound ____ relative ____ famous person ____ unknown ____ other _____	Name: _____ Reason chosen: ____ liked the sound ____ relative ____ famous person ____ unknown ____ other _____	Name: _____ Reason chosen: ____ liked the sound ____ relative ____ famous person ____ unknown ____ other _____
Name: _____ Reason chosen: ____ liked the sound ____ relative ____ famous person ____ unknown ____ other _____	Name: _____ Reason chosen: ____ liked the sound ____ relative ____ famous person ____ unknown ____ other _____	Name: _____ Reason chosen: ____ liked the sound ____ relative ____ famous person ____ unknown ____ other _____
Name: _____ Reason chosen: ____ liked the sound ____ relative ____ famous person ____ unknown ____ other _____	Name: _____ Reason chosen: ____ liked the sound ____ relative ____ famous person ____ unknown ____ other _____	Name: _____ Reason chosen: ____ liked the sound ____ relative ____ famous person ____ unknown ____ other _____
Name: _____ Reason chosen: ____ liked the sound ____ relative ____ famous person ____ unknown ____ other _____	Name: _____ Reason chosen: ____ liked the sound ____ relative ____ famous person ____ unknown ____ other _____	Name: _____ Reason chosen: ____ liked the sound ____ relative ____ famous person ____ unknown ____ other _____

FIG. 11.1. Data collection chart.

Perhaps because the topic was a simple one like names, or perhaps because the people being considered were their parents and grandparents, students began to understand that some things change just because fashion changes and not because people in the past couldn't see how stupid they were. After this project, whenever anyone in the class mentioned how unusual or perplexing something in history seemed, other students could be counted on to interject, "But it wouldn't seem that way to *them*, it just seems that way to us because we're not used to it." Moreover, students were quite conscious, even proud, of their change in understanding: they knew they hadn't quite gotten it before, and now they did. In addition to all the benefits of the process of historical inquiry, then, this project helped students begin to see how their own perspective differed from people in the past—a fundamental characteristic of historical understanding.

Students can understand that the perspectives of people in the past differ from their own.

CHANGES IN SOCIAL RELATIONS

There are, of course, more serious changes in perspective over time. Some of the most important involve the way people treat those who are different than themselves: attitudes toward differences in race, religion, and gender have been responsible for many of history's most enduring and dramatic struggles. As noted in chapter 7, however, none of Amy's students chose to investigate changes in social relations during their History Museum projects; instead, they focused on the aspects of everyday

Personal experiences provide an introduction to historical topics.

life they knew best—toys, clothes, cars, and so on. Amy knew that it would be her responsibility to expand students' understanding of changing perspectives on social relations, and for this she relied primarily on children's literature.

Amy began this unit by asking students if any of them had ever wanted to do something and not been allowed to. They all had examples, of course, and Amy listed these on the board, along with the reasons they had been given for not being able to do what they wanted. She then asked which reasons they thought were fair and which ones weren't. Most students saw that some reasons were fair even if they disagreed with them: not being able to have a slumber party until the same age as a sister, for example, or not being allowed to ride a motorbike because of the danger. Others they considered clearly unfair: one girl couldn't play soccer because she was a girl, while a boy couldn't stay overnight at his friend's house because he lived in a housing project.

Amy had meant to spend this entire first lesson simply exploring the concepts of "fair" and "unfair" treatment, and talking about how attitudes may influence people's treatment of each other. In the middle of the discussion, though, one student noted, "Hey, this sounds like prejudice and discrimination!" Several other students agreed with her, and Amy made the most of the opportunity—asking them if they knew of any times in history people had been discriminated against. One girl had recently read *Number the Stars* and *The Diary of Anne Frank,* and she explained how Jews had been treated unfairly "during the war"; another mentioned slaves being treated unfairly because of their color; yet another student had read *Journey to Topaz* and explained that "the China people were treated bad just like the Jews." Nor did students simply consider these a thing of the past: they knew many examples, both from personal experience and from current events, of racial and sexual discrimination in the present.

Lowry (1990); Frank (1967)

Uchida (1985)

Students recognize that prejudice and discrimination are contemporary problems.

Some students have learned about history at school, from relatives, from the media, and from their own reading. *Barton (1995), Levstik & Barton (1996), Seixas (1993b)*

This discussion indicates just how much historical knowledge children have. By fourth grade, many of them have encountered the topic of slavery while learning about Harriet Tubman, and have heard words like *prejudice* and *discrimination* when studying Martin Luther King. Sources outside formal instruction provide an even wider range of information. Students often read historical fiction on their own, and the girl who had just read *Number the Stars* wasn't the only one who had heard about the Holocaust: several others had recently seen news reports on television about its commemoration. Children sometimes also learn how women and minorities were treated differently in the past from their relatives or other adults outside of school. Of course, this information is often lacking in context and elaboration, and students will benefit from learning that it was Japanese Americans (not "the China people") who were put in concentration camps, and that both that internment and the Holocaust happened about 50 years ago, during World War II. The fact that children are already familiar with both the concept of prejudice and specific historical examples, however, makes it easier for them to examine new information on the topic.

Over the next few weeks, Amy read aloud a variety of books about people who had been treated differently because of racial, ethnic, political, or gender differences—books such as *Teammates* (about the integration of baseball), *The Lily Cupboard* and *The Number on My Grandfather's Arm* (about the Holocaust), *The Bracelet* and *Baseball Saved Us* (about the internment of Japanese Americans during World War II), *Bloomers!* (about the women's rights movement in the 19th century), *Nettie's Trip South* and *Christmas in the Big House, Christmas in the Quarters.* (about slavery in the American South) and *Katie's Trunk* (about a Loyalist family during the American Revolution). Amy wanted students to achieve two main things during this unit—to understand the attitudes and beliefs that led to unfair treatment in the past, and to explain some of the ways people responded to such treatment. Nearly all the books directly addressed attitudes, so it was relatively easy to keep an ongoing class record of this information on a wall chart; *Bloomers!*, for example, explained that men in the 19th century expected women to obey their husbands, and *The Number on My Grandfather's Arm* explained that many Germans thought Jews were to blame for all the country's problems. In most cases, students simply remembered what the books said and added that information to the chart. In a few cases, they suggested their own

Golenbock (1990)

Oppenheim (1992), Adler (1987)

Uchida (1993), Mochizuki (1993), Blumberg (1993), Turner (1987), McKissack & McKissack (1994), Turner (1992)

Wall charts help students keep track of information gained from ongoing units of study.

elaborations of these explanations; several, for example, thought that White Southerners were racist because it meant they could get other people to do their work for them, and others suggested men's attitudes toward women could be explained in much the same way. ("They didn't want to do anything around the house," as one student put it.) Although their understanding was still fairly simple and straightforward, their explanations indicate they were beginning to see the connection between beliefs and the wider social context—rather than thinking of racism or sexism as inexplicable idiosyncrasies.

Through reading and discusion, students can begin to see the connections among attitudes and social relations.

Interestingly, attitudes toward race and gender appeared easier for students to understand than other prejudices. Perhaps because these continue to be important issues today—or perhaps because they had learned more about them previously—students had few questions about such attitudes. They were interested in the specifics of slavery, in how Japanese Americans were treated in camps, and in what women could and could not do in the past, but none of them seemed to consider such treatment *confusing*; they knew that the beliefs of people in the past on these issues differed from their own. Both the Holocaust and the treatment of Loyalists during the American Revolution, though, inspired many more questions. Students didn't understand why the Nazis would single out a religion for their attacks, nor did they quite understand how they knew who was Jewish and who wasn't. And while the story of *Katie's Trunk* interested them, they were never sure who was on which side or what difference it made. In retrospect, Amy didn't consider their difficulties surprising, because understanding these episodes in history requires a much greater degree of background knowledge than they were likely to have. Moreover, we suspect that in regions where issues like religion form a more salient part of the community's diversity, students might more readily understand the prejudices that can accompany this aspect of identity.

Students' social backgrounds may influence their understanding of social relations.

The books Amy read to her class also provided an opportunity to compare the ways people respond to mistreatment. After reading *Teammates*, for example, students pointed out that Jackie Robinson's main response was to put up with the abuse of the fans and other players, and to keep on doing his job; Amy also explained that after he had established himself in the National League, Robinson began to speak out publicly on racial discrimination. The class recorded these responses on the wall chart, and when they read *Bloomers!*, they saw that women's reactions were similar to Robinson's: they put up with abuse, they kept on doing what they wanted, and they spoke out publicly. In several other books, on the other hand, the main response was either to hide or to run away; this led to a discussion of what circumstances made one course of action wiser than another. Similarly, several books addressed the response of people not directly affected by mistreatment—Pee Wee Reese in *Teammates*, for example, or Nettie and her brother in *Nettie's Trip South*—and the students discussed what people who witnessed discrimination could do about it. Studying such issues clearly relates to the civic ideals and practices which form a key element of national standards in the social studies.

National Council for the Social Studies (1994)

Students' initial response to most of the books was indignation: they were angry that anyone would mistreat others because of their race, religion, or gender. Amy encouraged them in their judgments about how wrong such actions were, but at first she worried their moral responses were so strong that they were failing genuinely to take the perspective of people in the past. Many of the activities she had planned for the class asked students to put themselves in the place of participants in these episodes and to make decisions about what they would have done—whether they would have tried to hide Jewish children in their homes during World War II, for example. At first, students saw absolutely no reason to think they would have done otherwise (and frequently imagined themselves endowed with supernatural powers, able to hide every Jewish child in the Netherlands or to lead all the slaves to freedom); they argued that people were stupid not to know that everyone is the same, and they were sure they wouldn't have been that stupid if they were around then.

See also Bardige (1988) and Levstik (1986b)

Such responses were similar to students' reaction to names like *Oliver*—why didn't they know any better? Rather than indicating a reversion to this earlier inability to understand the motivations of people in the past, though, Amy ultimately decided that they represented students' way of distancing themselves from the beliefs they were studying: they seemed to need this complete certainty as a way of demonstrating their own moral and ethical sensibility. Once they got past their initial discussions, students demonstrated a much more sophisticated perspective-taking ability. After reading *The Lily Cupboard*, for example, students worked in pairs to complete decision charts (see Fig. 11.2) listing the reasons for and against hiding Jewish families. Although all students ultimately decided they would have done so, they gave much more complicated reasons than they had initially, and they were careful to explain why they thought the benefits outweighed the potential dangers. Rather than seeing it as an obvious decision that no rational person could avoid, they came to consider it a very complicated one that would have been difficult to make. Similarly, all the girls in the class were at first convinced that they too would have been an advocate for women's rights in the 19th century; on further reflection, though, some realized that their own attitudes as women might have been different then. As one girl said, "If it were *me* going back in time, I would have fought for women's rights, but if I had been a woman *then*, I might have been too afraid of what people would think."

Amy's use of graphic organizers with students was an important part of helping students think about these issues in more sophisticated ways. After reading *Teammates*, for example, students were assigned to write a simulated journal entry from the perspective of either Jackie Robinson or Pee Wee Reese. Before having them do that, though, she had them complete character webs for both Robinson and Reese (see Fig. 11.3). Students had to take these characteristics into account in their writing; rather than simply a knee-jerk response, they had to try to make their journals reflective of the character traits they had identified. The webs, then, helped clarify how they could write from someone's perspective other than their own. Similarly, before writing a dialogue between Japanese Americans and the agents sent to detain them, students had to identify what goals each would have had, and how they might have tried to

Decision charts allow students to record reasons for and against a course of action.

In simulated journals, students write diary-type entries from the perspective of people in history.

On character webs, students record physical features, personality characteristics, and other traits of people.

In written dialogues, students work in pairs to create an imaginary conversation between two historical characters.

```
Question:



Reasons for:                    Reasons against:

_____                 _____

_____                 _____

_____                 _____

_____                 _____

_____                 _____

_____                 _____


Conclusion:

```

FIG. 11.2.   Decision chart (for other examples of decision charts, see Alvermann, 1991).

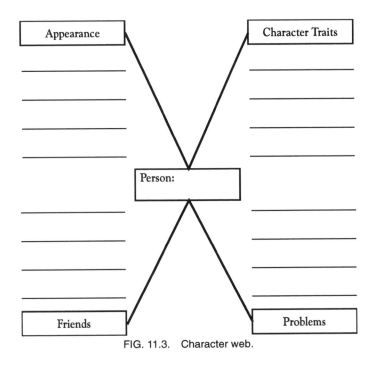

FIG. 11.3.   Character web.

reach them. Rather than stereotyping the characters as the embodiments of good and evil, students started to see them as real people who were probably concerned primarily with getting through the day. Instead of thinking that any sensible Japanese American would have started a violent confrontation (as they were at first sure they would have done themselves), they understood why many people might have gone along in the hopes that matters would be straightened out. It was the graphic organizers that Amy used that required students to stop, think, and organize what they knew instead of leaping to unhistorical conclusions.

Graphic organizers lead to more thoughtful written responses.

We should point out that Amy was careful about the kinds of perspectives she asked students to take. She never asked them to put themselves in the place of people whose behavior she condemned: students did not have to pretend to be Nazi soldiers, or racist baseball fans, or slaveowners. Although there may have been historical merit in having them try to take those perspectives, she considered such activities too manipulative, and we agree. Many educators seem enamored of the simulation in which a class of students is divided by eye color (or some other arbitrary characteristic), and one group is encouraged to mistreat the other for a day—purportedly so they will have firsthand experience with discrimination. We see no value, however, in encouraging students to act in ways that are ethically repugnant. We think Amy's pattern of asking students to imagine they are *witnessing* mistreatment—rather than engaging in it themselves—is much more likely to develop an ethic of caring while still retaining the validity of historical perspective-taking.

Students should not be required to imagine themselves acting in unethical ways.

Noddings (1992)

These response activities also demonstrate how teachers can avoid the temptation to "basalize" literature. Although many schools now buy trade books for use in classrooms, teachers often are at a loss as to what students can do with them. Traditional textbook programs come with a vast array of supplementary materials that can keep students busy for hours on end, but it's not always clear just what they should do after reading a chapter in a novel. Publishers have rushed in to fill this void, and teachers can now purchase dittos and blackline masters to accompany many well-known trade books. These materials too often mimic the worst features of textbook programs: they require students to copy definitions of vocabulary words, fill in blanks, and answer comprehension questions. With activities like these, students may learn to dislike reading good literature as much as they dislike reading textbooks.

121

Students read literature to learn about themselves and the world.

In dialogue journals, students respond to literature, and teachers respond to students' observations.

Open-ended questions stimulate students' responses in dialogue journals.

In Amy's class, though, students are asked to consider the content of what they read: they read literature to learn about themselves and the world. When the students have all read the same book, she has them write dialogues, perform skits, or write simulated journals—all activities in which they have to take what they have learned and extend their understanding by putting it in a new form. During their independent reading, on the other hand, students keep a dialogue journal in which they respond to the work they are reading. Since students often aren't sure what to write when journal assignments are completely unstructured, many teachers assign focused but open-ended questions for students to use in formulating their responses. Rhoda Coleman (see chapters 2 and 12), for example, assigns students to choose from among the following questions after reading each :

- What is your reaction to the events and words in this ?
- What questions do you have for the author or the characters?
- What would you want to say to the author or the characters?
- What predictions can you make about what will happen next?
- How does this relate to your own experience?

Authentic responses to literature call for an engagement with content.

Unlike commercial dittos, Amy's and Rhoda's activities help students understand what it means to engage with literature in authentic ways. When people read, they don't sit down and copy definitions or count syllables: they think about what they're reading—why an author wrote something the way she did, why a character acts as he does, how it relates to their own experiences. Students learn that reading is a way of grappling with issues that are significant and meaningful, not a prelude to easily graded school exercises.

This unit also encouraged students to see history itself as significant. We have sometimes heard people express hesitation at "exposing" young children to topics like the Holocaust or slavery, out of concern that they are too innocent to learn about such violence. In our experience, though, most children have grown up on a steady diet of violent cartoons, movies, and television shows, and are usually well acquainted with the most gory details of contemporary terrorism and warfare. Compared to the violence students see everyday in the media, children's literature is quite tame. What most students have not been exposed to, though, is what motivates people to mistreat others or what could be done to prevent such behavior. Without the kind of reflection Amy provides, students may come to think of violence as natural and inevitable; in this unit, however, they see that people make decisions about their actions—they choose to mistreat others or they choose to condemn or resist such mistreatment. Armed with this understanding, students are much better equipped to make their own decisions in the future.

Historical knowledge can help children analyze contemporary social issues.

SALEM WITCH TRIALS

Personal experiences provide an introduction to historical topics.

In studying the Salem witch trials, students encountered a set of beliefs that differed seriously from their own. Amy began this topic in much the same way as she had the study of social relations: with students sitting on the carpet in the front of the room, she asked if any of them had ever been accused of something they hadn't done. Needless to say, students had a number of examples to volunteer, and the discussion of unfair accusations and how to counter them took up most of the first day. Much of this discussion focused on the reasons a person might be accused and the kinds of evidence that would be necessary to support or refute such accusations.

The next day, Amy (herself a descendant of Rebecca Nurse, who was hung as a witch in Salem in 1692) began explaining the witchcraft accusations in 17th-century Salem Village to students. She focused primarily on the villagers' religious beliefs—not only that witches were real, but that idleness indicated a person was possessed by the devil. She also explained how a combination of physical disasters (such as an outbreak of smallpox and the death of livestock) and social tensions (revolving around the local church) made people particularly likely to look for someone to blame their problems on. Just as they had during previous lessons, students were eager to condemn these accusations—pointing out that witches don't really exist, and that being lazy "doesn't mean that the devil is in you." Many were particularly upset by the connection of witchcraft and religion: because they were convinced that the existence of witches is contrary to Christianity, they found it reprehensible that people justified their accusations by reference to the Bible. (In our experience, students often do not understand that beliefs within Christianity have changed over time, or even that beliefs vary from one denomination to another.)

Once again, however, this reaction seemed to be a way of distancing themselves from the people they were studying. Once they had demonstrated to their own satisfaction how much more logical (and theologically pure) they were than some of their ancestors, they were ready to enter more fully into the mindset of Salem villagers—a perspective necessary for the central activity of this unit, the creation of a fictional witchcraft trial. Amy assigned students various roles to play—accused and accusers, prosecutors, defense attorneys, witnesses for the prosecution and defense, and jury—and gave them general background information on their roles. (Since Amy's purpose was for students to learn about the perspective of people in the past—rather than the evolution of trial procedures—these roles more closely resembled contemporary courtrooms than the proceedings of 17th-century trials.)

There was no script for this trial; except for explaining procedures such as who got to call their witnesses first, Amy left the development of the trial to the students. For the next several days, they met in small groups to discuss their roles and what they entailed: jury members decided what kinds of evidence they would listen for, witnesses wrote depositions on their knowledge of the accused, attorneys planned their strategies. Of course, Amy was hardly idle during this time: she met constantly with students to help them perfect their plans. Through their discussions with her and their reading of the primary, secondary, and other sources she had provided, students largely were able to separate their contemporary perspectives from those of people at the time. Jury members, for example, decided that they would look for marks on the body of the accused, while defense attorneys prepared the accused to recite the Lord's Prayer as evidence of her innocence.

Students take responsibility for planning dramatic activities. *Fines & Verrier (1974)*

Students base role-plays on primary sources and other forms of evidence.

The trial itself was a big hit; several months later most students said it was their favorite activity the entire year. Many did their best to dress the part—judges wore black sweats to approximate robes—and several students used what they knew about the language of the time (with the occasional lapse, as when the defense attorney asked a witness why he thought the accused was "a slimeball"). The accused, meanwhile, repeatedly erupted into fits during the trial. But students' enthusiasm and flair notwithstanding, most of their learning had taken place before this point, during the discussion and planning that led up to it. It was while preparing what to say, what to ask, and what to listen for that students were most actively engaged in learning about the period.

Drama is one of students' favorite activities.

Preparing for role-play requires learning about the period under study.

In order for this kind of activity to be a meaningful learning experience, students must be given responsibility for creating the drama based on their investigation of the issues of the day. Telling students to "role-play" George Washington is unlikely to inspire in-depth research or consideration of alternative interpretations, and if they are simply enacting a predetermined script, they may learn something about acting but will probably gain little insight into the historical period under study. With a script, the story is already in place, the characters and themes already set, and students have nothing to do but play their parts; when they are involved in creating a drama, though, they obviously have a much more active role. Using role-play and simulations as opportunities to play out different interpretations or constructions of events can support the development of historical perspective-taking. This kind of drama demands historical inquiry, as students refine their questions, consult evidence and consider a range of responses, test possibilities, and examine the results. Without such inquiry, they could not have pulled off the performance: they would have had little

Effective drama involves students in inquiry. *Fines & Verrier (1974)*

idea what to say, could not have responded to unanticipated questions, would not have known where they were going or how to get there.

EXTENSIONS

Throughout this chapter, we have emphasized the importance of helping students gain insight into the perspectives of people in the past. Dramatic activities, simulated journals, and other responses to historical literature are particularly useful in involving students in a deeper interaction with history, and can easily be extended to a wide range of historical topics, events, and people. Although it is not always necessary to use literature as a springboard to role-playing, it does have some advantages. First of all, literature generally attempts to get inside the head of characters, and readers come to understand at least some of the ideas and emotions that motivated people in the past. In addition, historical literature often incorporates personal idiosyncrasies that enrich characterization.

Paul Fleischmann's *Bull Run*, for instance, consists of a series of monologues representing different perspectives on the Battle of Bull Run. A Southern officer recalls the first shots at Fort Sumter, a young boy tells of signing on as a drummer because he is too young to be a soldier, a Minnesota woman laments her father's harshness that sent her brother to war, and another young man signs on with the Confederacy because the army promises him a horse. This book lends itself very naturally to dramatic presentation. In Dee Hellau's fifth-grade class, for example, she asks students to role play characters from Fleischmann's book. "These are people who never met each other," she tells her class. "Given what you have read about each of them, what might they say to each other? What questions might they ask each other? What questions would you want to ask them?" Three students are selected and assigned roles. They come to the front of the room and sit at a table where they can see each other and be seen by their classmates. Dee asks the rest of the class to write questions on 3 x 5 index cards for the characters. She shuffles these, along with several questions she has written out, and then serves as moderator of the ensuing role-play.

Note that students are not simply asked to "act like" a particular character. Instead, they are given a specific task to resolve as they think their character would have responded. They are allowed to refer back to the book, but few of the questions can be answered only by reference to Fleischmann's novel. Instead, they have to think about what motivated a particular person and, given the time and circumstance, how that person might have answered a questions such as "If you had it to do over again, would you still join the Confederacy/Union?" or "How much do you think slavery had to do with this war?" As the students respond from their characters' perspectives, Dee periodically stops and asks the class if they think a particular response is supportable, given their reading of the book, and students are encouraged to give each other suggestions. In addition, Dee occasionally switches role-players so that most students have an opportunity both to ask questions and to take on the perspective of one of the book's characters.

Some teachers also use historical roundtables, in which students take on the roles of specific individuals from history, and other students serve as reporters who interview them. One roundtable discussion might include a mine worker, a family member, a union organizer, a mine owner, a scab, and a Pinkerton detective (hired to break up union activity). Using books such as *On Fire* and *The Thundering Voice of John L. Lewis* and movies like *Matewan* and *Harlan County U.S.A.*, students could investigate the personal and political goals that motivated each of these individuals, the practical concerns that restrained their actions, and the courses of action that they chose. Such roundtables can also be organized around themes rather than specific events; one such roundtable might involve dialogue about independence movements among Gandhi (India), Jinah (Pakistan), Mandela (South Africa), Bolivar (South America), and Sam Adams (United States). Just as in the Salem witch trial drama, students

Literature highlights the ideas and motivations of people in history.

Fleischmann (1992)

Students use what they know about specific characters to respond to questions.

In historical roundtables, students take on the roles of specific individuals from history.

Sebestyen (1985), Selvin (1969)

124

would need a thorough understanding of diverse viewpoints in order to be able to carry out these projects.

CONCLUSIONS

Understanding the perspective of people in the past is a fundamental aspect of historical understanding, yet students often have given the topic little thought—assuming, for example, that people were too stupid to know better than to mistreat others or to give their children names like Opal. But by reading and discussing literature, making comparisons to their own experiences, and engaging in response activities such as simulated journals, written dialogues, dialogue journals, and drama, students can come to understand the ideas, attitudes, and beliefs that underlay the actions of people in the past and see them as part of a larger social context.

Such a program of study is not merely an academic exericise, but an important means of helping students see history as meaningful and relevant. People still face the kinds of problems described in this chapter—how to get along with those from different backgrounds, how to explain social problems, whether to engage in warfare. Focusing on the motivations that influence such decisions helps students see history not as inevitable but as subject to human reason, and to see the *study* of history as a way of applying reason to contemporary problems. Many of Amy's students, in fact, drew precisely that conclusion: they thought people studied history so they would know what not to do in the future. They consistently pointed out that history was worth studying so that they would know not to mistreat African Americans, or women, or Jews, or immigrants. Although some elementary students have a limited perception of contemporary racism, prejudice, and discrimination, others know from the media or their own experiences that these are indeed enduring issues in society. When asked if she thought people's attitudes were different today than in the past, for example, one sixth-grade girl in a racially-mixed urban area—whose class had been reading literature on Holocaust—pointed to the skinheads, Klan, and "other kooks" in her neighborhood and concluded that not much had changed. "In my opinion," she said, "it could happen again."

Focusing on attitudes and be-liefs calls attention to the enduring human dilem-mas that are at the core of historical study.

Barton (1995)

Barton & Smith (1994)

CHILDREN'S AND ADOLESCENT LITERATURE

Women's Roles in Society

Blumberg, R. (1993). *Bloomers!* Bradbury Press.
Chang, I. (1991). *A Separate Battle: Women and the Civil War.* Lodestar.
Clinton, S. (1986). *The Story of Susan B. Anthony.* Children's Book Press.
Cullen-DuPont, K. (1992). *Elizabeth Cady Stanton and Women's Liberty.* Facts on File.
DePauw, L. G. (1975). *Founding Mothers: Women in America in the Revolutionary Era.* Houghton Mifflin.
Duffy, J. (1993). *Radical Red.* Scribner.
Hoople, C. G. (1978). *As I Saw It: Women Who Lived the American Adventure.* Dial Press.
Johnston, N. (1995). *Remember the Ladies.* Scholastic.
Landau, E. (1975). *Hidden Heroines and Women in American History.* Julian Messner.
Macy, S. (1993). *A Whole New Ball Game: The Story of the All-American Girls Professional Baseball League.* Holt.
ONeal, Z. (1990). *A Long Way to Go.* Viking.
Rappaport, D. (1990). *American Women: Their Lives in Their Words.* Crowell.
Sullivan, G. (1994). *The Day that Women Got the Vote: A Photo History of the Women's Rights Movement.* Scholastic.

World War II and the Holocuast

Abells, C. B. (1986). *The Children We Remember.* Greenwillow.
Adler, D. A. (1987). *The Number on My Grandfather's Arm.* Union of American Hebrew Congregations.
Adler, D. A. (1993). *A Picture Book of Anne Frank.* Holiday House.
Adler, D. A. (1994). *Hilde and Elie: Children of the Holocaust.* Holiday House.
Bacharach, S. D. (1994). *Tell Them We Remember: The Story of the Holocaust.* Little, Brown.
Chaikin, M. (1987). *A Nightmare in History: The Holocaust, 1933-1945.* Houghton Mifflin.
Drukcer, M., & Halperin, M. (1993). *Jacob's Rescue: A Holocaust Story.* Bantam Doubleday Dell.
Finkelstein, N. H. (1985). *Remember Not to Forget: A Memory of the Holocaust.* Franklin Watts.
Frank, A. (1967). *Anne Frank: The Diary of a Young Girl.* Doubleday.

Friedman, I. R. (1982). *Escape or Die: True Stories of Young People Who Survived the Holocaust.* Addison-Wesley.
Greenfeld, H. (1993). *The Hidden Children.* Ticknor & Fields.
Jules, J. (1993). *The Grey Striped Shirt: How Grandma and Grandpa Survived the Holocaust.* Alef Design Group.
Kerr, J. (1987). *When Hitler Stole Pink Rabbit.* Dell.
Koehn, I. (1977). *Mischling, Second Degree: My Childhood in Nazi Germany.* Greenwillow Books.
Laird, C. (1989). *Shadow of the Wall.* Greenwillow Books.
Leigh, V. (1986). *Anne Frank.* Bookwright Press.
Leitner, I. (1992). *The Big Lie: A True Story.* Scholastic.
Lowry, L. (1990). *Number the Stars.* Dell.
Matas, C. (1993). *Daniel's Story.* Scholastic.
Meltzer, M. (1976). *Never to Forget: The Jews of the Holocaust.* Harper and Row.
Meltzer, M. (1988). *Rescue: The Story of How Gentiles Saved Jews in the Holocaust.* New York: Harper and Row.
Oppenheim, S. L. (1992). *The Lily Cupboard.* HarperCollins.
Orlev, U. (1991). *The Man from the Other Side.* Houghton Mifflin.
Reiss, J. (1987). *The Journey Back.* HarperCollins.
Reiss, J. (1987). *The Upstairs Room.* HarperCollins.
Rosenberg, M. B. (1994). *Hiding to Survive: Stories of Jewish Children Rescued from the Holocaust.* Clairon Books.
Toll, N. S. (1993). *Behind the Secret Window: A Memoir of a Hidden Childhood During World War Two.* Dial.
van der Rol, R., & Verhoeven, R. (1993). *Anne Frank: Beyond the Diary, a Photographic Remembrance.* Viking.
Vogle, I., & Vogel, M. (1992). *Bad Times, Good Times: A Personal Memoir.* Harcourt Brace Jovanovich.
Volavkova, H.(Ed.). (1993). *I Never Saw Another Butterfly: Children's Drawings and Poems from Terezin Concentration Camp, 1942-1944.* Schocken.
Yolen, J. (1990). *The Devil's Arithmetic.* Puffin.

Internment of Japanese Americans During World War II

Hamanaka, S. (1990). *The Journey: Japanese-Americans, Racism, and Renewal.* Orchard.
Mochizuki, K. (1993). *Baseball Saved Us.* Lee & Low Books.
Salisbury, G. (1994). *Under the Blood-Red Sun.* Delacorte.
Savin, M. (1992). *The Moonbridge.* Scholastic.
Stanley, J. (1994). *I am an American: A True Story of Japanese Internment.* Crown.
Takashima, S. (1991). *A Child in Prison Camp.* Tundra Books.
Thesman, J. (1993). *Molly Donnelly.* Houghton Mifflin.
Uchida, Y. (1993). *The Bracelet.* Philomel Books.
Uchida, Y. (1985). *Journey to Topaz.* Creative Arts.

Racism, Discrimination, and Civil Rights in American History

Bealer, A. W. (1972). *Only the Names Remain: The Cherokees and the Trail of Tears.* Little, Brown, and Company.
Duncan, A. F. (1995). *The National Civil Rights Museum Celebrates Everyday People.* Bridgewater Books.
Golenbock, P. (1990). *Teammates.* Harcourt Brace.
Haskins, J. (1992). *The Day Martin Luther King, Jr. was Shot: A Photo History of the Civil Rights Movement.* Scholastic.
Haskins, J. (1993). *The March on Washington.* HarperCollins.
Haskins, J. (1994). *The Scottsboro Boys.* Henry Holt.
Herlihy, D. (1988). *Ludie's Song.* Dial Books.
Levine, E. (1993). *Freedom's Shildren: Young Civil Rights Activists Tell Their Own Stories.* G. P. Putnam's Sons.
McKissack, P., & McKissack, F. L. (1987). *The Civil Rights Movement in America.* Children's Press.
McKissack, P. C., & McKissack, F. L. (1994). *Christmas in the Big House, Christmas in the Quarters.* Scholastic.
Meltzer, M. (1984). *Black Americans: A History in Their Own Words.* Crowell.
Myers, W. D. (1991). *Now is Your Time: The African-American Struggle for Freedom.* HarperCollins.
Siegel, B. (1992). *The Year They Walked: Rosa Parks and the Montgomery Bus Boycott.* Four Winds Press.
Taylor, M. D. (1987). *The Friendship.* Dial Books for Young Readers.
Taylor, M. D. (1987). *The Gold Cadillac.* Dial Books for Young Readers.
Taylor, M. D. (1981). *Let the Circle be Unbroken.* Dial Books for Young Readers.
Taylor, M. D. (1990). *Mississippi Bridge.* Dial Books for Young Readers.
Taylor, M. D. (1976). *Roll of Thunder, Hear My Cry.* Dial.
Turner, A. (1987). *Nettie's Trip South.* Macmillan.
Walter, M. (1992). *Mississippi Challenge.* Bradbury Press.

For books on slavery, see the literature list at the end of chapter 12. For books on the Underground Railroad, and on the experience of immigrants in the United States, see the list at the end of chapter 5.

Colonial Witchcraft Beliefs and Trials

Dickinson, A. (1974). *The Salem Witchcraft Delusion, 1692: "Have You Made No Contract with the Devil?"* Franklin Watts.
Kohn, B. (1972). *Out of the Cauldron: A Short History of Witchcraft.* Holt, Rinehart, and Winston.
Lasky, K. (1994). *Beyond the Burning Time.* Scholastic.
Petry, A. (1991). *Tituba of Salem Village.* HarperCollins.

Rinaldi, A. (1992). *A Break with Charity: A Story About the Salem Witch Trials*. Harcourt Brace.

Speare, E. G. (1986). *The Witch of Blackbird Pond*. Houghton Mifflin.

van der Linde, L. (1992). *The Devil in Salem Village*. Middlebrook Press.

Other Works Mentioned in This Chapter

Flesichman, P. (1993). *Bull Run*. HarperCollins.

Fox, M. (1985). *Wilfred Gordon MacDonald Partridge*. Kane-Miller.

Freedman, R. (1980). *Immigrant Kids*. Scholastic.

Sebestyen, O. (1985). *On Fire*. Boston: Atlantic Monthly Press.

Turner, A. (1992). *Katie's Trunk*. Macmillan.

127

Chapter 12

Agency and Perspective in American History

After reviewing the changes in the Virginia colony that led to an increased demand for labor, Rebecca Valbuena asks her fifth-grade students what they think of when they hear the word *slave*. Many of them have clear but fairly simple ideas, which Rebecca records on a chart—"they were whipped," "Black," "they had no freedom," "it was a long time ago," "they were always in chains." She explains that they are going to find out which of their ideas are correct, and which they need to add to or change. After recording a list of their questions about slavery on another chart, she selects several students to perform Readers' Theater scripts based on firsthand accounts of the three passages of enslavement. After reading each selection, students brainstorm words to describe what slaves might have heard, seen, and touched, as well as what they might have said or felt. They then use these words and ideas to write poems from the perspective of enslaved Africans.

Over the course of this unit, students engage in several activities designed to extend and refine their understanding of slavery. In their second lesson, for example, they work in groups to develop a list of basic *human rights*—they suggest such things as privacy, being safe outside, speech, feelings, religion, clean air, nature, life, freedom, and "being yourself." She then shows them engravings of enslaved Africans and examples of slave codes from colonial Virginia; students compare these restrictions to their own list of rights and analyze why slaveowners considered such measures necessary. The class concludes this lesson by discussing contemporary examples of violations of human rights; some students' families come from Guatemala and El Salvador and can supply example from those countries, while others make comparisons to what they have learned at school about the Civil Rights movement, to media reports of events in Bosnia and Rwanda, or to their knowledge of topics—such as child abuse and sexual abuse—rarely discussed in school.

* * *

Rhoda Coleman's fifth-grade students begin their study of the Westward movement of the mid-1800s by reading two selections from their basal series—one a collection of tall tales from the American West, the other a set of first-person accounts by Native Americans about the loss of their land. Earlier in the year, the class had studied the cultures of several Native American peoples, as well as the earliest contacts between Europeans and Native Americans, and so most students readily contribute to a Venn diagram comparing the perspectives of Native Americans and settlers. Before recess, students plot the routes of several of the major trails—such as the Oregon Trail and the National Road—on individual maps. After recess, Rhoda leads the class in beginning a KWL chart on the Westward movement—recording what they know already and what they want to know.

After lunch, Rhoda reads aloud from *Cassie's Journey*, an account of the trip West based primarily on women's diaries, and stops frequently to discuss the book with students. Working in groups of three, students then develop a list of the hardships these settlers faced—either those they have just read about, or others they know about or can imagine. After compiling a class list of these problems, Rhoda selects several students to be on the "hot seat"—to come to the front of the room to portray men, women, and children traveling West, and to respond to questions from their classmates about the journey. They base some of their answers on what they have already learned today, while other questions are added to the KWL chart. Afterward, students write letters home from the perspectives of people on the journey, detailing where they are, what their hopes are, and what they think and feel. Over the next few weeks, students will continue to listen to *Cassie's Journey* and other books, and will use a variety of reference sources to investigate their questions and create simulated journals from the perspective of people on the trip West.

Many teachers do not have the choice of studying the topics they or their students consider important; they don't have the option of exploring the Holocaust, Japanese American internment, or the Salem witch trials. Particularly at the fifth- and eighth-grade levels, when most states require American history to be taught, teachers are expected to cover the events that textbooks and curriculum guides have traditionally identified as the major events in the nation's past—early explorers, colonial life, the American Revolution, the Westward movement, and so on. Of course, these expectations are not unreasonable: we certainly hope that by the end of the middle grades, students will know about topics such as Europeans' encounter with Native Americans, the enslavement of African Americans, and the constitutional basis of American government. No one could understand "how we got here" without having a thorough acquaintance with these historical issues. Many teachers must follow curriculum guidelines in teaching history.

Unfortunately, studying the content traditionally found in textbooks often means using methods of instruction that revolve around those texts: assigning students to read a chapter on Monday, define vocabulary words on Tuesday, answers questions at the end of the chapter on Wednesday, review on Thursday, and take a test on Friday. In some schools, principals even require this sequence, week after week after week, in order to guarantee that the required curriculum is covered. It should be clear from our discussion in chapter 2 of how people learn that this kind of slavish and unimaginative use of textbooks guarantees something else entirely—that students will fail to understand either the content covered or the reason for covering it. And in classrooms like Rhoda's and Rebecca's—where few students speak English as a native language—textbook reading in isolation would be practically unintelligible. Furthermore, because most of their students come from families who have immigrated to the United States only recently, the relevance of Jamestown or the Westward movement will need more explicit attention; few textbooks make it clear to a 10-year-old Tongan girl in Los Angeles what European Americans moving West in covered wagons have to do with her own life in the present. "Covering" content rarely leads to in-depth understanding.

But Rhoda's and Rebecca's teaching shows how theory- and research-based methods of instruction can help students understand the content that too frequently is only "covered," and shows that important historical principles can accompany such content. During the course of the year, for example, both Rebecca and Rhoda divide their social studies instruction into units that closely match the California state curriculum in history and social science—*The World and its Diversity* (including immigration and cultures around the world), *Cultures in Contact* (Native American cultures, European exploration, and Jamestown), *We the People* (slavery, colonial life, the American Revolution, and the development of the Constitution), and *New Frontiers* (life in the new republic and the Westward movement). But neither of these teachers relies primarily on textbooks, nor do they value the simple coverage of information or amassing of facts. Instead, both Rebecca and Rhoda rely on literature and primary sources to develop students' understanding of content; in addition, they devote systematic attention to aspects of American history that are frequently ignored in textbook treatments—the multiple and often conflicting viewpoints on events that exist at any one time, for example, and the agency of people involved in past events. For their students, most of whose families have immigrated only recently from Mexico, Central America, Southeast Asia, or the Pacific Islands, America's history really does become a story of *Nosotros La Gente* (We the People): they study the thoughts, feelings, and actions of real people, and they learn about the diversity of perspectives and experiences that have been—and continue to be—part of our history. California State Board of Education (1988) Although textbooks focus on events, most historians focus on people.

PEOPLE IN AMERICAN HISTORY

Although textbooks typically focus on *events*—the taking of Fort Ticonderoga, Pickett's charge, the Wormley House agreement—most historians focus on people. In particular, historians examine the decisions people made in the past, and the way Historians study people.

those decisions were affected by their beliefs, their hopes, and their fears. It's not that historians don't study events as well, but an essential part of understanding events is knowing how they affected real people. Why did families start having fewer children in the early 19th-century? Why did farmers join the Populist Party? How did Reconstruction affect the opportunities for former slaves in the South? For those who are not members of the academic discipline, the importance of people in history is even more pronounced. Without the emphasis on people, history would be a highly abstract—and not particularly interesting—subject.

In the past three chapters, we have drawn attention to the importance of helping students make *human sense* of history, particularly through the use of various forms of narrative. Rebecca's and Rhoda's classrooms show how this perspective can be applied to many of the topics traditionally covered in American history courses. Just as in Amy Leigh's classroom (chapter 11), many of their activities require students to use what they have learned to put themselves in the place of historical actors. After reading accounts of enslavement, for example, Rebecca's students wrote "I Am" poems in which they used a basic outline (see Fig. 12.1) to explain what slaves might have heard, seen, felt, and so on. The examples in Fig. 12.2 show how students were able to draw conclusions not only about the physical environment in which slaves found themselves, but about the way those circumstances affected their thoughts and feelings. And later, in studying slave codes in the antebellum South, Rebecca had students do "Open Mind" activities: using outlines of human heads, they listed potential ideas of slaves and slaveowners.

Rhoda's "Hot Seat" activity is similar to Dee Hallau's role-playing activity in chapter 11: after students had discussed the account of the Westward movement in *Cassie's Journey: Going West* in the 1860s, several of them took on the role of a family moving Westward and answered questions about their feelings, motivations, and hardships. In doing so, they had to demonstrate not only their understanding of the circumstances of these trips, but had to consider how they would have affected different members of a family. One of the main assignments for this unit, meanwhile, was for students to develop

In "I Am" poems, students follow an outline to explain what people in history may have heard, seen, felt, and thought.

In "Open Mind" activities, students use outlines of human heads to list the ideas people in history

Harvey (1988)

In a "Hot Seat," students take on the roles of people in history and respond to questions from other students.

I am _____

I wonder _____

I hear _____

I see _____

I want _____

I am _____

I pretend _____

I feel _____

I touch _____

I worry _____

I cry _____

I am _____

I understand _____

I say _____

I dream _____

FIG. 12.1. "I Am . . ." poem outline.

I am a Slave	I am a Slave

I am an African   I am a slave
I wonder if I'll ever go back home   I wonder what is going to happen with me
I hear the cries of relatives   I hear people crying
I see those evil people   I see dead people
I want my freedom   I want to be with my family
I am a slave   I am sad

I pretend it's not so bad though it is   I pretend I am somewhere else
I feel really miserable without my people I feel lonely
I touch nothing but chains   I touch people
I worry for my family   I worry about my family
I cry for the wooziness I feel   I cry all the time
I am a prisoner   I am African

I understand not a word they say   I understand nothing
I say you are the most hideous thing on Earth   I say I want to be home with my family
I dream that one day I'll have freedom   I dream I can be home with my family
        by Genoveva   by Vanessa

FIG. 12.2. "I am . . ." poems.

a simulated journal written from the perspective of someone moving West; these journals had to contain information on sights, weather, events, and the writer's reaction to these. Again, this assignment required that students understand not only the factual content of the unit but the way people reacted to their circumstances.

These perspective-taking assignments are basic features of instruction for most historical topics in Rhoda's and Rebecca's classrooms. In studying Jamestown, for example, students wrote broadsides advertising the colony to potential settlers in England; in doing so, they had to decide how to persuade a 17th-century Englishman to move to North America. (Phrases included "Dost thou want to get rich?" and "Come hither. Perchance you will hit the big one.") In another assignment, they took the perspective of Jamestown settlers, and wrote letters home to their families. And in studying the American Revolution, students wrote letters from the point of view of British soldiers stationed in Boston; created a colonial newspaper with news items, editorials, and interviews; and conducted debates between Patriots and Loyalists.

Most historical topics lend themselves to perspective-taking activities.

The "I Am" poems in Fig. 12.2 show the seriousness and passion with which students approached such assignments. In both classrooms, students consistently pointed to these kinds of perspective-taking activities as one of the primary reasons they enjoyed studying history. Several noted that they hadn't liked history in previous years, when they were just reading about it from a book or writing about it on paper; what they liked, as one girl pointed out, was acting things out, pretending to be people in the past. A classmate agreed: "It gives you a chance to be in their places—how did it feel, like the real thing."

Students generally enjoy taking the perspective of people in the past.

USING LITERATURE AND PRIMARY SOURCES TO UNDERSTAND PEOPLE

As we have noted, historical fiction is a particularly effective way of helping students take the perspective of people in the past. Fiction is inherently subjective in nature; it invites readers to put themselves in the place of the characters they read about. It is important to understand, however, that perspective-taking activities are not simply exercises in creative writing, nor is their purpose to instill some vague sense of sympathy for people in the past; their purpose is to develop historical understanding, and therefore they must be based on evidence. Without emphasizing the role of evidence, such activities might amount to little more than asking students to imagine that they're an elephant; because an elephant doesn't have human thoughts and feelings, anything students create is equally valid—there are no clear criteria for judging whether a student is *really* taking the perspective of an elephant. People, however, can explain what they're thinking, and they leave behind both direct and indirect evidence of their ideas; these expressions of their perspectives form the basis for historical interpretations.

Both Rhoda and Rebecca connect their perspective-taking activities to primary sources. Rebecca, for example, had students write their "I Am" poems after having read and discussed firsthand accounts of Africans describing enslavement; in another lesson, students used advertisements for escaped slaves to make inferences about the life of slaves—concluding, for example, that because the advertisements sometimes noted that a slave could read, most probably could not. Similarly, Rhoda's students based their "Hot Seat" role-play on literature based on the diaries of women who moved West in the mid-19th century, and their discussion of Native Americans' perspective on the loss of land was based on primary sources found in their basal readers and in *Bury My Heart at Wounded Knee.*

Of course, students' own experiences often provide a valid basis for attempting to imagine the thoughts and feelings of people in the past. Despite all the differences in world view and experience between a Mexican American 10-year-old in the 1990s and a West African adult in the 1600s, their feelings about being separated from their families probably have some important similarities. At the same time, however, teachers must stress that part of the reason for such perspective-taking activities is to understand both how attitudes are the same and how they are different across time and place—and that these conclusions must be based on evidence. When Rhoda asked students how Native Americans felt about their loss of land, they initially reacted with their own intuitive judgments—"sad," "mad"—but she consistently directed their attention back to the primary sources they had been reading—"What did they *say* they felt?" Of course, students will not always be able completely to separate their own contemporary perspectives from those of people in the past: as we saw in the last chapter, there is always a tension between imagining what someone 200 years ago might have thought, and what I would have thought if I had been alive then. Exercises in historical perspective-taking, however, help students expand their understanding so that they are no longer so limited to their own point of view. It is this emphasis on people—and the potential it holds for connecting them across time and space—that helps make the traditional topics in American history relevant for Rhoda's and Rebecca's students.

DIVERSITY IN AMERICAN HISTORY

North America has always consisted of widely diverse cultural groups, and the United States has been multicultural since its very inception as a nation. Even before the first European explorers arrived, the native inhabitants of the continent spoke thousands of different languages and displayed an enormous range of cultural variation. Once European settlers arrived, the variety of people here increased: Swedish, Dutch, German, English, French, and Scots-Irish settlers populated the East coast and interior waterways, while enslaved Africans further added to the Colonial population. By the mid-1800s, immigrants from Ireland, China, and Japan populated the coasts, and the conquest of Mexico resulted in the addition of millions of Latino residents in the Southwest. By the beginning of the 20th century, urban centers saw increasing numbers of residents from east and central Europe, and immigration from Mexico, Central America, the Caribbean, Asia, the Pacific Islands, and indeed, every region of the world continues to add to the greatest strength of the country—its diversity.

Historical perspective-taking depends on evidence.

Primary sources provide insight into the perspectives of people in the past.

Brown (1975)

Students' own experiences can help them take the perspective of people in the past.

Historical perspective-taking helps students make connections to people from different times and places.

America has always been multicultural.

Takaki (1993)

Diversity is America's greatest strength.

Many people do not think of American history as including such diversity, yet people from a wide variety of backgrounds have always been central to the development of American society. Ours would be a radically different society without the contributions of any of the above groups. European settlers could not have survived without the help of Native Americans; the southern plantation economy would never have developed without racial slavery; the American West would have taken a different course without the labor of its Chinese American, Japanese American, and Latino residents; the industrialization of the American economy has always depended on the labor of all segments of the population. And although it may come as a shock to some, women also have always contributed to the development of our society. We often have heard that women don't show up much in texts because they haven't really done much in history—an observation that would surely come as a surprise to the millions of women who have given birth, done housework, farmed, worked in factories, operated businesses, become professionals, participated in political movements, and done all the other things that have produced contemporary society.

People from all backgrounds have contributed to the development of American culture.

Although textbook publishers have begun to give increased attention to diversity, this attention is sometimes only at a superficial level; certainly most teachers cannot rely on their texts to present a significant account of the country's diversity. As long as women and minorities remain on the margins of the curriculum, the interactions and connections of the diverse people in our past will remain unclear. A meaningful understanding of American history requires the recognition that at any given time, the country consisted of both men and women; of people from many different racial and ethnic backgrounds; of those who were rich, those who were poor, and everything in between. Understanding American history means recognizing that people from these different backgrounds often had fundamentally different perspectives on the events of their day, and that these perspectives frequently came into serious—even violent—conflict. As we've said, teaching history cannot be limited to a single story about the past, a story in which it appears that everyone agreed with each other in a kind of happy consensus, free of exploitation, repression, or conflict. Teachers must consistently devote attention to the diversity found in society at any given time, and must take seriously the way perspectives on events differed among people.

Teachers must take responsibility for increasing attention to diversity.

People from different backgrounds had different perspectives on historical events.

This, too, is a constant feature of both Rebecca's and Rhoda's instruction. In all their historical units, they emphasize not only taking the perspective of people in the past, but taking the perspective of *different* people. In studying the Columbian encounter, for example, students write accounts from the perspective of Columbus, Columbus' crew, and Native Americans. In studying colonial Williamsburg, they learn about the lifestyles of the rich, poor, and "middling" segments of the population, and about the different kinds of work done by men and women. In learning about the American Revolution, they conduct debates between Patriots and Loyalists and write editorials from each viewpoint. In studying slavery, they examine the perspective of slaves and slaveowners. In studying the Westward movement, they look at the differences not only between settlers and Native Americans but the differences among settlers. (See the literature list at the end of this chapter for books from differing perspectives.)

Students study the variety of perspectives that existed at any given time in history.

Children often fail to see this diversity in history, and instead see the past as a matter of simple and linear development. As we pointed out in chapter 7, they often think that all people in the colonial era lived in log cabins, or that everyone in the 1800s dressed in formal clothes all the time. Such perceptions are hardly surprising, given that students are rarely exposed to differences within a given time period. But when teachers consistently emphasize diversity and conflicting perspectives, it becomes a basic part of students' understanding of the past. When students in Rebecca's classroom first examined pictures from colonial Boston, for example, they quickly noted features such as the presence of African servants, the different kinds of work done by men and women, and the variety of economic classes depicted in some pictures. Similarly, students reading about the Westward movement in Rhoda's class often stopped to point out how Native Americans would have viewed things differ-

Students learn to see diversity and conflicting perspectives as a basic characteristic of history.

133

ently—noting, for example, that what the settlers called a "new home" was already someone else's home. These are not the kinds of observations we have come to expect among students who have not been taught to look for such differences.

Examining diverse experiences and conflicting perspectives, however, does not mean simply reversing the traditional story of American history—portraying it as the story of pathetic victimization rather than noble conquest. Doing so reinforces the perception that there is a single story out there, one in which women, minorities, and the poor play a generally subordinate and inferior (albeit sympathetic) role. European American teachers are sometimes shocked, for example, when their African American students appear ashamed to hear about slavery: "It's their history," they ask, "so why aren't they proud of it?" They're not proud of it because slavery and segregation are typically the *only* time African Americans show up in school history; it's hard to be proud of your past when the only time you encounter it is in the context of someone beating up your forebears.

Portraying people exclusively as victims is neither historically nor pedagogically sound.

Portraying people as victims—without choice, control, or initiative—is neither historically nor pedagogically sound. Part of the solution lies in making sure that African Americans don't appear only when studying slavery, Latinos only when studying farmworkers, Japanese Americans only when studying World War II. The curriculum must reflect the actual diversity that has existed throughout American history, so that students see that African Americans have also been farmers and soldiers, women have been scientists and engineers, poor people have been politically active, and so on.

But just as importantly, people cannot be portrayed exclusively as victims. American slavery is one of history's worst violations of human rights, and those enslaved were ruthlessly and cruelly victimized in countless ways. But the victimization involved in the slave system is very different than thinking of individuals solely as victims; portraying slaves as hapless and servile—even when doing so sympathetically—is a caricature that does nothing to illuminate life under slavery. Despite their lack of basic political and economic freedoms, American slaves made lives for themselves—they married, had children, hunted, fished, raised gardens, learned skilled trades, and fought back against the slave system. Indeed, one of the most fascinating aspects of this period in history is the way people developed a vibrant and meaningful cultural tradition under trying circumstances—yet this is rarely a part of the way the topic is presented in school.

Enslaved Africans developed vibrant cultural traditions. *Joyner (1984), Levine (1977)*

In Rebecca's class, though, students studied not only how slavery violated human rights, but how slaves adapted and survived. An important part of the unit, for example, focused on storytelling. Rebecca began by talking about how slaves had to survive in a new environment, and how they passed on what they learned to each other and to their children. Students knew that some of the most important ways they themselves learn—schools and reading—weren't available to slaves, and Rebecca explained that storytelling fulfilled many of those same purposes. Students read several stories from *The People Could Fly* and other sources and discussed the lessons which each might have been meant to express. They concluded, for example, that one story explained the importance of not telling everything you know—a lesson they thought was as useful today as during slavery. After learning about the elements of stories and storytelling, students wrote and performed their own stories designed to teach a lesson.

Hamilton (1985)

These activities portrayed slaves not as stereotypical victims but as creative and insightful human beings, people who gained wisdom from their experiences and developed sophisticated art forms to convey those lessons. Through their own experience writing and performing stories, students saw just how difficult that was: they had to structure a story to teach a meaningful lesson, follow appropriate conventions, and learn techniques of performance. Finding out how much work and creativity was involved in such artistic products helped students see the richness and complexity of slave life, rather than perpetuating their initial stereotypes of slaves who were "always in chains." One student even pointed to this as his favorite activity during the course of the year: "It was something they did," he pointed out, "and we were doing the same thing."

Students see enslaved people not just as victims but as creative and insightful human beings.

BUILDING ON WHAT STUDENTS ALREADY KNOW

The lessons described here are interesting and intellectually stimulating, and students' enthusiasm about history makes it clear how effective they are in keeping them interested. Nonetheless, all these lessons required serious and sustained effort by teachers and students. Because of their diverse backgrounds, for example, neither Rhoda nor Rebecca could assume that their students would have the background knowledge to make sense of distant events in American history; as we pointed out in chapter 7, neither dates nor expressions like "the colonial era" are likely to call forth many specific associations for students from any background—much less those who have only recently immigrated to the country. Rhoda and Rebecca saw their first task, then, as helping students develop the schemas that would allow them to put topics like slavery and the Westward movement in context. An important step in building that understanding was finding out what students already knew; Rebecca, for example, recorded students' ideas about slaves on a web in the front of the classroom, while Rhoda listed what students knew about the Westward movement on a KWL chart. They did not limit such exercises to the beginning of new units, however; they also frequently structured individual lessons around students' prior knowledge—as, for example, when Rebecca had students develop a list of what they considered basic human rights before introducing slave codes, and then compare this to what they knew about contemporary human rights violations. Beginning lessons and units this way activates students' prior knowledge—it reminds them of what they already know.

> Teachers help students develop the schemas they need to understand history.

> A web (also known as a *semantic map*) shows relationships among concepts and ideas.

> On a KWL chart, students record what they know, what they want to know, and what they have learned. *Ogle (1986)*

> Beginning with discussion, KWL charts, and webs activates students' prior knowledge.

The collaborative nature of such activities is a critical part of this process. Asking an individual student what she knows about slavery or the westward movement will usually prompt the response, "Nothing." But when they work together, each student's contribution remind others of information they can add; often, students don't realize they have relevant knowledge until they hear their classmates' comments. In reading *Cassie's Journey*, for example, Rhoda asked students if they knew what buffalo chips were; only one student knew, but as soon as he explained what they were, other students realized that they knew what they were used for—they just didn't know the term. Meaningful reading in the content areas depends on students' ability to call forth their background knowledge, and collaboration yields a much greater store of such information than individual activities would produce.

> Students learn more when working collaboratively.

> Collaboration helps students activate their prior knowledge.

Such collaboration, we should point out, is often better accomplished in small groups—two to four students—than as a whole class (at least initially). Many students are hesitant to take risks before the entire class, and teachers sometimes find themselves calling on the same three or four students repeatedly. But working in small groups *before* coming together as a whole class helps more students contribute; those who are less confident—either of their language abilities or their knowledge—are more likely to take part in class discussion when they have had a chance to try out their ideas in small groups of peers first. Such collaboration, however, requires just as much direct instruction and scaffolding as academic content. Before Rhoda's students developed their list of hardships in small groups, for example, she asked them to review the standards of mutually respectful interaction which they had been practicing for months; they mentioned using quiet voices, listening to what others have to say, not hurting people's feelings, saying nice things, and "no idea's a bad idea."

> Small groups allow students to take more risks than whole-class discussion.

> Learning to work together requires explicit instruction, modeling, and practice. *Johnson, Johnson, & Holubec (1993), Slavin (1995)*

Activities like webbing and KWL charts also have a purpose beyond activating students' prior knowledge: they give the teacher insight into what she needs to address in upcoming lessons, and how much attention to devote to various aspects of the topic. Sometimes it becomes clear that students have already learned a great deal about a topic from relatives, the media, or their own reading. In chapter 11, for example, we saw how Amy discovered that her students were already so familiar with the concept of prejudice that some of the introductory content she had planned was unnecessary. Similarly, Rhoda had planned to spend more time developing students' understanding of transportation in the 1800s, but when she began by asking them if they could think of any differences between a covered wagon and a stagecoach, they

> Activites that activate prior knowledge provide teachers with insight into students' understanding.

When teachers encourage students to share what they know, they must take that knowledge seriously.

Webs, KWL charts, and discussion provide teachers with information on which misconceptions they need to address.

Webs and KWL charts help students see how their understanding has changed.

Teachers accept students' ideas as approximations. *Pappas et al. (1995)*

Vosniadou & Brewer (1987)

Students modify their understanding based on new experiences.

Students take responsibility for their learning.

Seixas (1993a)

quickly produced several dozen! These vehicles are apparently such a staple of cartoons, movies, and television shows that students had already developed extensive—and relatively accurate—background knowledge about them. It was only by allowing students to demonstrate this knowledge that Rhoda knew how much information to provide students. Effective instruction depends on giving students the opportunity to show what they already know, and taking that knowledge seriously.

Other times students' knowledge is inaccurate or—more frequently—incomplete, and webs and KWL charts alert teachers to the information they need to address in upcoming lessons. Experienced teachers can anticipate many of students' ideas—that there are no more Native Americans, for example, or that slavery only existed at one point in time—and already will have prepared lessons to address these misconceptions. Other times, discussions reveal unexpected aspects of students' understanding. A teacher might not know ahead of time that students think slaves were always kept chained to each other, for example—yet if she doesn't address that misconception, students will have trouble understanding how slaves lived. Because she had students web out their ideas about slaves, Rebecca knew that she would have to include more information (especially visual images) on the daily life of slaves in upcoming lessons. As a consequence, when the students returned to their web at the end of the unit, they were quick to point out that they had been mistaken about slaves always being kept in chains. They not only learned new content, but were able explicitly to track how their understanding of the topic had changed from the beginning of the unit to the end.

During such activities, teachers must accept students' ideas as approximations of more sophisticated understandings. Most of us are tempted simply to correct students whenever they say something that is factually inaccurate, but people don't modify their conceptual understanding just because someone tells them they're wrong. At best, they may place what they hear in school in a separate category of "school knowledge" unrelated to what they *really* know. (Young children, for example, often know that they're supposed to say that the world is round when they're at school, but remain convinced that it's actually flat, because that's what their experience tells them.) If school knowledge conflicts with the understanding students have gained elsewhere, they will believe it only if they can confirm it through new experiences. Reading firsthand accounts and looking at pictures of the daily life of enslaved families gives students new evidence about whether they always were kept in chains, and thus gives them the chance to modify their understanding. As a result, they are usually not only willing but even eager to point out their previous mistakes: they're proud that now they know more than they did before. If, on the other hand, Rebecca had simply told students, "No, slaves weren't always kept in chains, so I'm not going to write that on the web," she would have transformed a schema-building activity into nothing more than a pretest of factual details. Not only would students have learned little, but they probably would have stopped contributing to the discussion.

Finally, allowing students to decide on questions they want to answer during a unit helps place the responsibility for learning where it belongs—with the students. In previous chapters, we have explored the process of helping students develop questions to investigate; in most of those discussions, though, the topics under investigation were not ones usually covered by textbooks and curriculum guides—how medicine has changed over time, why people settled in our town, and so on. It would be difficult to learn about such topics *without* developing questions first; at first glance, however, it might appear that step is less important for "traditional" topics such as slavery or the Westward movement, which are already covered in textbooks. But one of the most serious problems with relying exclusively on texts is that it promotes the view that history—or any discipline—consists of a fixed body of knowledge, already discovered by others, and not open to investigation or interpretation. We hardly need to emphasize that such a perceptive is not psychologically, educationally, or historically valid: teaching students that studying history means remembering what someone else says about the past misrepresents the nature of history and fails to help them learn the content. Encouraging students to develop their own questions and take responsibility for finding the answers, on the other hand, builds on the concerns about history that students bring with them to school, and treats them as self-directed learners who can use a variety of resources to learn more. We have also pointed out that developing curriculum is not the sole job of either teacher or students, but is a joint responsibility. Students invariably are interested in some things that teachers may consider only marginally significant—Where did settlers go to the bathroom? What kind of snakes were there?—while teachers will want to emphasize some things—such as the concept of human rights—that students might not have initiated on their own.

Of course, for students to investigate questions of their own choosing, they need access to a wide variety of resources. Textbooks and encyclopedias are unlikely to contain answers to questions about how people went to the bathroom on the Oregon Trail, and such works have the added disadvantage of being written in a style that students find difficult. Trade books like *Pioneers*, *The Oregon Trail*, and *The Westward Movement and Abolitionism*, on the other hand, are well-illustrated, written in readable prose, and include information on many aspects of everyday life. Having an assortment of literature available for students at all times also allows them to find answers to more informal questions that emerge during a unit. While writing letters back home from the trail West, for example, several students in Rhoda's class began to wonder if people really did write letters, and whether there was any way for them to be delivered. A quick check of *If You Traveled West in a Covered Wagon* revealed a section on precisely that topic, and students stopped their work and listened attentively as Rhoda read; in looking that up, meanwhile, other students came across a passage on the Pony Express, and several others became interested in that topic as well. Teachers cannot always anticipate what topics will interest students, and so cannot plan lessons explicitly designed to address them; what they can do, though, is to make sure their classrooms have enough resources for students to find the answers they need. As Rhoda points out, "My room is more chaotic that way, but the learning is better."

SCAFFOLDING STUDENTS' UNDERSTANDING

As we have frequently noted, teachers must provide students with the structure they need to be successful. Creative and stimulating lessons sometimes fall apart when students begin independent or group assignments—hands fly up and the cry, "I don't know what to do" fills the room. The most imaginative, stimulating, creative assignments will yield little if students aren't given the scaffolding to complete them. To build on the enthusiasm that effective presentations can produce, teachers have to help students make the transition to their own work. Having students design colonial newspapers, write "I Am" poems, or perform stories that teach lessons will not go smoothly unless the teacher shows them how to use what they are learning to do those things.

One important aspect of scaffolding is class discussion. Although students may listen or read carefully, they invariably learn more when their interaction with texts is accompanied by discussion with the teacher and other students. Rhoda, for example, stopped frequently while reading *Cassie's Journey*—several times on each page—to ask questions. Some simply checked for comprehension—"Do you know what buffalo chips are?"—but most were calculated to stimulate thoughtful analysis and discussion among students—such as, "If you were a kid traveling West, and you could only take one thing, what would it be?" or "Why wouldn't you want to be at the end of the train of wagons?" Although some works benefit from uninterrupted reading, this kind of interaction is usually necessary when students are unfamiliar with the content. Especially with historical works—whether literature or primary sources—students depend on discussion to help them fully understand the context, to see the connection between events, and to gain insight into the perspectives of the people involved. The extremely high level of attention and participation when Rhoda and Rebecca read aloud is an indication of how much students benefit from such discussion; indeed, when we asked their students what advice they had for teaching

Teachers can encourage students to become self-directed learners.

Developing curriculum is the joint responsibility of teachers and students.

Beck & McKeown (1991)
Fisher (1990), Katz (1993), Sandler (1994)

Levine (1986)

Students understand texts better when they discuss them with teachers and with each other. *Pierce & Gilles (1993)*

137

history, several said that teachers shouldn't just read something out loud or tell students to read it—they should stop to talk about it so students will understand.

Another important aspect of helping students understand what they study is *concept development*. Although this has been considered a basic part of social studies instruction for many years, we find it frequently overlooked in teaching history. Even though students may be familiar with words for abstract concepts—*independence, religion, society,* and so on—they may not fully understand the ideas those words refer to. In preparing to study the American Revolution, for example, Rebecca knew that students would have to understand the concept *rebellion*; as a result, she devoted an entire lesson to exploring the topic with them. She read examples of people who had been dissatisfied with something and had taken action, and read examples of people who had not taken action; the class discussed the similarities and differences among the examples, constructed a Venn diagram comparing them, and worked in groups to develop their own definitions of rebellion. Finally, they took events from their own lives and from the news and considered whether they could be classified as examples of rebellion. When they moved into the events leading up the American Revolution, they frequently had occasion to refer back to these discussions. In order for historical topics to have meaning and relevance, students must have enough conceptual understanding to see how specific topics relate to broader themes and issues. Focusing on the concept of *human rights*, for example, helps students put their study of slavery into a broader context, one with relevance to many times and places.

Finally, graphic organizers are a key means by which both Rhoda and Rebecca help students build on what they know. Reading about enslavement may have produced a great many ideas, but most students would not have been able immediately to write a poem about an enslaved African's thoughts and feelings. Although the basic outline of the poem (Fig. 12.1) was one step in helping students get their ideas on paper, even more important was the graphic organizer the class filled out together: as they read and discussed each passage, they kept track of what a slave would have felt, seen, heard, and thought (Fig. 12.3). Similarly, even students who had studied the Westward movement in depth might have had trouble knowing what to write in a simulated journal. By leading students in webbing out their ideas beforehand, however (Fig. 12.4), Rhoda ensured that they would have many more words and ideas to draw on.

Enslaved Africans
What they might have...

	Felt	Heard	Seen	Said	Touched
First Passage					
Second Passage					
Third Passage					

FIG. 12.3. Enslavement graphic organizer.

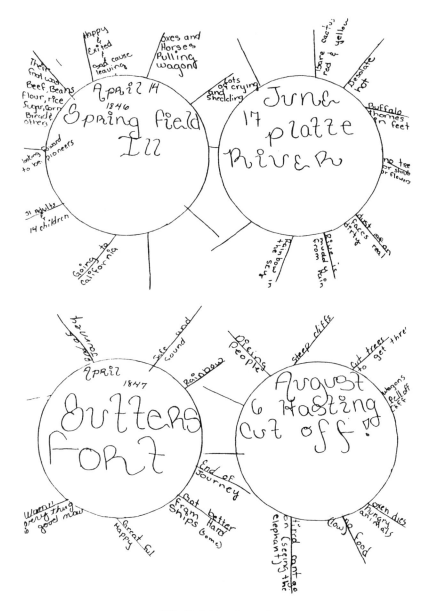

FIG. 12.4. Planning web.

EXTENSIONS

Throughout this chapter we have emphasized the importance of focusing on the agency of people in the past and the diversity of experiences that have characterized any moment in history. For any topic a teacher wishes (or is required) to teach, she should ask, "Who else was involved in this, and what did they think about it?" In teaching about World War II, for example, it is important not to limit the focus to the battles and political leaders that may quickly leap to mind. The wealth of rich literature on the Holocaust suggests one meaningful way of focusing on agency and diversity during the period; students would learn far more about humanity—and the relevance of history—by examining the personal choices people made in response to events than by re-enacting the Battle of Midway. In addition, students might study the effect of the war on daily life in the United States and other countries; that topic could include attention to the internment of Japanese Americans, the integration of

All historical topics should include the study of diverse perspectives and human agency.

139

the military, the changes in employment opportunities for women, American anti-Semitism and support for Hitler, and the economic consequences of the war. All these have more important and far-reaching implications than following colored arrows on a map to trace troop movements.

Barton (1994a), McKeown & Beck (1990)

Similarly, the American Revolution is one of the most frequently covered topics in both fifth and eighth grades, yet when asked about it later, students often remember only a string of unrelated people, events, and documents, and their understanding of its significance is limited to observations such as, "It's important so we wouldn't be bossed around by the queen anymore." Rarely do they learn that as many colonists opposed the war as supported it or that Patriots tarred and feathered Loyalists; rarely do they learn about the effect of the war on women, African Americans, or daily life in general. Nor do they learn that any account of the period is written from a particular point of view, that these perspectives vary from person to person, or that they change over time. Perhaps most significantly, students do not learn that creating such accounts requires the use of evidence, nor that such evidence can be examined critically. Rather than seeing the American Revolution as a pivotal and controversial event in their country's history, students are presented with a single, finished story—a story that has no clear immediacy and whose details they remember in only the most superficial way.

Students analyze and evaluate primary sources written from different perspectives. I. Bennett (1967)

Students' historical understanding benefits when their study of the Revolution includes methods similar to Rebecca's and Rhoda's. In Amy Leigh's class, for example, students read and evaluated a dozen accounts of the Battle at Lexington Green, each written from a different perspective. They enjoyed the chance to evaluate the sources for bias—noting, for example, that Patriots would be more likely to claim the British fired first, and newspaper articles in London would do the opposite; that accounts written a week after the battle would be more reliable than the recollections of a former soldier 50 years later; and that a captured British soldier might change his account to please his captors. Having seen just how many details of the battle were in dispute, students then become indignant whenever they found books that asserted more certainty than in fact existed. They were thus becoming adept at asking the basic question of critical thought—"How do I know if this is true?"

Collier & Collier (1974)
Collier & Collier (1984)
DeFord & Stout (1987)
Avi (1984)

Similarly, students will gain a more complete understanding of the Revolution if they examine novels on the period written from a variety of perspectives—works like *My Brother Sam is Dead*, about a Loyalist family in which the eldest son joins the Continental army; *War Comes to Willy Freeman*, about a freed African American girl searching for her mother during the war; *An Enemy Among Them*, about a Hessian soldier cared for by a German American Patriot family; *The Fighting Ground*, about a boy who learns that fighting is not as heroic as he had imagined. By working in literature response groups, students can analyze and compare these novels and the perspectives they represent. But as we described in chapter 9, narrative can be a very powerful medium: telling stories is a basic means by which people make sense of their world, and there is a tendency for students to regard what they have read without a critical eye. Students can thus use reference works like *The American Revolution, U.S. Kids History: Book of the American Revolution*, and *If You Were There in 1776* to investigate the accuracy of the books they are reading. By comparing the information in these sources, students will learn more both about historical inquiry and about the effect of the Revolution on diverse groups of people than they would be reading a text passage or seeing a filmstrip on the Boston Tea Party.

Brenner (1994), Carter (1992), Egger-Bovet & Smith-Baranzin (1994)

CONCLUSIONS

Many of the teachers in this book have almost complete control over their history curriculum, either because they teach in the primary grades—where there are few expectations for history content—or because their state curriculum focuses on outcomes rather than requiring specific topics at each grade level. Many teachers do not have that much responsibility for designing their curriculum; particularly in fourth grade and above, most teachers are required by official guidelines or informal (but very real) expectations to teach specific topics in state, American, or world history. As Rhoda and Rebecca demonstrate, however, teaching the required content of the curriculum does not mean following a textbook in lockstep fashion; principles of effective instruction and the elements of historical thinking can be applied to any topic a teacher wants or needs to teach.

At first glance, most of Rhoda's and Rebecca's students have little reason to be interested in the major events of American history. Most are immigrants from poor or working-class families; their ancestors rarely show up in stories of the British colonies, the Overland Trail, or the Civil War. But by focusing on human agency and multiple perspectives, Rhoda and Rebecca not only keep their students interested in American history but make it clear why the topic is relevant to them after all. Their students learn that America has always been diverse, that attention to any topic must include the experience of different ethnic groups, of men and women, of rich and poor. In addition, focusing on people—real human beings who live, work, play, create art, and make decisions—allows students to make connections across time and place, connections that might not at first be clear. By teaching history this way, Rhoda and Rebecca not only cover factual content but help students see what historical understanding is and how it relates to their own lives.

CHILDREN'S AND ADOLESCENT LITERATURE

Slavery

Berry, J. (1992). *Ajeemah and His Son*. HarperCollins.
Buss, F. L. (1991). *Journey of the Sparrows*. Lodestar.
Evitts, W. J. (1985). *Captive Bodies, Free Spirits: The Story of Southern Slavery*. Julian Messner.
Hamilton, V. (1985). *The People Could Fly*. Knopf.
Hansen, J. (1994). *The Captive*. Scholastic.
Hopkinson, D. (1993). *Sweet Clara and the Freedom Quilt*. Knopf.
Jacob, H. P. (1978). *The Diary of the Strawbridge Place*. Atheneum.
Johnson, D. (1993). *Now Let Me Fly: The Story of a Slave Family*. Macmillan.
Katz, W. L. (1990). *Breaking the Chains: African-American Slave Resistance*. Atheneum.
Lyons, M. E. (1992). *Letters from a Slave Girl: The Story of Harriet Jacobs*. Charles Scribner's Sons.
McKissack, P. C., & McKissack, F. L. (1994). *Christmas in the Big House, Christmas in the Quarters*. Scholastic.
Myers, W. D. (1991). *Now is Your Time: The African-American Struggle for Freedom*. HarperCollins.
Myers, W. D. (1994). *The Glory Field*. Scholastic
Palmer, C. A. (1995). *The First Passage: Blacks in the Americas, 1502-1617*. Oxford University Press.
Paulson, G. (1993). *Nightjohn*. Bantam Doubleday Dell.
Stepto, M, (Ed.). (1994). *Our Song, Our Toil: The Story of American Slavery as Told by Slaves*. Millbrook.
Turner, A. (1987). *Nettie's Trip South*. Macmillan.

For books dealing specifically with the Underground Railroad, see the literature list at the end of chapter 5.

Westward Movement

Brown, D. (1975). *Wounded Knee: An Indian History of the American West*. Adapted for young readers by Amy Ehrlich from Dee Brown's *Bury My Heart at Wounded Knee*. Dell.
Fisher, L. E. (1990). *The Oregon Trail*. Holiday House.
Freedman, R. (1983). *Children of the Wild West*. Scholastic.
Gregory, K. (1981). *Jenny of the Tetons*. Gulliver.
Harvey, B. (1988). *Cassie's Journey: Going West in the 1860s*. Holiday
Katz, W. L. (1993). *The Westward Movement and Abolitionism*. Steck-Vaughn.
Lasky, K. (1983). *Beyond the Divide*. Macmillan.
Lasky, K. (1988). *The Bone Wars*. Morow Junior Books.
Laurgaard, R. K. (1989). *Patty Reed's Doll*. Tomato Enterprises.
Levine, E. (1986). *If You Traveled West in a Covered Wagon*. Scholastic.
Russell, M.. (1993). *Along the Santa Fe Trail: Marion Russell's Own Story*. Whitman.
Sanders, S. R. (1989). *Aurora Means Dawn*. Bradbury Press.
Sandler, M. W. (1994). *Pioneers*. HarperCollins.
Steedman, S., & Bergin, M. (1993). *A Frontier Fort on the Oregon Trail*. Peter Bedrick Books.

Turner, A. (1993). *Grass Songs*. Harcourt, Brace, & Jovanovich.
van der Linde, L. (1993). *The Pony Express*. New Discovery Books.
Williams, D. (1993). *Grandma Essie's Covered Wagon*. Knopf.

Colonial America and the Revolutionary Era

Anderson, J. (1988). *A Williamsburg Household*. Clarion Books.
Avi. (1984). *The Fighting Ground*. J. B. Lippincott.
Avi. (1979). *Night Journeys*. Pantheon.
Brenner, B. (1994). *If You Were There in 1776*. Macmillan.
Carter, A. R. (1992). *The American Revolution*. Franklin Watts.
Collier, J. L., & Collier, C. (1976). *The Bloody Country*. Four Winds Press.
Collier, J. L., & Collier, C. (1981). *Jump Ship to Freedom*. Delacorte.
Collier, J. L., & Collier, C. (1974). *My Brother Sam is Dead*. Four Winds Press.
Collier, J. L., & Collier, C. (1984). *War Comes to Willie Freeman*. Dell.
Collier, J. L., & Collier, C. (1984). *Who is Carrie?* Delacorte Press.
Corwin, J. H. (1989). *Colonial American Crafts: The Home*. Franklin Watts.
Davis, B. (1992). *Black Heroes of the American Revolution*. Harcourt Brace.
DeFord, D. H., & Stout, H. S. (1987). *An Enemy Among Them*. Houghton Mifflin.
Egger-Bovet, H., & Smith-Baranzin, M. (1994). *U. S. Kids History: Book of the American Revolution*. Little, Brown, and Company.
Finlayson, A. (1974). *Greenhorn on the Frontier*. Frederick Warne.
Finlayson, A. (1971). *Redcoat in Boston*. Frederick Warne.
Fisher, L. E. (1966). *Colonial American Craftsmen: The Weavers*. Franklin Watts.
Meltzer, M. (Ed.). (1987). *The American Revolutionaries: A History in their Own Words, 1750-1800*. Thomas Y. Crowell.
O'Dell, S. (1980). *Sarah Bishop*. Houghton Mifflin.
Perl, L. (1975). *Lumps, Grunts, and Snickerdoodles: What Colonial Americans Ate and Why*. Clarion.
Rinaldi, A. (1994). *Finishing Becca: A story about Peggy Shippen and Benedict Arnold*. Harcourt Brace.
Rinaldi, A. (1993). *The Fifth of March: A Story of the Boston Massacre*. Harcourt Brace.
Turner, A. (1992). *Katie's Trunk*. Macmillan.

Chapter 13

Cognitive Pluralism in History Teaching and Learning

What makes a culture unique, where are the commonalties that we share if it isn't the arts? The arts make us all a part of humankind. When you think of learning as a whole instead of little pieces, the arts give you the whole picture. So, in seventh grade when I teach ancient civilizations, how could I teach about Greece and not teach about drama? How could I teach about Greece and not teach about architecture? And in eighth grade, it's really been interesting to watch the student who studied Mozart and found out that he was a contemporary of George Washington . . . The arts also give us a window. Sometimes, we don't give students an opportunity to share with us what they do know because we restrict their vehicle of expression. If I only accept what they know about the Bill of Rights in written form, then I've eliminated children that want to share that information with me in a picture or a drama or those kinds of things. The arts give them a vehicle to share with me what they really do know . . . And sometimes you help a child develop areas they wouldn't have otherwise. They would have said that's not my strong suit, that's not something I do, but because it is a way that we express ourselves in the classroom—sometimes its on some kind of assessment—that child makes an attempt to do it and becomes stronger as a result.

—Jeanette Groth, middle school teacher, Grades 6, 7, & 8

Jeanette Groth's classroom is always full of art, music, and movement. When studying the Constitution, eighth-grade students carve feather pens, make ink (after finding a period recipe), and try their hands at drafting resolutions. A recording of Mozart's music using period instruments plays in the background as they work. A few weeks later, seventh graders transform the classroom into a medieval castle. Jeanette removes the classroom door and installs a "drawbridge" for the duration of their study. In her sixth-grade class students make kente cloths and study the West African tradition of preserving history in the archives of a griot's memory. At other times, the arts of ancient Japan, Mali, and Mesopotamia compete for wall space with more recent images of American history. As one observer notes, the juxtaposition of images creates "harmonious chaos." Jeanette nods, "I like it because my room is mostly student created and so I think they feel comfortable with their own work, and I think it calls to mind things that they have learned." Three brief vignettes provide some of the flavor of Jeanette Groth's arts infused curriculum.

* * *

Garrett is, he says, doing a "non-research paper" on Ulysses S. Grant for his eighth-grade American history class. His task is to study the life of Grant, and then put together a "Jackdaw"—a packet of information and artifacts that will illuminate his subject. Jeannette's instructions direct him to "*visually represent* your topic, supply notes or photocopies of information with relevant details highlighted, provide pictures and replicas of relevant artifacts." "Then," Garrett says, "we get to present our Jackdaw to the class."

"Jackdaw" is also the trade name for a series of historical primary source and activity packets

Jeanette explains that this assignment involves gathering all the sources for a research paper, "except you don't write the paper." Garrett compares it to an archaeological dig in reverse: rather than presenting a written interpretation based on artifacts, he has to present interpretive artifacts based on written sources. So far he has decided to include a cigar and an empty whiskey bottle, along with a set of "letters from the field"—perhaps to Abraham Lincoln— and maps of Civil War campaigns.

The school choir is planning a program of Middle Eastern music that coincides with the sixth graders' study of the Middle East. Jeanette challenges her students: use what you have learned about the Middle East to help the choir director develop the concert. As a follow-up assessment, Jeanette asks the students to develop program notes explaining what they considered to be the distinctive elements of Middle Eastern music. Students compare the smaller intervals, different rhythms, and instrumentations common to Middle Eastern music with those used in European music and discuss vocal sound production—comparing the "loose" throat vocalizations of Western music with the "tighter" throat more common to Middle Eastern music.

* * *

Jeannette's seventh graders are deeply involved in studying Islamic influences on Spain. The Alhambra, a Moorish fortress, and castle in Granada, Spain, seems to be a perfect example of how war and conquest can disperse other aspects of culture, including art and architecture. Building a replica of the Alhambra might work, the students decide, but they really want visitors to be able to see, in detail, the kind of art introduced by the Moors—and they definitely want to try their hand at reproducing these artistic styles. Perhaps they could try some of the art and hang it around the room? Or, they could do what they had seen students do last year with the medieval castle! Before long, the students turn their classroom into a replica of the Alhambra, complete with examples of Islamic art. Student guides conduct visitors on a tour of historic Moorish art and architecture, explaining its political and religious significance as they point out the distinctive style of portrait painting and mosaics. While students are enthusiastic in their admiration for Islamic art and respectful of the culture that produced it, they are also impressed with their own production. Hannah smiles when complimented on her work, and says, "It really is beautiful, isn't it?" She then points out some details of the time period that they have included "because this style lets you know exactly when it was built."

Because she teaches all the sixth-, seventh-, and eighth-grade social studies in this small arts magnet school, Jeanette sees her students develop over time. She worries, too, about what will happen to them when they leave this school. "Some teachers are afraid to integrate the arts," Jeanette says. "They feel that they'll have more behavior problems. I think that the reverse is true, but I have trouble convincing people of that. They think they can't let children create a piece of music or a piece of art—that they'll miss some content because the arts are taking up their time. In reality, they are probably not going to be so frustrated in their learning. They see the whole picture. In other words, they may learn separate parts, but I want them to see how it fits in the whole. We may relate a concept from early in the year—early African and Indian slavery—and then that fits in with the picture of what happened in the Civil War, and then we might talk about what happens with a racial situation here."

In our view, the arts are an integral part of history—part of what makes civilizations unique. Think about how Rap music speaks to the life and experience of many young people today, how songs such as *Hair* or *Blowin' in the Wind* represented the counter-culture or antiwar movements of the 1960s and 1970s in the United States, or how Picasso's *Guernica* powerfully interprets the horrors of the Spanish Civil War. Think, too, about the variety of *official* uses of art: commemorative stamps, memorial statues and monuments, political campaigns, and the like. As you look at the historical art in Fig. 13.1, consider how each artist attempts to manipulate your emotions. By casting lurid red and orange firelight upward onto the faces of Hitler and Hirohito, emphasizing the whites of Hitler's hypnotic eyes, and the bit of liquid dripping from Hirohito's oversized teeth, one artist conjures up images of hell. Out of the black and red night, Hitler stares directly at the viewer; Hirohito shifts his view to the side, implying that he can see into the shadows. In the second example, the artist also uses red, but this time it directs your eye to a mother and child. The lines are softer, and the picture is meant to recall the sentimentality and safety of a Madonna and child. In this instance, too, textual graphics call attention first to safety—she's good enough to be your baby's mother—and then to the point of the illustration—and she's good enough to vote *with you.*

The impact of each poster is greater, too, if you consider the historical context as well as the artistry of the rendering. Who was the audience for each piece of art? To what fears did each speak? The first, of course, is a World War II propaganda poster;

The arts help students see the "whole picture."

Albert (1995), Williams (1991)

The arts are political as well as aesthetic.

Eisner (1988)
The arts exist in a historical context.

144

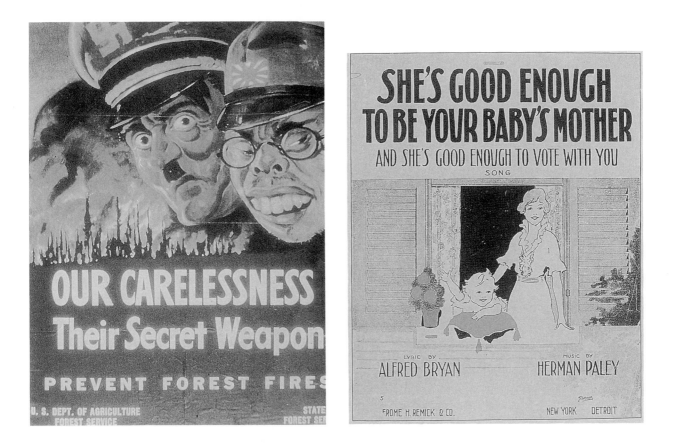

FIG. 13.1.

the second a 1918 song sheet used to promote women's suffrage. As Jeanette explains, the "arts are situated in a historical context, in a culture, in a society. I think the arts can help the students speculate about what the purpose of a specific art form in a particular historical context or a particular historical time might be."

THE ARTS ADDRESS SIGNIFICANT HISTORICAL QUESTIONS

The historical arts help students address different questions than do more traditional print sources. A variety of print sources, for instance, might help students respond to a question such as: "Could the conflicts between Native Americans and European Americans in the post Civil War era have been avoided?" Students might read U.S. and Canadian government documents and census records, analyze statements by military leaders such as General Philip Sheridan ("The only good Indian is a dead Indian"), study U.S. government policies intended to destroy tribal cohesiveness ("Kill the Indian, save the man"), and consider Sitting Bull's call for his people not to surrender the sacred Black Hills ("We want no white men here. The Black Hills belong to me. If the whites try to take them, I will fight"). Using these sources, students could build and defend positions regarding the inevitability of hostility, develop an expla-

Epstein (1994b, 1994d)

Welch (1994)

145

Historical arts complement and extend more traditional historical sources.

nation of culture clash and its aftermath, or suggest alternatives to U.S. policy based on the Canadian example. These are important, but limited, questions to consider in making sense of this historical era. By working with the historical arts, students' focus on a different—although related—sort of historical question: "What was it like to be a Sioux or one of their allies during the period surrounding the Battle of Little Big Horn?" This question deals more explicitly with a people's "way of being in the world." Consider what sources students might use to answer this question. They might study examples of the decorative arts—clothing, basketry, body art—that evoke aspects of Sioux culture. They could use photographs taken of Sioux and Cheyenne children as they first entered boarding schools (separated from their families, tribal communities, and home language) and again after their long hair was shorn and their familiar clothing replaced by European-style clothing. Photographs of an Arapaho camp, a Lakota woman or a young warrior on horseback, free on the plains, could be juxtaposed with images of reservation life. Further, photographs of the massacre at Marias River, cartoons expressing outrage at Custer's defeat, posters for Buffalo Bill Cody's Wild West show, and Sioux artwork showing the death of Sitting Bull and Crazy Horse all provide insight into the human experience behind the myth of "Custer's last stand" and the eventual subjugation of the Sioux (and other Native peoples). These historical arts provide different vantage points from which to view history, and make explicit the powerful emotions that often defy the power of words to fully express. This does not discount more traditional historical sources; rather, together they develop the "whole picture" that Jeanette seeks for her students.

Greene (1995)

The arts provide different historical vantage points.

Developing the whole picture is clearly important to Jeanette. Although her small classroom is often crowded with work from three different grades, she feels strongly that this apparent chaos really is harmonious. Students regularly see each other's work, borrow ideas from each other, and are reminded that the "separate parts" they study each year really do fit in a larger framework. In building this framework, Jeanette focuses on several aspects of the arts related to thinking and learning in history. First, she uses the arts as source material for historical study. This involves understanding and making judgments about art, as well as coming to appreciate art from different times and places. Second, she encourages (and regularly requires) students to use the arts as vehicles for the expression of their historical understanding. This is closely related to what Howard Gardner describes as the heart of arts education, "the capacity to handle, to use, to transform different artistic symbol systems—to *think with and in* the materials." While these processes are interrelated in the context of Jeannette's classroom, it is useful to consider the separate contributions of the arts both as historical data and as ways to "think with and in" history.

Brandt (1988), Eisner (1988), Gardner (1988), Renyi (1994)

The arts are data sources for history as well as vehicles for expressing historical understanding.

THE ARTS AS SOURCE MATERIAL FOR HISTORICAL STUDY

The arts are primary source documents that tell us about the time and place in which they were produced. As Jeanette says, it is hard to imagine teaching about ancient Greece without reference to its art, literature, and architecture. Indeed, it should be equally difficult to imagine ignoring the rich artistry of such African empires as Benin or Mali, or of the ancient Aztecs and Mayans. While much of Western knowledge of these civilizations was originally based on the reports of European explorers, each empire left at least a partial record of its *own* world view in its arts. An ivory mask from Benin, for instance, depicts a row of Portuguese sailors in a position intended to represent the power of the people of Benin over these strangers. Similarly, the art and architecture of the ancient Maya indicate a sophisticated understanding of math and astronomy, as well as a rich cosmology and elaborate social and political life. In North America, the art of Sioux and Cheyenne—pictures drawn in ledger books, and on fabric to explain events from the Native American perspective—provides eyewitness accounts of the Plains wars in the late 1800s (see Fig. 13.2). The arts are sources of information on the *content* of these cultures, from clothing and recreation to religious

Zevin & Evans (1993)

Both content and form in the arts are historically significant.

FIG. 13.2. An unknown Hunkpapa Lakota artist's rendition of the arrest and killing of Sitting Bull (North Dakota Historical Society).

beliefs and technology, from gender roles and child rearing practices to political and natural cataclysms. But the *form* of the arts is also historically important. Just as culture gives direction to art—by providing religious ideas, for instance—so art shapes our perceptions of the world by embodying ideas in sensory images—a Russian Orthodox icon, perhaps. Fully understanding history, then, means studying how the form and content of the arts express history.

Eisner (1988)

While World War II posters and ledger art are primary sources—artifacts of the times in which they were created—the arts also function as secondary sources, interpreting other times and places. Perhaps you have seen the movie *Dances With Wolves*. It is certainly not a firsthand account of life among the Lakota or the U. S. cavalry. Instead, it is a modern interpretation of the past, operating much as textbooks do by reinterpreting the past to a modern audience. In doing so, *Dances with Wolves* provides a commentary on what modern Americans are willing to tell themselves about this part of their past. In contrast to early "Westerns" where Native peoples were generally villainous and the cavalry rode to the rescue of white settlers, *Dances with Wolves* presents the Lakota as a heroic people stalked by the evil U.S. Cavalry. Such an interpretation probably tells us more about modern American society than it does about the complex lives of either the cavalry or the Lakota. Yet our students encounter history interpreted through the visual arts—pictures, films, art and artifacts, the built environment, television—all the time. While we tend to emphasize the literary arts in school, our students' ideas of life on the American frontier or during the Civil War or Eisenhower administration are at least as likely to be shaped by television shows such as *Little House on the Prairie* and *Happy Days* , or by movies such as *Dances with Wolves* or *Glory* as by anything in a history text.

The arts function as both primary and secondary historical sources.

Welch (1994)

Barton & Levstik (1996), Levstik & Barton (1996)

In Jeannette's classroom, she draws on music, dance, drama, literature, and the visual arts, and feels strongly that each makes a contribution to her students' understanding of history and social studies. Her students expect the arts to be an integral part of their historical study. On the day that students try writing amendments to the U.S. Constitution using their newly carved quill pens and homemade ink, Jeanette turns down the lights. ("I would have used candles, but we aren't allowed to have them in school.") She plays a tape of Mozart's music to help establish a tone for student work. The class has already talked about Mozart and Washington as contemporaries, the kind of instruments available at the time, the places where that music might have been available, and the importance of music in the social life of the Revolutionary era. As the tape ends, students look up in the sudden stillness. "What happened?" asks one boy. "We need the music!" Jeanette restarts the tape, and the class goes back to its labors, immersed in some of the sensory experiences of the age they are studying.

Albert (1995)

During the same unit on the Constitution, Jeanette reads excerpts from one of Jean Fritz' books, *Shh! We're Writing the Constitution*, shows a video of a play from the period, and requires that students report on at least one source of information on the Constitution not already used in class. "What picture do you get from each of these sources?" she asks. "What images come to mind?" The students immediately respond with sensory images: "hot and muggy," "a lot of white-haired, white men," "flies buzzing around, windows closed," "secretive." At this point, Jeanette introduces a large print of the signing of the Constitution, and says:

Fritz (1987)

The arts develop sensory images of historical people, places, and events.

> What we are looking at is a painting of the immediate setting of the writing of the Constitution. Now, when you look at this painting, I want you to use some of the work we have done with costume, with clothing, art and things of the time period. You know there wasn't any CNN back during the writing of the Constitution. After the fact an artist did a rendering of what he thought it would look like if you had been at the Constitutional convention. Now, you are the art critic. I want you to look at the painting and to evaluate it in terms of [she writes on the board]:
>
> What kind of job do you think the artist did? Did he make an accurate portrait of what happened at that time? Inaccurate? Why?
>
> Where is attention focused in the painting? What do you think the artist is trying to do here? What are the aesthetic elements of this painting? What are the political uses this painting might be put to?

Working in small groups, the students begin noting details that conflict with other sources they have used. The men in the painting seem cooler and less uncomfortable than other sources indicated; curtains and windows are open, also contrary to most sources. They notice that George Washington is centered in the painting, the light focusing on him so that "he becomes the main figure" while the men who did most of the writing are minor figures in the painting. Carter explains that seeing the painting helped him visualize what the delegates looked like: "It really assisted me . . . knowing which figure was which." Interestingly, he also mentions that despite "knowing" how many delegates had been in attendance, "I didn't realize just how many delegates participated . . . until I saw that picture. There were quite a few, you know."

Seeing often supports believing.

Carter's experience may be familiar to you. Think back to the first time you saw a favorite ballet, heard a soul-stirring concert, or stood before a powerful piece of art—not on film, or reproduced in a textbook, but *live*, perhaps in a theatre, concert hall, gallery, or museum. Perhaps the experience jolted you out of familiar ways of seeing. You understood, to some degree, not just an event or idea, but a world of feelings. As you gained experience—perhaps heard a recording of the concert, or saw the play performed a second time, you noticed dimensions of the work you missed the first time. These experiences enriched your feelings for the work; perhaps you also shared it with someone else, and re-experienced it through their eyes. In a sense, this kind of aesthetic experience is a bit like unraveling a mystery—one in which there is no final scene where all is made clear. It engages both your intellect and your emotions, and often moves beyond the power of words to explain. As Isadora Duncan said, "If I could *tell* you what I mean, there would be no point in dancing."

Epstein (1994b, 1994c), Greene (1995), Kosma (1991), Neuman (1992), Winner (1982)

Goodman (1984)

Rockefeller (1977), Selwyn (1995)

In history, too, there is an element of mystery, of searching for some key to explain not just *what* happened, but *why* it happened—what web of emotions, values and

148

ideas connects a set of events. Perhaps because of this air of mystery, students are likely to recognize voice and intention in the arts more readily than in textbooks. As students think about the mind behind the historical image, however, it is important to consider not only the viewpoint represented but how the artist used her medium to express that viewpoint. An increasing number of children's books explore just this connection between artist and art, intention and action (see literature list at end of chapter). In *A Young Painter: The Life and Paintings of Wang Yani—China's Extraordinary Young Artist*, for instance, the relationship between Wang Yani's prodigious paintings, her life with her father, and her experiences growing up in China are explored. *Follow the Drinking Gourd*, a picture book for younger readers, explains how a song provided directions for African Americans escaping from slavery.

History and the arts share an element of mystery.

Brown, Collins, & Duguid (1989), Kosma (1991)
Epstein (1994b, 1994c), Gabella (1994)

Zhensun & Low (1991)

Winter (1988)

Unfortunately, the very thing that students find appealing—the emotion and intentionality of the arts—sometimes leads them to discount the arts as "biased." Students may assume that the world view of a textbook is "objective" precisely because it has, from their perspective, no recognizable voice or intention. This is not an argument against using the arts; rather, we think that an arts infused curriculum in which children analyze the intentional nature of *all* modes of expression will help children think more carefully about the nature of historical perspective, wherever encountered.

Epstein (1994b, 1994c), Levstik & Pappas (1987)

Students should learn to recognize the voice and intention of all modes of expression.

Analyzing visual sources has several advantages for students. Unlike the events they represent, for instance, visual images are fixed in time. When you analyze a still image (or stop a moving one) you are undisturbed by the changing moment, by movement or the emotional fluctuations that were part of the actual event. You can go back to an image repeatedly, searching its multiple dimensions, asking new questions, bringing new information and experience to bear. Of course, this presents its own set of problems. Something that was, in fact, ephemeral, can gain undue significance simply because it was preserved. Think how easily a single photograph from your family album, taken out of context, could misrepresent your family history. We have all learned how powerfully a single image can capture public attention, either for good or ill. The photograph of a firefighter holding an injured child in the wake of a bombing speaks volumes about the tragic dimensions of this event. On the other hand, a photograph of Gerald Ford falling down a staircase during a campaign stop becomes emblematic of a larger political "clumsiness."

Levstik & Barton (1996), Mazur (1993), Olson (1974)

Visual images allow students to examine and re-examine historical moments.

Taking a historical moment out of context can lead to incomplete interpretations.

Children enter school having been exposed to an enormous variety of visual images. Although they may be more adept at making sense of animated computer art or cartoons than historical art, they already have a store of visual clues at their disposal. From their earliest years, sighted and hearing children infer relationships between visual and aural data and their own social situations and background experiences. In fact, many children communicate through the arts long before they achieve fluency with reading and writing, and may prefer drawing to writing despite increasing fluency in writing. In addition, children often have a rich visual symbology that helps them interpret their own and others' art. In Fig. 13.3, for instance, a 7-year-old's response to the *Little House* books uses only one word, but incorporates many details from the story—high button shoes, water pails, a barn with square nails, Laura's clothing—along with more iconographic symbols that were already part of the child's artistic shorthand—the imaginary house and yard and the bird.

Winner (1982)

Dyson (1989)

Gardner (1982)

As children gain more background knowledge in history (often from nonprint media), they use that information in their own artistic productions and in interpreting the historical arts. In general, they are more fluent in describing and interpreting material culture—technology, clothing, architecture, food—where they can make connections between the historical image and their own lives—or the lives they see displayed on television, or in movies and books. Children looking at a photograph of a Victorian schoolroom, for instance, associated it with Samantha, a character (and doll) from the *American Girls* books, and recognized various elements in the photograph based on their experience with these dolls and books. They also mistakenly identified a group of Iroquois as Romans because they mistook the blankets draped

Historical information can be garnered from many sources, including the media.

Barton & Levstik (1996)

FIG. 13.3.

over the Iroquois' shoulders as "robes like Roman times." Their visual experience with Native peoples did not include wearing blankets in the way pictured, but they had recently seen illustrations of Roman togas in a history display created by older students.

It is clear that children in a variety of settings find the arts a rich part of their historical study. Old Town Elementary, a school not too far from the arts magnet school where Jeanette teaches, draws on one of the poorest populations in the city. Old Town has no special arts programming, and few of its teachers began their teaching careers with more than the rudimentary background in the arts provided by introductory undergraduate courses, yet the school overflows with art. Murals of pioneer life stretch down one hall, a display of masks produced by different cultures around the world hang from the ceiling in the entryway, a huge three-dimensional dragon left over from a study of China lingers in a corner, and photographs of an Indonesian visitor demonstrating a lion dance to a group of primary children are displayed on a classroom door. In the first grade, students invite a guest to try her hand at brass rubbing. Several classmates are carefully rubbing crayons across paper-covered brass reliefs. The reliefs (raised images on a flat background) represent British historical figures, and as the children rub their crayons across the surfaces of the reliefs, they comment on the images emerging on their paper, reminding each other of medieval symbology:

Erin: This one is a king.

David: He's a knight, cause he's got a sword, see?

Levstik (1993)

The arts can speak across race, class and cultural differences.

150

Erin:	Yeah, but there's a . . . see down by his feet.
Aggie:	A lion.
Erin:	Uhhuh. That lion means he's a king. Kings get lions [this had been a small note on a picture seen earlier in the year].
Catrina:	The lady's got something.
Jake:	A dog.
Catrina:	Yeah, a dog. She's not a queen, I don't think.

As the children continue their work, they rearrange these visual elements for their own purposes. Two of the boys label their rubbings in Norse (one of the artifacts they have been working with includes a Norse alphabet). Another girl turns her rubbings into stick puppets, and several others follow suit, intent on turning their work into a puppet show. David cuts each of his figures out, and pastes them on different backgrounds, creating a picture that looks much like a medieval tapestry.

Students use visual arts for their own purposes.

In surrounding themselves and their students with the visual arts, these teachers, along with Jeanette, are learning to read the historical arts as well as teach with them. Their students analyze the arts from historical and aesthetic perspectives and learn to associate specific questions with each of these analytical stances. From a historical perspective, for instance, students look for the details of daily life, asking:

Students learn to read the arts historically and aesthetically.

Geoghegan (1994), Sautter (1990)

- What parts of life are shown? Young children studying changes in childrearing practices might study art for information on child labor, recreation, family activities, religious events, or schooling.
- What are the artist's feelings about these activities? A Norman Rockwell picture, for instance, celebrates certain aspects of family and small town life, while another artist might poke fun at small town insularity.

Students also consider the arts as social and political commentary. They ask questions such as:

- How do artists shape historical and political thinking? Older students might consider what works of art such as The Rake's Progress, Guernica, or The World Upside Down tell them about the social and political world of the artists.
- What themes seem to come in for the most artistic comment at any particular time? Students might compare political cartoons over time and chart common themes.
- How controversial might this commentary have been in its own time? Now? This question might send students to other sources to provide a context for their interpretations.

From an aesthetic perspective, students study how the elements of the art relate to each other and to the historical content, and ask:

- How does each artist approach the subject (style and technique)? Students might compare different artists' interpretations of the same idea, event, or emotion, as Jeanette's students did with the Constitutional Convention.
- What do these styles and techniques say about the world view of the people who create them? Younger children might study a group of cartoons of, say, Abraham Lincoln, and discuss how each cartoonist has interpreted this historical figure.

As students apply these questions to the historical arts, they become better able to interpret the arts from historical and aesthetic perspectives.

151

IMAGING IN YOUR MIND:
LEARNING TO READ THE HISTORIC ARTS

You'd have to take this picture, imagine it in your mind and go through time . . . based on what you know, you come to a conclusion

—Rodney, Grade 5

[Looking at a picture of a mass gathering in front of a large building] You have like protests about race . . . the soldiers uniforms, well it could be about like black rights. . .but I don't see any black people, but I guess they could be carrying the signs.

—Evan, Grade 5

[After looking at pictures of antebellum America] It looks real interesting because there's a lot of stuff in it that makes you think its older, like it has lots of boats and old buildings in it, and a hot air balloon and it makes you think that its older because the hot air balloon was invented a long time ago . . . and a lot of the people, it looks like they're homeless, they lost their homes. . . . I think it would just be neat to see what they did and talk to them and see what they'd look like and see what the land would look like without anybody on it.

—Haveli, Grade 6

Each of these students is eager to look carefully and "imagine in their minds" what might be going on in a piece of art. Students can become equally immersed in the details of a medieval tapestry, an intricately carved ivory sculpture from China, or Seurat's Pointillism. Yet we have all followed along on museum tours where docents find it hard to keep children focused on even the most exquisite works of art. Feet get sore, attention wanders, the gift shop beckons, and art is ignored. Interest and attention to art, as with so many other things that adults think are good for children, has much to do with context—with attending to children's purposes.

Authentic tasks encourage close attention to the arts.

As the teachers described in this chapter began making more use of the arts, they discovered that context really was crucial. Their students were more likely to immerse themselves in art if there was a reason for close attention. Each of the children cited here, for example, had been asked to think about the time sequence of a set of visual images. They pored over the details of each picture, analyzing them for clues to the mystery of time. Other primary, intermediate, and middle school students enthusiastically responded to the same task, discussing the historical images, comparing pictures, and making reference to other sources of historical information. In other classes, students focus critical attention and discussion on selecting the images for a comparative time line.

Barton & Levstik (1996), Levstik & Barton (1996)

Making sense of the arts, like making sense of a written text, does not come automatically. While we are probably born able to perceive patterns in different sensory modalities, experience and culture clearly influence how we interpret the arts. To a large extent what we expect to see (or hear) influences what we do see (or hear). When something violates our expectations we try to impose order on it, seeking to make sense out of our experiences. While students certainly recognize some cultural ways of representing an object, idea, or emotion (downward curving lines indicate sadness, the forward lean of a figure indicates motion), there are others that are quite confusing. Young children who assume a Japanese print depicts a wedding because the people wear white would certainly make a more supportable interpretation if they knew that, in Japan, white is generally the color of death and mourning. In the same way, children who learn some of the complex language of hand gestures typical of traditional Indonesian dancing are better able to appreciate the performance of an Indonesian dancer.

Gombrich (1994), Winner (1982), Kennedy (1974)

Eisner (1988)

Helping students make sense of the arts requires attention to background knowledge

The kind of teacher mediation necessary to help students accomplish these tasks varies, of course, with the degree of familiarity the students have with the arts and their background knowledge of the history depicted. When Liza Flornoy was assigned

152

to teach fourth grade, she knew her students would be studying their state's history. Because she had only recently arrived in the state, she was very nervous about her competence in handling this curriculum. She had been quite successful in using the arts in her old school, but had few resources for this new assignment. In addition, she was worried because she had been told that her school was "in transition"—redistricting was shifting the school population to include a more even balance of low and middle income students. Many of her students would be unfamiliar with the school and the surrounding neighborhood, and some, she had been told, would be actively hostile. When Liza expressed her concerns to her team teacher, Mrs. Kadahota suggested she look at state history materials developed by a local heritage group. Liza liked the emphasis on public art and thought that, with a few adjustments, the materials might work well. She decided to start with the built environment surrounding her school. This had several advantages. Because the school was located in the state capital, there were a number of buildings and monuments with obvious political and aesthetic significance. The school bordered an area of newly gentrified older homes, a small business and shopping district, and a public housing development, so there would be a variety of public art, from signs and gardens to architecture and graffiti. Liza did some background reading and began adapting the materials from the heritage council.

Public art is generally free and accessible.

As she had expected, her students had little experience either with buildings and monuments as sources of historical information, or with the neighborhood around the school, so Liza planned two introductory experiences on data retrieval. She began with a set of five slides of different types of public and private buildings and monuments in the area, and introduced several themes that might be related to each building: privacy, values, culture, change over time, social behavior, creativity, and history. As she showed the slides, students identified evidence of each theme: an ornate plaster ceiling medallion for creativity, an electrified gas lamp as change over time, a recreation room for social behavior, family photographs as history, art and sculpture as both values and culture, and so forth. Liza then distributed data retrieval charts for the children to use in collecting information from a place of their own choosing—their own home, a favorite vacation spot, a store or recreation area. The data retrieval charts consisted of one sheet of paper. On the front, students filled in columns headed with each theme. On the back, they answered three questions about the building they selected: What is the purpose or function of the place you selected? How does the look, feel, and smell of this place make you think and feel? How important are the social things that happen there—how you are treated, whom you are with, what you do together (or apart)?

Teachers need to help students collect and organize data.

Built Environment Education Consortium (1990)

Specific questions help students organize data collection.

Not surprisingly, the children found that the categories listed on the data retrieval chart often overlapped. Two children listed the Bible as evidence of values, for instance, while another listed it as social behavior. Several children indicated that separate bedrooms for children was evidence of privacy. "Isn't that a value, too," asked another child. "And what's the difference between history and change over time? Aren't they pretty much the same things?" Another child declared that "all of it is culture." As a result, the students altered the chart, limiting their categories to privacy, values, change over time, social behavior, and creativity. They also categorized buildings by use—commercial, educational, governmental, industrial, recreational, religious, residential, and transportation related—and compared how each theme was represented in each category. They noted that several buildings had changed categories over time. A former gas station, for instance, was now an ice cream parlor, and several residences had become commercial buildings. They began compiling a list of questions they wanted to investigate: What caused buildings to change use? Why were older buildings more elaborately decorated? Why were people paying so much more to move into older buildings, rather than buy newer houses in the suburbs? What did the graffiti on some of the buildings mean?

Initial data collection often generates more researchable questions.

Next, Liza organized a study of two buildings within walking distance of the school. Each student received a research guide—directions for observations and data collec-

Corwin (1991)

tion, as well as follow-up activities—a clipboard, and materials for sketching and texture rubbings, as well as a camera. Working in small groups, students collected data on each building. As you look at the task outlined in Fig. 13.4, notice that, while it includes elements of the arts, it also uses other forms of historical documentation such as interviews and printed information. Liza also asks her students to use this combination of data sources in their final product, requiring that students express their historical interpretations through visual images as well as different written genres.

The arts should be an integral part of historical study.

When the arts are an integral part of historical study, students are surrounded by a rich array of images that let them see what things looked like, what people did, how they did them, how people saw themselves or were seen by others. Art is studied as a product of human intention through which an artist or artists create alternate worlds and respond to the worlds created around them. From this perspective, making sense in art—just as in history—requires careful observation and a willingness to consider

Baggett (1989), Goodman (1984)

multiple interpretations. It is not enough, however, for children to be consumers of

---

Step One: Observe

Carefully examine the building from as many angles and sides as possible. Look for the details and study the overall shape and size. Identify any sounds, smells, and tastes that may be associated with the building. Try to recognize the variety of building materials and textures related to the building. Look for any changes that may have occurred since its construction.

Step Two: Document

Answer as any of the following questions as possible from your observations.

1. Name of the building

2. Describe the location and setting of the building

3. What is the foundation material?

4. What are the building materials?

5. Sketch or film the different types of windows and doors, as well as decorative materials and designs used on the building.

6. Make texture rubbings of different parts of the building (check with me first!)

7. Are there any chimneys? How many? Draw a picture of the chimney.

8. Describe any signs or words on the building

9. What was the building built for?

10. How many stories (floors) does the building have?

11. Describe, draw or film any evidence of each of our themes.

12. What is the current use of the building?

13. Sketch a floor plan of the first floor of the building.

Step Three: Research

Be a historical detective! Find out as much as you can about the history of our buildings. You will have a chance to talk to a local historian, so think carefully about what questions you might want to ask her. You may also use materials in the folder marked "Built Environment."

Step Four: Interpret

We will be writing and producing a documentary on these buildings. As you plan your work, think about including the following:

1. A drawing or model of what you think the original setting of the building was.

2. Reenactments of some of the historical events this building "lived through."

3. An interview with the builder and/or original owners, discussing what the building meant to each of them.

4. Pictures and discussion of what this building means to the community today.

5. A poem or reader's theater showing what is unique or special about the building.

FIG. 13.4. Read-a-Building (adapted from materials developed by the Built Environment Education Consortium, 1990).

the historical arts; as they experience the multiple worlds expressed in the arts, they also need to express their own historical perspectives through the arts.

Epstein (1994a)

THE ARTS AS VEHICLES FOR EXPRESSING HISTORICAL UNDERSTANDING

Nathan stands before the class, about to present his report on the French Revolution: "I kind of thought of it as looking like *The Highwayman* sounds . . . sort of dark and dangerous." He holds up a charcoal drawing of a street scene in Paris. The paper is black, with white buildings whose faces (literally) stare down into the street or lean back with their windows (eyes) shut. In the street, white figures out of Munch's *The Scream* gather around a red guillotine.

* * *

Jeanette asks her students "What picture comes to your mind when you hear the words, 'living Constitution? I'd like you to find different ways to express your ideas . . . show why the Constitution has lasted so long. For us to be living we need water, air, food, light. . . . What kind of things does it take for the Constitution to be living?" One student responds by drawing the Constitution as an eagle in flight, with legs, wings and beak. Another student writes:

Concepts of freedom

Open minds

Nation as one

States as a union

Timeless set of laws and rights

Ideas accepted

Thoughts spread

Understanding of citizen's desires

Time of brainstorming

Indifferent laws

Outstanding results

No one's rights denied

Each of these students is learning to *think with* and *in* the arts. As they blend feeling and ideas to create art, they make their inner conceptions public. At the same time, the very process of selecting representations for their inner conceptions shapes students' historical understanding. Where otherwise students might have relied largely on written language to convey ideas, they now have a wider repertoire of forms and symbols available to them. And, as Jeanette notes, when class work includes the arts "you can't remain an observer very easily. You have to become a participant and when you become a participant, you have a way of learning by doing."

Gardner (1990)

The arts provide a wider expressive repertoire.

Opportunities to produce art are as important as opportunities to view art.

Producing your own historical art is quite different from using the arts as historical data. It is like the difference between reading a novel and writing one. Making historical art, in particular, can seem like a very risky business to a youngster. Faced with the problem of combining the symbology of art and the requirements of history, students will need plenty of supportive instruction. It helps, then, to think of producing historical arts as both problem solving and intellectual risk taking, components of the inquiry-based approach to history used throughout this book.

Art is a form of problem solving and intellectual risk taking.

THE ARTS AS PROBLEM SOLVING

Jeanette has asked her eighth graders to represent a portion of the Constitution in some way that will make clear its most significant elements. She tells them to think first about what information they want to convey, and then how best to represent it to their peers. Students work in four groups, first discussing the task, then drawing sketches to illustrate to each other how their ideas might best be presented. One group discusses the use of circles "because these things keep repeating." Another debates the appropriateness of cartoon characters that represent the different sides of an issue; a third sketches ideas, playing with spatial relationships, symbols, and colors. Individual groups divide up the work, sending a couple of students off to draw pictures, others to compose the text and still others to mock up the full presentation on a piece of poster board. Jeanette moves between the groups, asking them questions and making suggestions. She asks one group if the Senate has ever chosen a president who did not receive "a majority of the actual votes." She mentions to another group that all people did not receive equal rights in the original Constitution. "Look through the amendments. Whose rights are guaranteed later?" She also comments that one group "has a very good idea, here. Their chart gives you two alternatives; it tells you what happens when there is a majority and what happens when there isn't. How has this changed from the way the Constitution was originally written?" She asks another group if they copied an idea from another source or made it up themselves. "What does this mean?" she asks them. "Tell us about that."

The final products are an interesting mix of art and text. One group presents an illustrated flow chart of the twelfth amendment to the U.S. Constitution (election of president and vice president). They have arranged a series of branching choices that must be made in electing the president and vice president. At each decision point, they have an illustration showing some actual historical event that coincides with the decision that must be made. A hand dropping a vote into a ballot box illustrates the first step when electors meet. Further down the chart, an illustration of what happens when there is a majority vote shows Richard Nixon with his arms above his head, his fingers making the "V" for victory sign. A bubble over his head says "I am not a crook." Another illustration shows angry Congressmen negotiating the election of Thomas Jefferson.

Clearly, Jeannette's students do not do art as an afterthought to inquiry or as icing on an otherwise less palatable cake. Rather, art is fundamental to the way in which students solve problems in history. The problems that Jeanette sets for her students sometimes require a particular medium—perhaps a dramatization or the selection of music to fit a historical event or period—but more often require that students select their own form of representation. Notice that Jeanette has developed a vocabulary for this type of assignment. Her use of "represent," for instance, operates on several levels: it signals an arts inclusive activity, refers back to the language used in students' arts-specific classes, and finally, reminds the students that, in this instance, the arts are intended to represent historical content. As she moves between groups she challenges students to better develop both the art and the history in their representations. This can be a real challenge for a teacher, especially when one piece of the work is clearly stronger and better grounded than another. In one group, for instance, the students want to get on with the art without having to carefully construct the history. They confuse the statement of equality in the Declaration of Independence with the Constitution, and are preparing an illustration that credits the Constitution with guaranteeing equal rights "to everyone." Jeanette sends them back to their historical sources, and leaves them with the more complicated problem of deciding how to visually represent the *ideal* of universal political equality with the reality of inequity.

Note, too, how the students use the potential for double entendres in their art. The text on the chart for the Twelfth Amendment, for instance, is quite straightforward, explaining that when a majority of members of the electoral college vote for a candidate, that person becomes president or vice president. The accompanying illustration, however, shows Richard Nixon declaring both his victory and his innocence of wrongdoing. The juxtaposition of text and image speaks volumes about the students' perceptions of the challenges of the democratic process.

As historical problem solvers, then, Jeannette's students often transform linguistic information into visual representation. In doing so they select and retrieve relevant information, generate ideas and form new concepts. They ponder the organization of shapes and ideas, play with how colors influence each other, how to create spatial as well as historical depth, and how to indicate structural as well as historical relations. It takes courage for children to risk all this, especially in the face of possible misinterpretation by the adults who assess them.

Art is not an afterthought. It is fundamental to historical problem solving.

Juxtaposing text and image can be a powerful tool for expressing historical understanding.

Albert (1995), Arnheim (1981)

156

THE ARTS AS INTELLECTUAL RISK TAKING

Representing ideas through the arts can seem quite risky, particularly to students used to more linguistic modes of expression. They may be unsure of the parameters within which they are working, of the language of interpretation or the symbol systems open to them. In her work with high school students, Epstein found that students became more willing to discuss and use the arts as they observed that their teacher accepted and encouraged a range of interpretations. They also gained confidence as they listened to and learned from their peers. Our observations indicate that this is true of younger students as well. Elementary and middle school teachers find that students with little experience with the arts become quite concerned with "getting it right." In fact, some children become so uncomfortable with their inability to render an image with photographic accuracy that they are stymied in their ability to express themselves.

Epstein (1994b)

Gardner (1982)

It is not particularly useful at this point to tell students that there is more to art than realism. What seems to work more effectively is to give students choices in terms of medium, practice in using different media, and specific help so that they can create art that is satisfying to them. Dehea Smith found that her students loved to use the overhead projector to trace images that they then manipulated for their own purposes. They would draw the background to a picture, for example, and then use the overhead to trace a car or people, and so forth. This worked well early in the year, but their teacher also wanted them to be a bit more adventurous. For one project, then, she helped the students to develop a shadow puppet theatre and play. She demonstrated how shadow puppets worked, showed them examples of shadow puppets from different cultures, and then set them to work making their own puppets. It soon became clear that their tiny figures with details drawn on were not going to show up effectively as shadows. Freed from the need to draw realistically, the students began paying attention to shape and space. They experimented with different materials, sizes of puppets and distance from the screen. With well-timed suggestions from their teacher, the children developed an interesting set of props and puppets using a much wider array of materials than they had tried before. As the children became more confident with these images, their teacher encouraged them to add music and movement to their plays. She also asked the art teacher to teach the students specific techniques to satisfy their desire for realism. He worked with two-point perspective and figure drawing. Later in the year, a parent with some experience in stage design took the students to his studio and demonstrated simple techniques to make images feel peaceful, spooky, dangerous, and so forth. By the time the students painted their own stage sets for a series of historical skits they were able to use some of the techniques they had learned, and were more confident in expressing themselves artistically.

Collaboration with teachers in the arts enriches historical study.

The art in children's literature can also serve as a beginning point in helping children experiment with different techniques. You might share a book with a distinctive technique—collage, charcoal, crayon resist—and then let students try their hand at the same technique. One class, fascinated with pop-up books, created pop-up illustrations for stories about early settlement in their community. Another class, after reading George Littlechild's *This Land Is My Land*, in which the artist combines photographs, painting, resists, and realia, tried their hand at combining these elements. Littlechild's book is autobiographical, describing his life as a Cree and an artist. The children did much the same thing. They brought in family photographs or cut pictures from magazines that represented the story they wanted to tell. The teacher photographed children in class, too. She then photocopied the pictures so her students could cut out the parts they wanted to use without ruining the originals. The students drew illustrations in crayon resist and paint and glued the pieces of photographs to their pictures. They added shells and bits of lace, as had Littlechild. One girl glued sand below a picture of a bare foot (cut from a magazine). She scratched birds into the crayoned sky, glued on cotton puff clouds, and titled her picture "My first walk on the beach." The result delighted her and inspired her classmates to try some of her techniques.

Children's literature can be a rich source of visual art

Kiefer (1995)

Littlechild (1993)

In a fifth-grade classroom where students had studied the ledger art of the Sioux and Cheyenne, they decided to see if they could show what they knew about a historic event using only pictures. One group decided that they would tell the story of the first Norse explorations of North America. Another gave a child's eye view of the Plimoth Colony, and a third presented a Chinese immigrant's view of building the transcontinental railroad. In creating these images, they went back through their history text as well as other sources they had used in studying American history. Their teacher suggested they also review some of the literature they had read on each of these topics, such as *Strange Footprints on the Land: Vikings in America, Meet the Real Pilgrims: Everyday Life on a Plimoth Plantation in 1627, The Seekers,* and *Dragon's Gate.* While these books were not all richly illustrated, they reminded the students of the feelings as well as facts that might be represented in their drawings. A couple of the finished pictures were stick-figure renditions of battles, but most provided interesting perspectives on how the students understood the events they had studied thus far. From a child's eye view, for instance, adults in Plimoth are huge, the forest threatening, plates and bowls often empty; Vikings sail between icebergs, beneath a vast sky of stars with arrows pointing in the direction of a tiny North American island; Chinese men in baskets dangle next to ice-covered mountains while their bosses sit warm and safe inside.

An important feature of arts infused classrooms is that children's artwork is on display. Teachers carefully mount and arrange students' work, honoring the intensity of effort and trust that went into its production. They find that art, like writing, thrives when it has a respectful audience, and especially when that audience goes beyond the teacher. One Boston school displays children's art and writing so that adults will see it as they walk their youngsters to class each morning. As a father stops to admire a mural of life on the Great Plains, his daughter begins to explain her work to him, pointing out the decorations on tipis, the place where a smudged bear became a large bush, and so forth. Her classmates join her, eagerly sharing other features of the mural, and explaining how each element matched something they had learned about the people who lived on the Plains: "See, this is a buffalo. The tipis are made out of buffalo hide, and they use the horn and everything. That's why there's a buffalo painted on this tipi. It has a zigzag lightning thing going from its mouth. We saw that in a book we read. Want to see the book?" Meanwhile, another parent compliments a child on how realistic the buffalo looks. "Oh," the child smiles. "We looked at lots of pictures. It was hard to find one that had a whole buffalo, though. At first it looked just like a horse with a very big head. Buffaloes have very strange shapes." Her friend explains that chickens are easier to draw, but she didn't think these Indians had chickens.

By displaying student work, teachers provide multiple audiences as well as multiple opportunities for students to discuss the aesthetic and historical choices they have made. Through these discussions, they are encouraged to be more experimental—turn bears into bushes if need be, care about historical accuracy, and not worry about an experiment that did not come out entirely as planned. In our experience, when student's artwork is displayed and discussed, students become more confident and produce much more interesting, historically sound artwork. As Jeanette explains:

> The arts give children who learn in a different way a lot of different opportunities to learn. I think that it gives them a chance to integrate material or to review what they learn in another way too. None of us has a single learning style. If I learn in a visual way and then again get to repeat it in an audio way, it's just strengthening my learning. I have another chance to learn. Sometimes you watch that here in the classroom. A child will seem to be over their head, and when you use a different form, it becomes something they can learn. It certainly provides more interest to teaching. It's more fun for me as a teacher and I think that makes it more interesting for the students. With the arts . . . you take what you learn into your being.

CHILDREN'S AND ADOLESCENT LITERATURE

Dillon, E. (1986). *The Seekers.* Scribner's.
Fritz, J. (1987). *Shh! We're Writing the Constitution.* Putnam.

Margin notes:

Dillon (1986), Irwin (1980), Loeb (1979), Yep (1994)

Literary imagery can inspire visual imagery.

Displaying student art honors the students' problem solving and risk taking in an authentic way.

Displaying student art provokes discussion and promotes confidence.

Irwin, C. (1980). *Strange Footprints on the Land: Vikings in America*. Harper.
Lawrence, J. (1992). *The Great Migration: An American Story*. The Museum of Modern Art, The Phillips Collection & HarperCollins.
Littlechild, G. (1993). *This Land is My Land*. Children's Book Press.
Wilder, L. I. (1953). *Little House on the Prairie*. Harper & Row.
Winter, J. (1988). *Follow the Drinking Gourd*. Knopf.
Yep, L. (1993). *Dragon's Gate*. HarperCollins.
Zhensun, Z., & Low, A. (1991). *The Life and Paintings of Wang Yani—China's Extraordinary Young Artist*. Scholastic.

Other Literature on the Historical Arts

Arenas, J. (1990). *The Key to Renaissance Art*. Lerner.
Braun, B. (1994). *A Weekend with Diego Rivera*. Rizzoli.
Chaucer, G. (1988). *Canterbury Tales*. (Selected and adapted by B. Cohen and illustrated by T. S. Hyman). Lothrop.
Davidson, R. (1994). *Take a Look: An Introduction to the Experience of Art*. Viking.
Everett, G. (1992). *Li'l Sis and Uncle Willie: A Story Based on the Life and Paintings of William H. Johnson*. Rizzoli.
Fisher, L. E. (1993). *Gutenberg*. Macmillan.
Freedman, R. (1992). *An Indian Winter*. Holiday House.
Garfunkel, T. (1994). *On Wings of Joy: The Story of Ballet from the Sixteenth Century to Today*. Little, Brown.
Gaughenbaugh, M., & Camburn H. (1994). *Old House, New House: A Child's Exploration of American Architectural Styles*. Preservation.
Glenn, P. B. (1993). *Under Every Roof: A Kids' Style and Field Guide to the Architecture of American Houses*. Preservation.
Highwater, J. (1978). *Many Smokes, Many Moons: A Chronology of American Indian History Through Indian Art*. Lippincott.
Hunt, P. (1989). *Illuminations*. Bradbury.
Isaacson, P. M. (1993). *A Short Walk Around the Pyramids and Through the World of Art*. Knopf.
Lattimore, D. N. (1991). *The Sailor Who Captured the Sea: The Story of the Book of Kells*. HarperCollins.
Macaulay, D. (1977). *Castle*. Houghton Mifflin.
Monceaux, M. (1994). *Jazz: My Music, My People*. Knopf.
Moore, R. (1994). *Native Artists of Africa*. Muir.
Morley, J. (1994). *Shakespeare's Theater*. Bedrick.
Nickens, B. (1994). *Walking the Log: Memories of a Southern Childhood*. Rizzoli.
Niemark, A. E. (1994). *Diego Rivera: Artist of the People*. HarperCollins.
Orozco, J. (Selector/Arranger). (1994). *De Colores: And Other Latin-American Folk Songs for Children*. Dutton.
Ross, S. (1994). *Shakespeare and Macbeth: The Story Behind the Play*. Viking.
Silverman, J. (1994). *Songs and Stories from the American Revolution*. Millbrook (See also *The Blues, Work Songs. African Roots* and *Slave Songs*).
Sullivan, G. (1994). *Mathew Brady: His Life and Photographs*. Cobblehill.
Turner, R. M. (1994). *Dorothea Lange*. Little.
Willard, N. (1991). *Pish, Posh, Said Hieronymous Bosch*. Harcourt Brace Jovanovich.
Wilson, E. B. (1994). *Bibles and Bestiaries: A Guide to Illuminated Manuscripts*. Farrar.
Woolf, F. (1993). *Picture This: An Introduction to Twentieth Century Art*. Doubleday.
Yeck, J. L., & McGreevey, T. (1994). *Movie Westerns*. Lerner.

Chapter 14

Constructive Assessment in History

Assessment and *evaluation* are used interchangeably throughout this chapter.

Johnston (1987)

Assessment, evaluation, testing, and worst of all, *grading:* For many educators, these are four of the most unpleasant words in their professional vocabulary. They conjure up a host of negative associations—from stanines and percentiles to long evenings spent poring over countless versions of the same assignment, redlining and correcting ridiculous mistakes, pleading for insight into why students just don't get it. Considering how much importance schools attach to grades and other forms of evaluation, students are usually shocked to discover that their teachers don't enjoy the process and would just as soon jettison the whole enterprise. For most of us, it's not evaluating but *instructing*—the scaffolding we've discussed throughout this book—that provides our image of what teaching is all about. Evaluation seems, at best, a necessary evil to be tacked onto the end of units so we can come up with a grade for report cards. At worst, it can ruin a perfectly good relationship between a teacher and her students.

Evaluation can be meaningful and even enjoyable.

But it doesn't have to be that way. Instead of an unpleasant add-on, evaluation can be a meaningful and sometimes—believe it or not—*enjoyable* task, a set of practices at the very heart of teaching and learning. To fulfill such lofty expectations, though, evaluation must play a very different role than we usually imagine. If the primary purpose of classroom evaluation is to produce a set of grades, then neither students nor teachers are likely to see much benefit in the practice. When gradebooks, rather than students' needs, determine the form of assessment, assignments become little more than an attempt to trip students up, to force them into revealing what they don't know so the grades will resemble a normal distribution. This obsession with sorting students out virtually guarantees that evaluation will be a negative experience, one designed to uncover the deficiencies in students' knowledge and understanding.

Hart (1994), Johnston (1992), Shepherd (1991)

Johnston (1992)

In the kinds of classrooms described in this book, the primary characteristic of evaluation is that it is *constructive*. By constructive evaluation, we mean first and foremost that it serves a constructive purpose—it has beneficial effects on teaching and learning. For students, this means that evaluation tasks allow them to show what they know rather than what they don't know. The teacher is not an adversary who tries to ferret out what they have failed to accomplish, but an advocate who helps them demonstrate their achievement. Most teachers at one time or another worry that students' performance doesn't accurately reflect what they have learned; they believe (or hope) that students know more than they have been able to show on tests or other assignments. Constructive assessment confronts this problem head-on by giving students as many ways of showing what they know as possible—through formal and informal measures, through tasks chosen by both teacher and student, through speaking, writing, and other forms of presentation (see also chapter 13). When students and teachers work together like this—looking for the best means of demonstrating what's been learned—students' self-esteem benefits because they have every chance to live up to their potential. The teacher's instruction is better, meanwhile, because she gains more complete insight into what students know and what they still need to learn.

Teachers are student advocates in constructive evaluation.

Wiggins (1989)

Hart (1994)

In order to gain this kind of insight, the teacher needs more than one way of tapping into students' achievement; by combining several means of assessment, she can be more confident of finding out what students know and can do. Three of the most useful ways of finding out about students are through their discussion, their writing, and their performances or presentations. Think back to the History Museum projects in chapter 7, for example. Amy's students spent several weeks talking to her and each other about what they were learning, they constructed museum displays on their topics, they gave presentations to other students, and they wrote essays. No one of these tasks would have provided a complete picture of their learning: some students might have remained silent during discussions but written fine essays, some might have given insightful presentations but never finished their writing, and so on. Relying on just one measure would have meant that students who did well in that medium—writing, speaking, drawing, or whatever—would have done well, but those whose strengths lay elsewhere would have seemed deficient. Using multiple means of assessment gave each student a chance to show what he or she knew.

Hart (1994), Johnston (1992)

Multiple assessments provide a more complete picture of student progress.

Providing choices makes the evaluation process more illuminating for teachers and students alike. In some cases, students may choose the form their assessment will take; in the "History of Me" projects in chapter 4, for example, Tina's students choose from a variety of forms of presentation: some made posters, some wrote essays, some wrote scripts and recorded audio- or videotapes, one gave a tour through a museum of his life. Other times, it may be the topic of study that students choose; in chapter 7, Amy's students picked the aspects of everyday life they wanted to learn about, and in chapter 11, Rhoda's selected the questions about the Westward Movement they wanted to investigate. When given choices, students are more likely to make the most of their opportunities than if they are simply answering questions posed by the teacher, using the forms assigned by her.

Harp (1993)

These examples point to another characteristic of constructive evaluation—its continuity with instruction itself. Traditionally, teachers think of assessment as what comes *after* instruction: you teach students about something (or they read about it on their own), and then you test them to see if they learned it. In most classrooms, it's easy to tell the difference between teaching and assessment. In fact, schools often go to great lengths to make the two situations as different as possible: when students are being tested, they don't talk, they don't move around, they don't work together, they don't get help from the teacher. But in the kinds of classrooms described in this book, there is no such split between instruction and assessment. An observer walking into one of these classes would not be able to tell whether it was a "teaching" day or a "testing" day, since they're one and the same thing. Teachers take notes while students are talking, they observe their presentations, review their projects, and read their written reports; all these are part of the ongoing assessment of learning. There are few separate times set aside for assessment because assessment is always taking place.

Hart (1994), Johnston (1992)

Constructive evaluation is also consistent with a constructivist perspective on teaching and learning. As we discussed in chapter 2, people learn new information by linking it to what they already know; their understanding, then, is never a simple reproduction of the information they encounter, but always an interpretation in light of prior understanding. A student's understanding at any given time represents the interaction between external sources of information and her prior knowledge; as a result, no two adults' understanding will be identical, nor will a child's understanding be the same as an adult's. Anyone's understanding of history will vary depending on what she brings to her studies; learning about history is not an all-or-nothing process in which you either "know" a topic or you don't, but a lifelong process of schema-building in which not only the quantity of information but also the connections and relationships among information are important. Constructive evaluation seeks to provide teachers and students a picture of how this schema-building process is going, rather than assessing whether students have "caught" discrete pieces of factual information.

Constructive assessment requires more than the reproduction of information.

Historical understanding develops in the interaction between new sources of information and prior experience.

Learning in history is a process of schema building.

Johnston (1987)

Assessment tasks should involve authentic historical
activity.

Hart (1994), Wiggins (1992)

And finally, in order for evaluation to be consonant with a constructivist approach to teaching and learning, the activities should be authentic—they should be similar to tasks people do in their communities, in businesses, or in scholarly disciplines. When the only audience for an assessment task is the teacher, students have little motivation to show what they know. When children retell a story they have heard to someone who doesn't know the story, their explanations are much more complete than when they know the listener has heard it as well. Similarly, when students communicate for a real audience, they perform at a much higher level than when they complete an assignment only to turn it in to the teacher. Throughout this book, we have seen students directing their studies toward an audience—creating a History Museum for other students and for parents and grandparents, for example, or making presentations on their own histories and their families' histories for classmates. In these situations, students are motivated to show what they know because of the necessity of getting their audience to understand them.

Good assessments promote
self-reflection.

Hart (1994)

Rubrics establish performance standards.

The ultimate goal of this kind of assessment is for students to understand the standards of achievement well enough to evaluate their own work meaningfully and productively. As we pointed out in chapter 2, a key characteristic of effective instruction is the promotion of metacognition—helping students learn how to plan, implement, and assess their own learning. When students constantly look to the teacher for her judgment of their work, they show they have little ability to evaluate their own efforts. In Amy's classroom, on the other hand, explicit scoring rubrics accompany all major assignments, and a generic writing rubric is posted on the wall; Amy devotes enough class time to explaining these rubrics so that students are aware of what constitutes good work. When students ask her how they are doing, she first calls their attention to these rubrics; although students are not always sure whether they have met the standards yet or not, Amy's ultimate goal is to transfer responsibility for evaluation to them.

Constructive assessment is
consistent with disci-
plined, reflective inquiry.

Students express what they
know through discussion,
writing, and the arts.

Instead of searching for "correct" answers, then, constructive assessment requires students to use multiple forms of communication to conduct their inquiries and report their findings. Throughout this book you have read about teachers who do just that. Their students use primary and secondary sources, read visual as well as verbal texts, express themselves through role-plays and simulations, and tell others what they have learned through discussion, writing, and the arts. In contrast to the limited means of expression allowed by fill-in-the-blanks and multiple-choice tests, these activities require students to elaborate on what they know and are learning.

Extended discussion is crucial
to developing communi-
ties of inquiry.

Discussion is at the heart of many of these assessment activities. The teachers in this book work hard to build communities of inquiry that engage students in extended and substantive discussion. As you can see from reading the vignettes in each chapter, discussion involves testing different points of view, expressing feelings, making judgments about history, and applying historical information to new contexts. This can be a challenging experience. Most often students find these discussions exhilarating. Dehea's students love to argue, and debate is nurtured by a classroom environment in which different types of discussion and argument are understood as necessary parts of inquiry. In this classroom context, *argument* does not mean a free-for-all in which students or their ideas are denigrated. Instead, debate is a carefully monitored opportunity for students to jointly construct new historical understanding. Some-times, however, students find debate and argument threatening. When issues of race and gender moved from the past into the complexities of current dissension, some of Jim Farrell's students wanted him to "just tell us the information." They were uncomfortable when their assumptions were challenged, or they found themselves in disagreement with their peers.

Debate and argument can be
assesed.

Pierce & Gilles (1993)

Through discussion, students
jointly develop historical
understanding.

Listening in on some of these discussions, however, it becomes clear that students are developing richer and more sophisticated historical schemas as they participate in discussion with their peers. In Amy's class, for instance, extended conversation helped students better understand the perspective of historical actors. Students who began by assuming people in the past were either ignorant or tasteless came to recognize that perceptions (and taste) change over time. In Walt Keet's classroom, discussion moved students from thinking that apartheid was a distant problem with little connection to their lives to recognizing parallels to their own history and current situation.

Discussion is clearly an important part of disciplined, reflective inquiry in history. Yet little consideration is given to evaluating this schema building process. Obviously you cannot collect every classroom discussion for later contemplation and evaluation. It is also difficult to juggle participating in discussions and recording them for assessment purposes. Finally, it may seem that assessing discussion is adding another burden to an already heavy load of accountability requirements. As we said earlier, however, when assessment and evaluation are integral parts of ongoing instruction they can facilitate rather than impede instruction. And, with some attention to organization, they can be relatively simple to manage.

Assessing discussions need not be a burden.

Pierce & Gilles (1993)

To begin with, it is worth remembering that students can learn to assess their own class discussions. They usually know when a discussion is working and when it degenerates into an exercise in killing time, when they are learning from each other and when they are simply going through the motions. Or, they can at least learn to make these distinctions with a little help from their teachers. Abby Mott works with her students to establish criteria for successful class discussions. She found that students had very strong ideas about how a discussion should go and were relieved when classroom protocols supported their sense of fair play in discussion. After a lively exchange of ideas, Abby's students settled on these criteria for a good discussion:

- Everyone participates
- There are no times when nobody is talking
- Comments are interesting and to the point
- No one dominates the whole discussion

Students can help establish performance criteria for their discussions.

Immediately after establishing these criteria, Abby suggested testing the criteria on the discussion they had just had. The students decided that the four points seemed to work well. Abby asked them to self-assess after each of the next several discussions, and then they would re-evaluate their criteria. After doing as she asked, the students decided that they needed to add a new criterion: *In a good discussion, you learn something you didn't already know.* They also decided that formally evaluating each discussion was cumbersome and detracted from discussion. Abby agreed and made two additional suggestions: that students use the criteria to evaluate their individual contribution to discussions, and that rather than evaluate every discussion, students include a weekly assessment as part of their portfolios. This record helped her assess student progress and was useful in reporting to parents and guardians.

Students need to test their criteria on their own work.

Whole-class discussions such as Abby conducted can be monitored by a single teacher, but it is more difficult to keep track of small group work. Billie Davis finds that asking students to audiorecord small group discussions frees her to move around the room while discussion is occurring. Later, she can go back to the recordings to check on how individual discussions went in her absence. In addition, Billie keeps sample tapes as a method of monitoring change over time. Again, this is an occasional practice. At the beginning of each year, Billie finds that some students are reluctant to be taped while others find the tape distracting or an opportunity to fool around. But because Billie keeps a class archives—a collection of photo albums, videotapes, and artifacts representing each of the years that she has taught— her students quickly adjust to being video- and audiotaped; in fact, they *want* a record of their work. Students from previous years sometimes stop by to check the archives, and her current students love to see what other classes have done, comparing their own performances to those in the past. They ask to have their best work put in the archives, and frequently consult work from other years to get ideas for projects.

Recording small group discussions allows for better monitoring.

Class archives keep the class' history alive and available to students for reference.

Another simpler approach is to take quick notes during class discussions. Dehea keeps a note pad handy and frequently and very visibly takes notes, modeling the kind of thing she wants students to do. She shares what she has written down as part of

Quick notes help organize observations.

163

debriefings with the students, and asks students to do the same. Walt and Viktor both use "post-it" notes attached to a clipboard. At the end of the day they transfer the notes to student folders, maintaining a running record of student participation in discussion. These notes are useful in conferences with students as well as parents and guardians, but they also help Walt and Viktor recognize problem areas, select learning resources to address particular topics raised in discussion and keep track of the development of particular aspects of historical thinking.

WRITING

Daley (1989), Tierney, Carter, & Desai (1991)

Written language is one of the most common forms of evaluation and, in our experience, students often learn by writing in history. When combined with other forms of assessment, then, writing has tremendous potential for providing insight into what students know and can do. The chief requirement for meaningful written assignments is that they be open-ended—that they allow for a variety of correct responses. Good instruction (and good literature) usually presents more information than any single student can be expected to remember; an open-ended assignment allows each student to draw from that body of information to reach conclusions or make evaluations. Each student will respond differently, yet each response has to make use of the facts, concepts, and relationships that form the topic of discussion. This is not the same as saying that any answer is equally correct; for a question to be an effective means of assessment, there must be a range of possible responses, from insightful to shallow.

Meaningful written assignments are open-ended.

While responses to open-ended questions may differ, all must make use of appropriate facts, concepts, and relationships.

As students write, teachers assess both the strategies or processes that students employ in making sense of history and the final analyses or products that grow from these strategies. *Process assessment* documents how students construct historical understanding over time. As Pamela's students pieced together Hugh McKay's life, their writing provided a written record of how they understood historical sources, as well as how they were reconstructing their understanding of the Civil War. Because Pamela had access not just to her students' written interpretations of history but to the sources they were using, she could trace student progress in selecting what was historically and personally significant from primary and secondary sources. She could see when the swashbuckling romance of war gave way to the grim realities of rain, tent hospitals, and lives lost in a sea of mud. In addition, students' first person narratives made clear how well they were able to take on the perspectives of historical actors. While some struggled to give voice to Hugh, most made good use of other soldiers' diaries and letters and tried to make their writing true to Hugh's time and place. Her students wanted to "get it right."

Process assessment can document growth over time.

Access to students' written work as well as their historical sources helps in tracing their progress in making supportable interpretations.

Given good support from teachers and an audience for their work, students want to their history to be accurate.

Peer editing helps students recognize alternative interpretations.

As they struggled to get it right, students made use of peer editing, often making important changes in their interpretations and assumptions after consulting with another student. Deciding how Hugh sustained the injury that destroyed his hand, for instance, elicited considerable debate and demonstrations of alternate scenarios—Hugh raising his hands in surrender, lifting his hand as he pulled the ramrod out of his rifle, or as he flicked ink from a quill pen as he wrote a letter home to his mother, and so on. Another discussion centered on whether Hugh was literate, and what internal evidence the primary sources provided to support assumptions either way. Controversy swirled around the reasons for Hugh's joining the Union Army. Initially, some students were sure the only thing that would have compelled Hugh to join up would have been the draft, and their writing reflected this conclusion. Through peer editing, however, they were referred to other documents that made that interpretation seem unlikely—Hugh's home state of Ohio was not even accepting recruits, much less drafting them, so Hugh had to go to Cairo, Illinois, to enlist. Students altered their stories, looking more closely at pro-Union newspaper stories from Hugh's hometown, trying to understand his feelings—was he an abolitionist or just anti-secessionist?—as he and his brothers left home. Further peer editing and discussion with

Peer editing includes referring students to other sources.

164

Pamela suggested places where interpretation was either not supported or supportable—and provided Pamela with a "paper trail" of multiple drafts. Because she collected these multiple drafts of student writing, Pamela could better assess how interpretations changed over time, what documents or discussions seemed most compelling to students and what progress students were making in synthesizing data into a coherent, supportable account.

One quick, basic way of assessing students' understanding through writing is the use of Magic Words. Magic Words (see Table 14.1) are subordinating conjunctions and prepositions; they're called *magic* not only because that sounds more exciting but because their use magically improves the quality of writing—and even though preschoolers know and use most of these words in speech, they are rarely part of the writing of students of any age. These words call attention to the relationships that lie at the heart of history—how one thing causes another, what events came before or after others, and so on—and using them requires that students demonstrate their understanding of relationships. At the end of a lesson or unit, for example, Rebecca Valbuena's students (chapters 5 and 12) write several sentences about what they've learned; they can write anything at all about the topic, but each sentence has to contain a Magic Word. They thus have the opportunity to search through all the information they have gained in order to show what they know about time, causation, and so on. The following examples of Magic Word sentences come from her class and others:

> Because the ground [at Jamestown] is watery, they can't plant corn.
> Because Francis Drake stole money and land, he was a hero to England.
> In a new settlement, slaves were in high demand because the colonists needed a lot of work done.
> Although the Indians were not lazy and stupid, the Spanish thought they were.
> Whenever a slave was bought, almost everytime a family was split up.
> Although the Indians lived here first, the Spanish said they owned the land.
> After a woman was bought as a slave she begged her master to buy her children too.

This strategy is a clear example of giving students the chance to show what they know rather than what they don't know, and it also gives the teacher insight into the information that was most salient, interesting, or memorable for the class.

A somewhat more structured task is the use of open-ended questions. Such questions also allow for a range of possible answers, but require a more focused response than magic words. Productive open-ended questions generally ask students

Table 14.1
Magic Words

about	because	for	though
above	before	from	through
across	behind	if	to
after	below	in	unless
against	beneath	in order that	until
along	beside	like	when
although	between	near	whenever
among	beyond	of	where
around	by	on	wherever
as	down	past	while
as if	during	since	with
at	except	so that	

Note. Adapted from Barton (in press)

Open-ended questions ask students to identify patterns, draw conclusions, or make evaluations.

to pull together different aspects of what they have learned in order to identify patterns, draw conclusions, or make evaluations. After having studied the encounter between Native Americans and Columbus, for example, Rebecca asked students to explain what kind of personality Columbus had. One wrote that he was greedy, and pointed to his quest for gold; another noted he was curious, because he wanted to find a new way to Asia; yet another suggested he was hopeful, because he kept going when he ran out of supplies. Each student responded differently, yet each had to use what he or she had learned to support a judgment about Columbus' personality. Similarly, Amy followed her History Museum projects by having students explain how the United States had changed over the last 100 years. Although each student used different examples, each had to draw on information to support a generalization about patterns of change.

Processes result in products or *performances*—opportunities for students to present supportable interpretations.

In the end, of course, writing provides a product as well as a process. Such products are sometimes referred to as *performances* and when used as assessment they are sometimes called *performance tasks*. Where process assessment looks at how students learn to organize, synthesize, interpret and hypothesize, *product assessment* evaluates whether the final product or performance sustains a supportable interpretation given the available information (and the level of experience of the writer). A finished piece of historical writing, for instance, should be an original piece of work rather than the reproduction of someone else's information or analysis. The writing should be clear and coherent (again, given the level of experience of the writer), rich in the kind of details that support the writer's interpretation but also engage the reader in the historical account. Historical writing, then, is more than creative storytelling. Historical writing must be grounded in substantial historical knowledge. This is not just a matter of getting the facts right, but of showing how those facts are related to each other and to the writer's larger interpretation. This is true even with the youngest writers. When LeeAnn's primary students wrote about Columbus, they included such telling details as Columbus "trading fake jewels for real gold" and kidnapping the Taino as support for their interpretation of his claim to fame. While an older student might make a more complex argument, these young children are novices, and the fact that they marshal evidence to support a position is an important beginning point.

Assessment focuses on originality, clarity, coherence, and richness of details in a product or performance.

Historical writing must be grounded in substantial historical knowledge. *Newmann et al. (1995)*

Daley (1989), Graves (1983)

Newmann et al. (1995)

Oftentimes, good written tasks ask students to organize what they have learned into forms other than expository sentences and paragraphs. After studying the Columbian encounter, for example, Rebecca had students write dialogues between a reporter and a student who was protesting either a school's Columbus Day celebration or a school's cancellation of such a celebration. In writing the dialogue, students had to draw upon their knowledge of why Columbus is regarded either as a villain or a hero—they had to use historical information to support a position on a contemporary social issue. Similarly, Amy had students write a dialogue between a Japanese American during World War II and the government agent sent to detain him or her; again, students had to use what they had learned to support a position in a real-life setting. *Using* information in this way leads to more meaningful writing—and better assessment—than simply trying to get students to *reproduce* a set of facts, definitions, or concepts.

Through writing, students can bring historical information to bear on contemporary issues.

Historical writing uses rather than reproduces information.

You would, of course, expect more sophisticated arguments and interpretations from older students. One of Walt's students, for instance, wrote a paper arguing for an "honest look at the evils of apartheid" by all South Africans. She used the U.S. post-Reconstruction experiences as a counterexample, showing how ignoring or misrepresenting the past made it more difficult to correct historic injustices. Her paper showed her grasp of the major perspectives of participants in South Africa and the United States, as well as the degree of agency those participants might have in effecting change in race relations in their respective countries. Her writing was a credible piece of work, making good use of available sources and reflecting her richer experience with historical analysis. It is our observation that students like these who have many opportunities to read and write in a variety of genres in the context of indepth inquiry create interesting, sophisticated historical writing that is more representative of authentic historical thinking than is ever demonstrated on a standardized test.

Experience with a wide variety of genres encourages richer historical thinking.

THE ARTS

There are many resources to help teachers assess reading and writing in their classrooms that can be adapted to address historical writing. Most of the teachers with whom we work are reasonably comfortable assessing writing processes and products, and often have established routines for selecting portfolio pieces and sharing student progress with parents and guardians. Although many of these teachers have also used the arts in teaching history, they are less sure of how to assess this aspect of their curriculum. In fact, many of the assessment issues teachers fear in the arts are similar to ones they are already successfully handling in writing. Just as with writing, one issue is how to draw the line between credible and incredible interpretations or renditions. Sometimes, despite everyone's best efforts, students create artwork that reproduces stereotypes, ignores supportable historical interpretations or is just silly. The work may be attractive or interesting artwork, but it is poor history. When you have worked hard to encourage students to take the risk and use the arts, this can be a real dilemma. How do you respond to the art without encouraging bad history, and to the history without discouraging good art? This is particularly problematic when the teacher is insecure about assessing nonrepresentational art. At this point it may seem easier to rely on linguistic modes of expression—just let students tell you what they know. But that, of course, is exactly what they *are* doing. They are letting you know that something is missing in their historical thinking. Epstein's work with high school students provides a useful way of thinking about responding to student's historical art. She argues that, just as with any written historical interpretation, students' work must be historically plausible or possible. In other words, the work must be both historically sound and historically bound.

Historically sound interpretations are those that are credible in terms of the history represented in the art. A picture depicting a bus driver happily inviting Rosa Parks to sit in the front of the bus (and not intended as satire) would not be true to events surrounding the Montgomery bus boycott. Such an interpretation, no matter how aesthetically pleasing, cannot be historically sound.

Historically bound interpretations are those that make sense within the broader historical context in which an event takes place. In other words, the interpretation is plausible, given the time period and culture being studied. While Jeannette's students did not know for sure that delegates to the Constitutional Convention listened to music by Mozart, it is plausible that they might have done so. In the same way, a fifth grader's representation of cowboys in the 1800s enjoying a televised football game is not historically bound—it would have been impossible for this activity to have taken place.

Jeannette deals with these issues in two ways. First, students participate in a number of activities that are presented to peers for discussion and suggestion. Although few of her students make blatant errors with historical soundness, they do sometimes have difficulty with historical boundedness. They have the specific events right, but there are anachronisms—usually items of material culture that would not have appeared in the particular time and place represented. By asking students to explain their work, and respond to suggestions, Jeannette provides opportunities for students to self-correct, or to put nonrepresentational art into historical context. Students also receive written peer evaluations of their work. These evaluations are based on a scoring rubric jointly developed by Jeannette and the students. The rubric addresses both the artistic and historical aspects of each performance. One expectation, for instance, is that the art must expand on any written information, not simply illustrate it. Thus, a poster explaining the electoral college has a straightforward text, but its illustrations comment on and expand the text through political cartoons. In another instance, a dance performance gives emotional weight to a reading from the Constitution.

After peer evaluation, Jeannette also provides feedback on the content as well as the form of presentation. She will compliment students for creative imagery on the one hand and tell them to recheck their historical interpretation on the other. Her

Hiebert & Hutchinson (1991)

Assessment in writing and the arts is often quite similar.

Epstein (1994a)

Epstein (1994a, 1994b, 1994c)

As with other historical genres, historical art can be assessed on its use of historical evidence.

Historical art can be assessed on its relationship to a broader historical context.

Anachronisms are ideas, events, or situations that are out of their proper historical time.

In explaining their own work, students have an opportunity to put that work in historical perspective—or to correct anachronisms.

Kornhaber & Gardner (1993)

Assessment addresses both historical and aesthetic aspects of a performance.

students seem to understand the distinction and expect her critique to include both parts of their work. These are, after all, the same distinctions they are asked to make when they analyze other forms of historical art. In this sense, Jeannette insists that students give their own artwork the same respect and close reading accorded other artists.

Student work is worthy of the same respect and close reading accorded to other artists.

Dyson (1987)

Sometimes it is not essential that aesthetic merit be assessed, even when the arts are the medium of expression. Younger children especially may be able to say what they know through the arts in ways they are not yet able to do linguistically. Thus, providing students with the opportunity to use the arts frees them to say more than they could otherwise manage. Especially with younger students, some teachers find "Sketch to Stretch" activities useful in helping students think about the historical soundness of their ideas. A sketch to stretch activity involves creating at least two different images of the same concept, event or era. At the beginning of their study, children are asked to draw things they associate with some aspect of history. In one classroom, primary students drew things they associated with Africa long ago and things they associated with Africa now. Initial pictures combined elements of Disney's *The Lion King* with jungle scenes, grass huts, and masks. One or two pictures included images of war and starvation. For the most part, however, there was little distinction between "long ago" and "now." As they studied the history and culture of three different countries within Africa, students compared what they were learning with these first pictures. Sometimes they found elements that were accurate for a particular time and place. More often they found that many of the countries they were studying were quite different from their old ideas.

"Sketch to Stretch" activities demonstrate schema restructuring. *Pappas et al.* (1995)

Sokoni (1991), Stanley & Vennema (1988), Stock (1993), Wesniewski (1992)

As the unit progressed, the children drew new pictures of long ago and now for each of the countries. These new pictures combined images drawn from children's literature (*Shaka Khan, King of the Zulus, Where Are You Going, Munyoni? Sundiata,* and *Mchesi Goes to Market*), slides, and photographs of each country. As children drew their new pictures, it was clear that their view of Africa was changing. Their "now" pictures concentrated on the contrast between urban and rural communities, whereas several of the "long ago" pictures depicted historical figures such as Shaka Khan and Sundiata. Follow-up discussions allowed children to explain why they had included particular things in their pictures or left others out. There were still misunderstandings. One child drew a "now" picture of a young man from Chad who had visited the class. In the drawing the young man and his sister ride an elephant to the student's school. As he shared his picture, the child explained: "I hope he comes visit our school again, but next time I want him to bring his sister and ride an elephant."

"Sketch to Stretch" pictures allow teachers to see where students' misconceptions persist.

As you may have noticed by now, we are not describing assessment in terms of tests and quizzes. Although you might decide (or be required) to include such tools in your repertoire of assessment strategies, they can only provide a limited view of your students' historical thinking. Instead, we are suggesting an approach to assessment that is consistent with the kind of history instruction that we advocate throughout this book. This means that process and content are inextricably linked, and both must be assessed. It is not enough to know isolated bits of historical information or even be able to recite someone else's historical interpretation or analysis. Rather, we want to encourage students to articulate and test different theories or points of view, consider the implications and applications of what they are learning, and interpret the role of people, ideas, and events in history. To do so requires attention to *doing history* as well as knowing historical data. From our perspective, then, historical thinking must be assessed in the context of historical inquiry.

Process and content are inextricably linked.

This need not be a more burdensome requirement than current assessment practices. In fact, we hope it will free teachers from the necessity to drill and test in favor of the more historically authentic practice of assessing historical thinking in the context of historical inquiry and interpretation. Almost all the activities described in this book provide opportunities for assessing historical thinking in practice. Your "kid-watching" skills and a willingness to document your observations are the best tools you have for assessing the development of historical thinking. And, you are not

Historical thinking is assessed in the context of historical inquiry.

Pappas et al. (1995)

168

in this alone. As we have already explained, students need to learn to monitor their own learning. It makes sense then, for them to share in the task of assessment. Initially, peer and teacher review, self-assessment, and portfolio construction may take more time, but as students become more independent in self-assessment, and our record-keeping tasks become more organized, this approach to assessment frees up more instructional time.

Keeping track of this kind of writing takes attention to organization. Again, we suggest that students can manage much of the organization on their own *if they understand the established protocols*. Make sure students know what records must be kept, where they are kept, and how they will be used. Take time weekly (sometimes daily checks are necessary) to make sure the system is working. Most of the teachers with whom we work use portfolios as a means of organizing collections of assessment data. Portfolios help them trace progress over time and make better judgments about how to best support students' developing historical understanding. In general, they organize student portfolios into three levels. The first is a *learning portfolio*. Teachers and students jointly decide what should be included in these ongoing collections representing student work either across the curriculum (usually in elementary classrooms) or for one content area (more common at the middle school level). These portfolios are organized to correspond to the categories used in reporting student progress. Documenting historical thinking within a learning portfolio might include the kinds of things we have already mentioned—audio- and videotapes, samples of different genres of historical work, self-assessments, and the like. At the end of each week, then, students, in cooperation with their teacher, select a *Friday Portfolio* of work to share with parents and guardians. Although some teachers do not require the return of these materials, most ask that parents respond to the portfolios and that students return them on the next school day. If you use this technique, you might want to talk with students a bit about how to share their work with their family.

Ruby Yessin, for instance, describes trying to help her first graders decide what should go in their "Friday Portfolios." It had been a busy week, and she wanted to make sure they would share something about the Russian dance company performance, learning Russian folk dances, or perhaps the maps they had worked on that showed some of the geography of Russia. "What" she asked them, "will you say when your parents ask you what happened this week?" Almost as one her students responded, "the Russian kissed Melissa."

In response, Ruby and her students developed some conversation starters to help students share their "Friday Portfolios." They might want to start with "something I am proud of because, . . ." "something I did for the first time, . . ." or "something I didn't know before. . . ." In addition, because not all the adults in her students' lives could read, and it was good practice for her students in any case, Ruby asked students to read one piece of their writing to someone else. In this way, the "Friday Portfolios" became a source of communication between home and school, and the students had a way of sharing what they were learning.

A third level of organization is an *assessment portfolio*. Like the "Friday Portfolio," this is a subset of the learning portfolio. It, too, is jointly constructed by the students and the teacher. Once this portfolio is completed, it becomes the grounds for whatever formal evaluation is required by the school or district. Students have an opportunity to select and explain what they consider to be their best work in different categories for inclusion in the assessment portfolio. In addition, the teacher requires the inclusion of certain items. Pamela, for instance, required that all students include their work on Hugh McKay. Jeannette asks for student self-assessments along with the videotapes of their Bill of Rights productions.

Assessment portfolios also provide a good opportunity for teachers to conduct conferences with students about their work. Abby goes over the assessment portfolio with each child, discussing strengths and areas that need to be worked on in the coming weeks. Her students write up a set of goals for the upcoming grading period; the goals are then put in the learning portfolio as a way of organizing for the next

Students need to monitor their own learning.

Teachers can establish clear protocols to keep assessment manageable. *Hart (1994)*

Pappas et al. (1995), Wexler-Sherman, Gardner, & Feldman (1988)

Portfolios function at three levels: as ongoing collections of student work, as a source of regular feedback to parents and students, and as the grounds for formal progress reports.

Fredericks & Rasinski (1990)

Portfolios help structure reporting to parents and guardians.

"Friday Portfolios" and "assessment portfolios" are subsets of each student's learning portfolio.

Portfolios help structure student–teacher conferences.

When students help develop their own portfolios they have a clearer understanding of their own performance.

grading period. Besides the obvious advantage of emphasizing evaluation as an opportunity to plan for the future, these conferences allay student fears about report cards. By the time the report cards are distributed there are rarely surprises. The students have a pretty clear understanding of their progress to that point and what they can do in the upcoming term.

CONCLUSIONS

Johnston (1987), Newmann et al. (1995)

Constructive evaluation shifts the focus from a remediation model for teaching and learning to the construction of a community of inquiry in which students rehearse, refine and revise, and communicate in a distinctive "voice" or style while solving substantive intellectual problems. Such an approach is closer to the way in which adults operate when they are working and is certainly more congruent with the ways in which teachers and students work throughout this book.

We have emphasized that the best assessment exercises have an authentic audience, and much of the work students have done in these classrooms clearly are directed at audiences beyond the teacher. We should also point out that some of the most meaningful assessment occurs when students are writing for themselves. The benefit of magic words and of good open-ended questions or performance tasks is often that they give students a chance to demonstrate to *themselves* what they have learned. During a lesson or a unit, students may have picked up a great deal of information, but it often remains in a somewhat vague or disorganized form. Constructive evaluation provides a chance for students to reflect on their learning in order to identify organizing themes, patterns, and structures—it becomes a way for them to say, "Hey, I know what's going on here, and here's how I know it."

CHILDREN'S AND ADOLESCENT LITERATURE

Books on Africa

Benin

Cowen-Fletcher, J. (1994). *It Takes a Village*. Scholastic.

Cameroon

Grifalconi, A. (1986). *The Village of Round and Square Houses*. Little, Brown.

Cote d'Ivoire

Tadjo, V. (1988). *Lord of the Dance: An African Retelling*. HarperCollins.

Ethiopia

Levitan, S. (1987). *The Return*. Fawcett/Ballentine.
Negash, A. (1990). *Haile Selassie*. Chelsea House.

Kenya

Kanjoyah, J. N., & Mulima, S. (1989). *Our Location (Pupil Book for Standard 2)*. Longmans Kenya.
Sokoni, M. A. (1991). *Mchesi Goes to Market.*. Nairobi, Kenya: Jacaranda Designs, LTD.

Liberia

Bess, C. (1982). *Story for a Black Night*. Houghton Mifflin.

Malawi

Williams, K. L. (1990). *Galimoto.* Lothrop, Lee & Shepard.

Mali

Wesneiwski, D. (1992). *Sundiata.* Clarion.

South Africa (for additional titles, see chapter 10)

Gordon, S. (1990). *The Middle of Somewhere: A Story of South Africa.* Orchard.
Isadora, R. (1991). *At The Crossroads.* Greenwillow.
Kristensen, P., & Cameron, F. (1985). *We Live in South Africa.* Franklin Watts.
Meltzer, M. (1986). *Winnie Mandela: The Soul of Africa.* Viking.
Stanley, D., & Vennema, P. (1988). *Shaka Khan: King of the Zulus.* Morrow.

Tanzania

Lundgren, G. (1983). *Malcolm's Villge.* Annick.
Margolies, B. (1990). *Rehema's Journey: A Visit to Tanzania.* Scholastic.

Zimbabwe

Cheney, P. (1990). *The Land and People of Zimbabwe.* HarperCollins. (Additional volumes in this series deal with Kenya
   and South Africa)
Jacobsen, K. (1990). *Zimbabwe.* Chicago: New True Books, Children's Book Press.
Stark, A. (1986). *Zimbabwe: A Treasure of Africa.* Dillon.
Steptoe, J. (1987). *Mufaros' Beautiful Daughters.* Lothrop, Lee & Shepard.
Stock, C. (1993). *Where Are You Going, Manyoni?* Morrow.

General Africa

Haskins, J. (1989). *Count Your Way Through Africa.* Carolrhoda.

References

ᚲᚱᛏᛇᚾ

Adler, D. (1987). *The number on my grandfather's arm.* New York: Union of American Hebrew Congregations.

Adler, D. (1990). *A picture book of Helen Keller.* New York: Holiday House.

Ahlberg, J., & Ahlberg, A. (1986). *The jolly postman.* Boston: Little, Brown.

Albert, M. (1995). *Impact of an arts-integrated social studies curriculum on eighth graders' thinking capacities.* Unpublished doctoral dissertation, University of Kentucky, Lexington.

Aliki, M. (1983) *Medieval wedding.* New York: HarperCollins.

Alvermann, D. (1991). The discussion web: A graphic aid for learning across the curriculum. *The Reading Teacher, 45*, 92–99.

Anderson, L. (1990). A rationale for global education. In K. Tye (Ed.), *Global education: From thought to action* (pp. 13–34). Alexandria, VA: Association for Supervision and Curriculum Development.

Appleby, J., Hunt, L., & Jacob, M. (1994). *Telling the truth about history.* New York: Norton.

Arnheim, R. (1981). *Visual thinking.* Berkeley: University of California Press.

Atwell, N. (1987). *In the middle: Writing, reading, and learning with adolescents.* Upper Montclair, NJ: Boynton/Cook.

Atwell, N. (1990). *Coming to know: Writing to learn in the intermediate grades.* Portsmouth, NH: Heinemann.

Avery, P., Bird, K., Johnstone, S., Sullivan, J. L., & Thalhammer, K. (1992). Exploring political tolerance with adolescents. *Theory and Research in Social Education, 20*, 386–420.

Avi. (1984). *The fighting ground.* Philadelphia: Lippincott.

Baggett, P. (1989). Understanding verbal and visual messages. In H. Mandle & J. Levin (Eds.), *Knowledge acquisition from text and pictures* (pp. 101–124). Amsterdam, NY: Elsevier.

Bakhtin, M. M. (1986). *Speech genres and other late essays* (V. W. McGee, Trans.). Austin: University of Texas Press.

Baldwin, J. (1988). A talk to teachers. In R. Simonson & S. Walker (Eds.), *Multicultural literacy* (pp. 3–12). Saint Paul, MN: Graywolf Press.

Barber, B. (1992). *An aristocracy of everyone: The politics of education and the future of America.* New York: Ballantine.

Bardige, B. (1988). Things so finely human: Moral sensibilities at risk in adolescence. In C. Gilligan, J. V. Ward, & J. M. Taylor (Eds.), *Mapping the moral domain: A contribution of women's thinking to psychological theory and education* (pp. 87–110). Cambridge, MA: Harvard University Press.

Barton, K. C. (1994a). *Historical understanding among elementary children.* Unpublished doctoral dissertation, University of Kentucky, Lexington.

Barton, K. C. (1994b, November). *History is about people: Elementary students' understanding of history.* Paper presented at the annual meeting of the College and University Faculty Association, National Council for the Social Studies, Phoenix, AZ.

Barton, K. C. (1995, April). *"My mom taught me": The situated nature of historical understanding.* Paper presented at the annual meeting of the American Educational Research Association, San Francisco.

Barton, K. C. (in press). Using magic words to teach social studies. *Social Studies and the Young Learner.*

Barton, K. C., & Levstik, L. S. (1996). "Back when God was around and everything": The development of elementary children's understanding of historical time. *American Educational Research Journal, 33*, 419–454.

Barton, K. C., & Smith, L. A. (1994, November). *Historical fiction in the middle grades.* Paper presented at the annual meeting of the College and University Faculty Assembly, National Council for the Social Studies, Phoenix, AZ.

Beck, I. L., & McKeown, M. G. (1991). Social studies texts are hard to understand: Mediating some of the difficulties. *Language Arts, 68*, 482–490.

Bennett, C., & Spalding, E. (1992). Teaching the social studies: Multiple approaches for multiple perspectives. *Theory and Research in Social Education, 20*, 263–292.

Bennett, P. S. (1967). *What happened on Lexington Green: An inquiry into the nature and methods of history* (teacher and student manuals). Washington, DC: Office of Education, Bureau of Research. (Eric Document Reproduction Service No. ED 032 333).

Bestor, A. (1953). Anti–intellectualism in the schools. *New Republic, 128*, 11–13.

Beyond the Barricades: Popular Resistance in South Africa. (1989). Washington, DC: Aperture.

Blyth, J. (1989). *History in primary schools: A practical approach for teachers of 5- to 11-year-old children.* Philadelphia: Open University Press.

Blos, J. (1993). Perspectives on historical fiction. In M. O. Tunnell & R. Ammon (Eds.), *The story of ourselves: Teaching history through children's literature* (pp. 11–18). Portsmouth, NH: Heinemann.

Blumberg, R. (1993). *Bloomers!* New York: Bradbury Press.

Boatner, M. M. (1969). *The Civil War dictionary.* New York: David McKay.

Boner, P. (1995). New nation, new history: The history workshop in South Africa, 1977–1994. *Journal of American History, 81*, 977–985.

Bradley Commission on History in Schools. (1989). Building a history curriculum: Guidelines for teaching. In P. Gagnon & The Bradley Commission on History in the Schools (Eds.), *Historical literacy: The case for history in American education* (pp. 16–47). New York: Macmillan.

Brandt, R. (1988). On assessment in the arts: A conversation with Howard Gardner. *Educational Leadership, 45*(4), 30–34.

Brenner, B. (1994). *If you were there in 1776.* New York: Macmillan.

Bresnick-Perry, R. (1992). *Leaving for America.* Chicago: Children's Book Press.

Brooks, J. G., & Brooks, M. G. (1993). *In search of understanding: The case for constructivist classrooms.* Alexandria, VA: Association for Supervision and Curriculum Development.

Brophy, J. (1990). Teaching social studies for understanding and higher-order application. *The Elementary School Journal, 90,* 351–417.

Brophy, J., VanSledright, B. A., & Bredin, N. (1992). Fifth graders' ideas about history expressed before and after their introduction to the subject. *Theory and Research in Social Education, 20,* 440–489.

Brophy, J., VanSlredright, B., & Bredin, N. (1993). What do entering fifth graders know about U. S. history? *Journal of Social Studies Research, 16/17,* 2–19.

Brown, D. (1975). *Wounded Knee: An Indian history of the American west.* New York: Dell.

Brown, J. S., Collins, A., & Duguid, P. (1989). Situated cognition and the culture of learning. *Educational Researcher, 18*(1), 32–42.

Bruer, J. (1993). *Schools for thought: A science of learning in the classroom.* Cambridge, MA: MIT Press.

Bruner, J. (1986). *Actual minds, possible worlds.* Cambridge, MA: Harvard University Press.

Built Environment Educational Consortium. (1990). *Assessment tasks submitted to the Kentucky Council on School Performance Standards.* Unpublished report.

Bunton, L. S. (1992). *Cultural consciousness and response to literary texts among African-American and European-American high school juniors.* Unpublished doctoral dissertation, University of Kentucky, Lexington.

Caine, R. N., & Caine, G. (1994). *Making connections: Teaching and the human brain.* New York: Addison-Wesley.

California State Board of Education. (1988). *History–social science framework for California public schools, kindergarten through grade twelve.* Sacramento: California State Department of Education.

Carey, S. (1985). *Conceptual change in childhood.* Cambridge, MA: MIT Press.

Carretero, M., Jacott, L., Limón, M., Manjón, A. L., & León, J.A. (1994). Historical knowledge: Cognitive and instructional implications. In M. Carretero & J. F. Voss (Eds.), *Cognitive and instructional processes in history and social sciences* (pp. 357–376). Hillsdale, NJ: Lawrence Erlbaum Associates.

Carter, A. R. (1992). *The American revolution.* New York: Franklin Watts.

Carlisle, M. (1995). Talking history. *OAH Magazine of History, 9*(2), 57–59.

Casanova, U. (1995). An exchange of views on "The great speckled bird." *Educational Researcher, 24*(6), 22.

Cazden, C. B. (1988). *Classroom discourse: The language of teaching and learning.* Portsmouth, NH: Heinemann.

Cheney, L. V. (1987). *American memory: A report on the humanities in the nation's public schools.* Washington, DC: National Endowment for the Humanities.

Chi, M. T. H. (1976). Short-term memory limitations in children: Capacity or processing deficits? *Memory and Cognition, 4,* 559–572.

Chi, M. T. H., Feltovich, P., & Glaser, R. (1981). Categorization and representation of physics problems by experts and novices. *Cognitive Science, 5,* 121–152.

Children of Yugoslavia Staff. (1994). *I dream of peace.* New York: HarperCollins.

Clarke, A. C. (1974). Drummer boy of Shiloh. In D. Roselle (Ed.) *Transformations II: Understanding American history through science fiction* (pp. 13–23). Fawcett.

Coerr, E. (1994). *Sadako.* New York: Putnam.

Cohen, D. W. (1994). *The combing of history.* Chicago: University of Chicago Press.

Collier, J. L., & Collier, C. (1974). *My brother Sam is dead.* New York: Four Winds Press.

Collier, J. L., & Collier, C. (1984). *War comes to Willy Freeman.* New York: Dell.

Collingwood, R. G. (1961). *The idea of history.* London: Oxford University Press.

Conley, R.J. (1992). *Nickajack.* Garden City, NJ: Doubleday.

Cook, L. W. (1965). *When great-grandmother was a little girl.* New York: Holt, Rinehart & Winston.

Conrad, P. (1991). *Prairie visions: The life and times of Solomon Butcher.* New York: HarperCollins.

Cope, B., & Kalantzes, M. (1990). Literacy in the social sciences. In F. Christie (Ed.), *Literacy for a changing world* (pp. 118–142). Hawthorne, Victoria: Australian Council for Educational Research.

Cornbleth, C. (1995). *The great speckled bird: Multicultural politics and educational policymaking.* New York: St. Martin's Press.

Cornell, K. (1993). *These lands are ours: Tecumseh's fight for the Old Northwest.* New York: Steck-Vaughn.

Corwin, S. (1991). *Art as a tool for learning United States history.* Champaign–Urbana: National Arts Education Research Center, University of Illinois.

Cox, J. K. (1993). *Teaching about conflict and crisis in the former Yugoslavia:The Case of Bosnia-Hercegovina.* ERIC Digest. (ERIC Document Reproduction Service No. ED377139).

Crook, J. B. (1988). Where have all the heroes gone? In V. Rogers, A. D. Roberts, & T. P. Weinland (Eds.), *Teaching social studies: Portraits from the classroom* (Bulletin No. 82, pp. 36–41). Washington, DC: National Council for the Social Studies.

Cushman, K. (1994). *Catherine called Birdy.* New York: Clarion.

Cuthbertson, G. (1995). Racial attraction: Tracing the historiographical alliances between South Africa and the United States. *Journal of American History, 81,* 1123–1136.

Daley, E. (Ed.). (1989). *Monitoring children's language development: Holistic assessment in the classroom.* Portsmouth, NH: Heinemann.

Danto, A. C. (1965). *Analytical philosophy of history.* Cambridge: Cambridge University Press.

DeFord, D. H., & Stout, H. S. (1987). *An enemy among them.* Boston: Houghton Mifflin.

Degenhardt, M., & McKay, E. (1988). Imagination and education for intercultural understanding. In K. Egan & D. Nadaner (Eds.), *Imagination and education* (pp. 237–255). New York: Teachers College Press.

Dewey, J. (1933) *How we think: A restatement of the relation of reflective thinking to the educative process.* New York: D. C. Heath.

Dewey, J. (1956). *The child and the curriculum* and *the school and society*. Chicago: University of Chicago Press.

Dickinson, A. K., & Lee, P. J. (1984). Making sense of history. In A. K. Dickinson, P. J. Lee, & P. J. Rogers (Eds.), *Learning history* (pp. 117–153). London: Heinemann.

Dickinson, J. (1993). Children's perspectives on talk: Building a learning community. In K. M. Pierce & C. J. Gilles (Eds.), *Cycles of meaning: Exploring the potential of talk in learning communities* (pp. 99–116). Portsmouth, NH: Heinemann.

Dillon, E. (1986). *The seekers*. New York: Scribner's.

Donaldson, M. (1978). *Children's minds*. New York: Norton.

Downey, M. (Ed.). (1982). *Teaching American history: New directions* (Bulletin No. 67). Washington, DC: National Council for the Social Studies.

Downey, M. (1994, April). *After the dinosaurs: Elementary children's chronological thinking*. Paper presented at the annual meeting of the American Educational Research Association, New Orleans.

Downey, M., & Levstik, L. S. (1991). Teaching and learning history. In J. Shaver (Ed.), *Handbook of research on social studies teaching and learning* (pp. 400–410). New York: Macmillan.

Downs, A. (1993). Breathing life into the past: The creation of history units using trade books. In M. O. Tunnell & R. Ammon (Eds.), *The story of ourselves: Teaching history through children's literature* (pp. 137–146). Portsmouth, NH: Heinemann.

Dunn, R., & Griggs, S. A. (1988). *Learning styles: Quiet revolution in American secondary schools*. Reston, VA: National Association of Secondary School Principals.

Duckworth, E. (1987). *"The having of wonderful ideas" and other essays on teaching and learning*. New York: Teachers College Press.

Dyson, A. H. (1987). Individual differences in beginning composing: An orchestral vision of learning to compose. *Written Communication, 9,* 411–442.

Dyson, A. H. (1989). *Multiple worlds of child writers: Friends learning to write*. New York: Teachers College Press.

Egan, K. (1983). Accumulating history. *History and Theory, Belkeft 22,* 66–80.

Egan, K. (1989). Memory, imagination, and learning: Connected by the story. *Phi Delta Kappan, 70*(6), 455-459.

Egan, K., & Nadaner, D. (Eds.). (1988). *Imagination and education*. New York: Teachers College Press.

Egger-Bovet, H., & Smith-Baranzin, M. (1994). *U.S. kids history: Book of the American Revolution*. Boston: Little, Brown.

Eisner, E. (1988). *The role of discipline-based art education in America's schools*. Los Angeles: Getty Center for Education in the Arts.

Elshtain, J. B. (1981). *Public man, private woman: Women in social and political thought*. Princeton, NJ: Princeton University Press.

Engle, S. (1970). The future of social studies education and the National Council for the Social Studies. *Social Education, 34,* 778–781.

Epstein, T. L. (1991). Equity in educational experiences and outcomes. *OAH Magazine of History, 6,* 35–40.

Epstein, T. L. (1993). Why teach history to the young? In M. Tunnel & R. Ammon (Eds.), *The story of ourselves: Teaching history through children's literature* (pp. 1–8). Portsmouth, NH: Heinemann.

Epstein, T. L. (1994a). "America Revised" revisited: Adolescents' attitudes toward a United States history textbook. *Social Education, 58,* 41–44.

Epstein, T. L. (1994b). The arts of history: An analysis of secondary school students' interpretations of the arts in historical contexts. *Journal of Curriculum and Supervision, 9,* 174–194.

Epstein, T. L. (1994c, April). *Makes no difference if you're black or white? African-American and European-American adolescents' perspectives on historical significance and historical sources*. Paper presented at the annual meeting of the American Educational Research Association, New Orleans.

Epstein, T. L. (1994d). Sometimes a shining moment: High school students' representations of history through the arts. *Social Education, 58,* 136–141.

Epstein, T. L. (1994e). Tales from two textbooks: A comparison of the civil rights movement in two secondary history textbooks. *The Social Studies, 85,* 121–126.

Evans, R. W. (1988). Lessons from history: Teacher and student conceptions of the meaning of history. *Theory and Research in Social Education, 16,* 203–225.

Filipovic, Z. (1994). *Zlata's diary*. New York: Viking.

Fines, J., & Verrier, R. (1974). *The drama of history: An experiment in co-operative teaching*. London: New University Education.

Fisher, L. E. (1990). *The Oregon Trail*. New York: Holiday House.

Flack, J. D. (1992). *Lives of promise: Studies in biography and family history*. Englewood, CO: Teacher Ideas Press.

Fleischmann, P. (1992). *Whipping boy*. Boston: HarperCollins.

Forbes, E. (1943). *Johnny Tremain*. Boston: Houghton Mifflin.

Fox, M. (1985). *Wilfred Gordon MacDonald Partridge*. New York: Kane-Miller.

Frank, A. (1967). *Anne Frank: The diary of a young girl*. Garden City, NY: Doubleday.

Fredericks, A. D., & Rasinski, T. V. (1990). Involving parents in the assessment process. *The Reading Teacher, 44,* 346–349.

Freedman, R. (1980). *Immigrant kids*. New York: Dutton.

Freedman, R. (1983). *Children of the wild west*. New York: Clarion.

Freedman, R. (1990). *Franklin Delano Roosevelt*. New York: Clarion.

Freedman, R. (1993). *Eleanor Roosevelt: A life of discovery*. New York: Clarion.

Freedman, R. (1994). *Kids at work: Lewis Hine and the crusade against child labor*. New York: Clarion.

Freeman, E., & Person, D. G. (Eds.). (1992). *Using nonfiction trade books in the elementary classroom: From ants to zeppelins*. Champaign–Urbana, IL: National Council of Teachers of English.

Fritz, J. (1967). *Early thunder*. New York: Putnam.

Fritz, J. (1983). *The double life of Pocahontas*. New York: Putnam.

Fritz, J. (1987). *Shh! We're writing the Constitution*. New York: Putnam.

Fulwiler, T. (1982). Writing: An act of cognition. In C. W. Griffin (Ed.), *New directions for teaching and learning, No. 12, Teaching writing in all disciplines* (pp. 15–26). San Francisco: Jossey-Bass.

Gabella, M. S. (1994). Beyond the looking glass: Bringing students into the conversation of historical inquiry. *Theory and Research in Social Education, 22,* 240–263.

174

Gagnon, P., & the Bradley Commission on History in the Schools. (Eds.). (1989). *Historical literacy: The case for history in American education.* New York: Macmillan.

Gallie, W. B. (1964). *Philosophy and the historical understanding.* New York: Schocken.

Gardner, H. (1982). *Art, mind, and brain: A cognitive approach to creativity.* New York: Basic Books.

Gardner, H. (1983). *Frames of mind: The theory of multiple intelligences.* New York: Basic Books.

Gardner, H. (1988). Toward more effective arts education. *Journal of Aesthetic Education, 22,* 158–166.

Gardner, H. (1990). *Art education and human development* (Occasional paper no. 3.) Eric Document Reproduction Service. No. ED 336 325.

Gardner, H. (1991). *The unschooled mind: How children think and how schools should teach.* New York: Basic Books.

Gardner, H., & Boix–Mansilla, V. (1994). Teaching for understanding in the disciplines—and beyond. *Teachers College Record, 96,* 198–218.

Garfield, S. (1991). Building self-esteem through poetry. *The Reading Teacher, 44,* 616–617.

Garza, C. L. (1990). *Family pictures/Cuadros de familia.* Chicago: Children's Book Press.

Gauch, P. L. (1974). *Thunder at Gettysburg.* New York: Coward, McCann & Geohegan.

Geertz, C. (1983). *Local knowledge: Further essays in interpretive anthropology.* New York: Basic Books.

Geoghegan, W. (1994). Re-placing the arts in education. *Phi Delta Kappan, 75,* 456–458.

Golenbock, P. (1990). *Teammates.* New York: Harcourt Brace.

Gombrich, E. H. (1974). The visual image. In D. R. Olson (Ed.), *Media and symbols: The forms of expression, communication, and education* (Yearbook of the National Society for the Study of Education, New Series No. 73, part 1; pp. 241–270). Chicago: University of Chicago Press.

Gonzales, C. T. (1987). *Quanah Parker: Great chief of the Comanches.* Austin, TX: Eakin Press.

Good, T. L., & Brophy, J. E. (1994). *Looking in classrooms* (6th ed.). New York: HarperCollins.

Goodman, N. (1984). *Of mind and other matters.* Cambridge, MA: Harvard University Press.

Gordon, L. (1988). *Heroes of their own lives: The politics and history of family violence.* New York: Viking.

Gordon, L. (1990). U. S. women's history. In E. Foner (Ed.), *The new American history* (pp. 185–210). Philadelphia: Temple.

Graves, D. (1983). *Writing: Teachers and children at work.* Exeter, NH: Heinemann.

Greene, M. (1993a). Beyond insularity: Releasing the voices. *College ESL, 3*(1), 1–14.

Greene, M. (1993b). The passions of pluralism: Multiculturalism and the expanding community. *Educational Researcher, 22*(1), 13–18.

Greene, M. (1995). Art and imagination: Reclaiming the sense of possibility. *Phi Delta Kappan, 76,* 378–382.

Greenfield, E. (1977). *Mary McLeod Bethune.* New York: HarperCollins.

Griffin, A. F. (1992). *A philosophical approach to the subject-matter preparation of teachers of history.* Washington, DC: National Council for the Social Studies.

Gutman, H. G. (1976). *The black family in slavery and freedom: 1750–1925.* New York: Pantheon.

Gutmann, A. (1987). *Democratic education.* Princeton, NJ: Princeton University Press.

Hahn, C. L., & Tocci, C. M. (1990). Classroom climate and controversial issues discussion: A five nation study. *Theory and Research in Social Education, 18,* 344–362.

Hamilton, V. (1985). *The people could fly.* New York: Knopf.

Hammond, T. (1988). *Sports.* New York: Knopf.

Hansen, J.(1993) What keeps writing alive in our classrooms? *Reading and Writing Quarterly: Overcoming Learning Difficulties, 9*(2) 197–205.

Harp, B. (1993). Principles of assessment and evaluation in whole language classrooms. In B. Harp (Ed.), *Assessment and evaluation in whole language programs* (pp. 37–52). Norwood, MA: Christopher-Gordon.

Harste, J. C., & Short, K. G. (1988). *Creating classrooms for authors: The reading–writing connection.* Portsmouth, NH: Heinemann.

Hart, D. (1994). *Authentic assessment: A handbook for educators.* Menlo Park, CA: Addison-Wesley.

Harvey, B. (1988). *Cassie's journey: Going west in the 1860s.* New York: Holiday House.

Harvey, K. D., Harjo, L. D., & Jackson, J. K. (1990). Introduction. In K. D. Harvey, L. D. Harjo, & J. K. Jackson (Eds.), *Teaching about Native Americans* (Bulletin No. 84; pp. 1–7). Washington, DC: National Council for the Social Studies.

Henson, J. (1993). The tie that binds: The role of talk in defining community. In K.M. Pierce & C. J. Gilles (Eds.), *Cycles of meaning: Exploring the potential of talk in learning communities* (pp. 37–57). Portsmouth, NH: Heinemann.

Hepler, S. (1991). Talking our way to literacy in the classroom community. *The New Advocate, 4,* 179–191.

Hertzberg, H. W. (1989). History and progressivism: A century of reform proposals. In P. Gagnon & the Bradley Commission on History in the Schools (Eds.), *Historical literacy: The case for history in American education.* Boston: Houghton Mifflin.

Hesse, K. (1992). *Letters from Rifka.* New York: Henry Holt.

Hiebert, E. H., & Hutchinson, T. A. (1991). Research directions: The current state of alternative assessments for policy and instructional uses. *Language Arts, 68,* 662–668.

Hirsch, E. D. (1987). *Cultural literacy: What every American needs to know.* Boston: Houghton Mifflin.

Holt, T. C. (1990a). African-American history. In E. Foner (Ed.), *The new American history* (pp. 211–232.). Philadelphia: Temple University Press.

Holt, T. C. (1990b). *Thinking historically: Narrative, imagination, and understanding.* New York: College Entrance Examination Boards.

Holtze, S. (1988). *A circle unbroken.* New York: Clarion.

Huck, C., Helper, S., & Hickman, J. (1987). *Children's literature in the elementary school.* New York: Holt, Rinehart & Winston.

Hudson, J. (1989). *Dawn rider.* New York: Philomel.

Hudson, J. (1990). *Sweetgrass.* New York: Philomel.

Hyde, A. A., & Bizar, M. (1989). *Thinking in context: Teaching cognitive processes across the elementary curriculum.* New York: Longman.

Irwin, C. (1980). *Strange footprints on the land: Vikings in America.* New York: Harpers.

Jennings, F. (1975). *The invasion of America: Indians, colonialism, and the cant of conquest.* Chapel Hill: University of North Carolina Press.

Johnson, D. W., Johnson, R. T., & Holubec, E. J. (1993). *Circles of learning: Cooperation in the classroom* (4th ed.). Edina, MN: Interaction Book.

Johnston, P. (1987). Teachers as evaluation experts. *The Reading Teacher, 40,* 744–748.

Johnston, P. (1992). *Constructive evaluation of literate activity.* New York: Longman.

Joliffe, D. A. (1987). A social educator's guide to teaching writing. *Theory and Research in Social Education, 15,* 89–104.

Jordan, W. D. (1968) *White over Black: American attitudes toward the Negro, 1550–1812.* Chapel Hill: University of North Carolina Press.

Jorgensen, K. L. (1993). *History workshop: Reconstructing the past with elementary students.* Portsmouth, NH: Heinemann.

Joyner, C. (1984). *Down by the riverside: A South Carolina slave community.* Urbana: University of Illinois Press.

Kammen, M. (1991). *Mystic chords of memory: The transformation of tradition in American culture.* New York : Knopf.

Kansteiner, W. (1993). Hayden White's critique of the writing of history. *History and Theory, 32,* 273–293.

Katz, W. L. (1993). *The westward movement and abolitionism.* Austin, TX: Steck–Vaughn.

Keating, C. (1994). Promoting growth through dialogue journals. In G. Wells (Ed.), *Changing schools from within: Creating communities of inquiry.* Portsmouth, NH: Heinemann.

Keefe, J. W. (1987). *Learning style: Theory and practice.* Reston, VA: National Association of Secondary School Principals.

Keller, C. W., & Schillings, D. L. (1987). *Teaching about the constitution* (Bulletin No. 80). Washington, DC: National Council for the Social Studies.

Kelly, T. E. (1986). Discussing controversial issues: Four perspectives on the teacher's role. *Theory and Research in Social Education, 14,* 113–138.

Kennedy, J. M. (1974). Icons and information. In D. R. Olson (Ed.), *Media and symbols: The forms of expression, communication, and education* (Yearbook of the National Society for the Study of Education, New Series No. 73, part 1; pp. 241–270). Chicago: University of Chicago Press.

Kentucky Council on School Performance Standards. (1991). *Kentucky's learning goals and valued outcomes* (Tech. rep.). Frankfort, KY: Author.

Kentucky's Six Learning Goals, Revised, 1994, KRS #158.6451.

Kerber, L. (1993). Some cautionary words for historians. In M. J. Larrabee (Ed.), *An ethic of care: Feminist and interdisciplinary perspectives* (pp. 102–107). New York: Routledge.

Kermode, F. (1980). Secrets and narrative sequence. *Critical Inquiry, 7,* 83–101.

Kessler–Harris, A. (1990). Social history. In E. Foner (Ed.), *The new American history* (pp. 163–184). Philadelphia: Temple University Press.

Kiefer, B. (1995). *The potential of picturebooks: From visual literacy to aesthetic understanding.* Englewood Cliffs, NJ: Merrill.

Kobrin, B. (1988). *Eyeopeners: How to choose and use children's books about real people, places, and things.* New York: Viking.

Kornhaber, M., & Gardner, H. (1993). *Varieties of excellence: Identifying and assessing children's talents* (Opinion paper BBB12599). Pleasantville: Aaron Diamond Foundation.

Kosma, R. (1991). Learning with media. *Review of Educational Research, 61,* 179–211.

Kraus International Publications. (1992). *Social studies: Curriculum resource handbook.* Millwood, NY: Author.

Lave, J., & Wenger, E. (1991). *Situated learning: Legitimate peripheral participation.* New York: Cambridge University Press.

Lee, P. J. (1978). Explanation and understanding in history. In A. K. Dickinson & P. J. Lee (Eds.), *Historical teaching and historical understanding* (pp. 72–93). London: Heinemann.

Lemke, J. (1991). Making meaning: The principles of social semiotics. In J. Lemke (Ed.), *Talking science: Language, learning, and values* (pp. 183–213). Norwood, NJ: Ablex.

Levine, E. (1986). *If you traveled west in a covered wagon.* New York: Scholastic.

Levine, E. (1993). *If your name was changed at Ellis Island.* New York: Scholastic.

Levine, L. W. (1977). *Black culture and Black consciousness: Afro-American folk thought from slavery to freedom.* New York: Oxford University Press.

Levinson, R. (1985). *Watch the stars come out.* New York: Dutton.

Levinson, R. (1992). *I go with my family to grandma's.* New York: Dutton.

Levstik, L. S. (1986). The relationship between historical response and narrative in a sixth-grade classroom. *Theory and Research in Social Education, 14,* 1–19.

Levstik, L. S. (1989). Historical narrative and the young reader. *Theory into Practice, 28,* 114–119.

Levstik, L. S. (1993). Building a sense of history in a first grade classroom. In J. Brophy (Ed.), *Advances in research on teaching, vol. 4, Research in elementary social studies* (pp. 1–31). Greenwich, CT: JAI Press.

Levstik, L. S. (1995). Narrative constructions: cultural frames for history. *The Social Studies, 86,* 113–116.

Levstik, L. S., & Barton, K. C. (1996). "They still use some of their past": Historical saliences in elementary children's chronological thinking. *Journal of Curriculum Studies, 28,* 531–576.

Levstik, L. S., & Pappas, C. C. (1987). Exploring the development of historical understanding. *Journal of Research and Development in Education, 21,* 1–15.

Lexington answer book. (n.d.) Lexington, KY: Lexington–Fayette Urban County Government.

Lindquist, T. (1995). *Seeing the whole through social studies.* Portsmouth, NH: Heinemann.

Linenthal, E. (1995). Struggling with history and memory. *The Journal of American History, 82*(3), 1094-1101.

Linenthal, E. T. (1994). Committing history in public. *Journal of American History, 81,* 986–991.

Littlechild, G. (1993). *This land is my land.* Chicago: Children's Book Press.

Loeb, R. (1979). *Meet the real Pilgrims: Everyday life on a Plymouth plantation in 1627.*

Lowry, L. (1990). *Number the stars.* New York: Dell.

Lybarger, M. B. (1990). The historiography of social studies: Retrospect, circumspect, and prospect. In J. Shaver (Ed.), *Handbook of research on social studies teaching and learning* (pp. 3–26). New York: Macmillan.

Macaulay, D. (1977). *Castle.* Boston: Houghton-Mifflin.

Mazur, J. (1993). *Interpretation and use of visuals in an interactive multimedia fiction program.* Unpublished doctoral dissertation, Cornell University, Ithaca, NY.

McGinnis, K. (n.d.). *Educating for a just society: Grades 7–12.* St. Louis: The Institute for Peace and Justice.

McKeown, M. G., & Beck, I. L. (1990). The assessment and characterization of young learners' knowledge of a topic in history. *American Educational Research Journal, 27,* 688–726.

McKinley, R. (1989). *The outlaws of Sherwood.* New York: Berkely.

McKissack, P., & McKissack, F. (1994). *A long hard journey: The story of the pullman porter.* Boston: Walker.

McKissack, P. C., & McKissack, F. L. (1994). *Christmas in the big house, Christmas in the quarters.* New York: Scholastic.

Megill, A. (1989). Recounting the past: "Description," explanation, and narrative in historiography. *American Historical Review, 94,* 627–653.

Meltzer, M. (1994). *Cheap raw material: How our youngest workers are exploited and abused.* New York: Viking.

Mitchell, M. K. (1993). *Uncle Jed's barbershop.* New York: Simon & Schuster.

Mizell, L., Benett, S., Bowman, B., & Morin, L. (1993). Different ways of seeing: Teaching in an anti–racist school. In T. Perry & J. W. Fraser (Eds.), *Freedom's plow: Teaching in the multicultural classroom* (pp. 27–46). New York: Routledge.

Mochizuki, K. (1993). *Baseball saved us.* New York: Lee & Low.

Naidoo, B. (1986). *Journey to Jo'burg A South African story.* New York: Harper.

Naidoo, B. (1989). *Chain of fire.* Philadelphia: Lippincott.

National Council for the Social Studies. (1994). *Expectations of excellence: Curriculum standards for social studies* (Bulletin No. 89). Washington, DC: Author.

National Council for the Social Studies Focus Group on the NEH History Standards. (1993). *Response to the history standards.* Unpublished report.

National Council of Teachers of Mathematics. (1989). *Curriculum and evaluation standards for school mathematics.* Reston, VA: Author.

National History Standards Project. (1994a). *National standards for United States history: Exploring the American experience.* Los Angeles: National Center for History in the Schools.

National History Standards Project. (1994b). *National standards for world history: Exploring the American experience.* Los Angeles: National Center for History in the Schools.

National Research Council. (1996). *National science education standards.* Washington, DC: Author.

Neuman, S. (1992). Is learning from media distinctive? Examining children's inferencing strategies. *American Educational Research Journal, 29,* 119–140.

Newkirk, T. (1989). *More than stories: The range of children's writings.* Portsmouth, NH: Heinemann.

Newmann, F. M., Secada, W. G., & Wehlage, G. G. (1995). *A guide to authentic instruction and assessment: Vision, standards and scoring.* Madison: Wisconsin Center for Education Research.

Noddings, N. (1992). *The challenge to care in schools: An alternative approach to education.* New York: Teachers College Press.

Novick, P. (1988). *That noble dream: The "objectivity question" and the American historical profession.* New York: Cambridge University Press.

O'Dell, S. (1980). *Sarah Bishop.* Boston: Houghton Mifflin.

Ogle, D. M. (1986). K–W–L: A teaching model that develops active reading of expository text. *Reading Teacher, 39,* 564–570.

Olson, D. R. (Ed.). (1974). *Media and symbols: The forms of expression, communication, and education* (Yearbook of the National Society for the Study of Education, New Series No. 73, part 1). Chicago: University of Chicago Press.

Oppenheim, S. L. (1992). *The lily cupboard.* New York: HarperCollins.

Pappas, C. C. (1991). Fostering full access to literacy by including information books. *Language Arts, 68,* 449–462.

Pappas, C. C., Kiefer, B., & Levstik, L. (1995). *An integrated language perspective in the elementary school: Theory into action.* White Plains, NY: Longman.

Parker, W., Mueller, M., & Wendling, L. (1989). Critical reasoning on civic issues. *Theory and Research in Social Education, 27,* 7–32.

Parker, W. C. (1991a). A final response: Searching for the middle. *Social Education, 55,* 27–28, 65.

Parker, W. C. (1991b). Helping students think about public issues: Instruction versus prompting. *Social Education, 55,* 41–44.

Parker, W. C. (1991c). *Renewing the social studies curriculum.* Alexandria, VA: Association for Supervision and Curriculum Development.

Parker, W. C. (1991d). Teaching an IDEA. *Social Studies and the Young Learner, 3*(3), 11–13.

Parks, R. (1992). *Rosa Parks: My story.* New York: Dial.

Peck, R. N. (1972). *A day no pigs would die.* New York: Knopf.

Peetoom, B. (1991, August). *The Bible and whole language.* Paper presented to the Whole Language Umbrella Conference, Phoenix, AZ.

Pelta, K. (1991). *Discovering Christopher Columbus: How history is invented.* Minneapolis, MN: Lerner.

Person, D. G., & Cullinan, B. E. (1992). Windows through time: Literature of the social studies. In E. Freeman & D. G. Person (Eds.), *Using nonfiction trade books in the elementary classroom: From ants to zeppelins.* Champaign–Urbana: National Council of Teachers of English.

Piaget, J. (1952). *The origins of intelligence in children.* New York: International Universities Press.

Pierce, K. M., & Gilles, C. J. (Eds.). (1993). *Cycles of meaning: Exploring the potential of talk in learning communities.* Portsmouth, NH: Heinemann.

Portal, C. (1987). Empathy as an objective for history teaching. In C. Portal (Ed.), *The history curriculum for teachers* (pp. 89–99). London: Falmer.

Portal, C. (1990). Empathy. *Teaching History, 58,* 36–38.

Prawat, R. S. (1989a). Promoting access to knowledge, strategy, and disposition in students: A research synthesis. *Review of Educational Research, 59,* 1–41.

Prawat, R. S. (1989b). Teaching for understanding: Three key attributes. *Teaching and Teacher Education, 5,* 315–328.

Purves, A. C. (1990). *The scribal society: An essay on literacy and schooling in the information age.* New York: Longman.

Rabinowitz, P. J. (1987). *Before reading: Narrative conventions and the politics of interpretation.* Ithaca, NY: Cornell University Press.

Ravitch, D., & Finn, C. E. (1987). *What do our 17-year-olds know? A report on the first national assessment of history and literature.* New York: Harper & Row.

Ravitch, D., & Schlesinger, A. (1990). Statement of the committee of scholars in defense of history. *Perspectives, 28*(7), 15.

Reardon, S. J. (1988). The development of critical readers: A look into the classroom. *The New Advocate, 1*, 52–61.

Reiff, J. C. (1992). *Learning styles.* Washington, DC: National Education Association.

Renyi, J. (1994). The arts and humanities in American Education. *Phi Delta Kappan, 75*, 438–445.

Resnick, L. B. (1987). The 1987 presidential address: Learning in school and out. *Educational Research, 16*(9), 13–20.

Richards, J. J. (1993). Classroom tapestry: A practitioner's perspective on multicultural education. In T. Perry & J. W. Fraser (Eds.), *Freedom's plow: Teaching in the multicultural classroom* (pp. 47–63). New York: Routledge.

Ricoeur, R. (1984). *Hermeneutics and the human sciences: Essays on language, action, and interpretation* (J. B. Thompson, Trans.). New York: Cambridge University Press.

Rockefeller, D. (1977). *Coming to our senses.* New York: McGraw-Hill.

Rogoff, B. (1990). *Apprenticeship in thinking: Cognitive development in social context.* New York: Oxford University Press.

Rowland-Warne, L. (1992). *Costume.* New York: Knopf.

Sadker, M., & Sadker, D. (1994). *Failing at fairness: How America's schools cheat girls.* New York: Scribner's.

Sancha, S. (1990). *The Luttrell village: Country life in the Middle Ages.* New York: Crowell.

Sandler, M. W. (1994). *Pioneers.* New York: HarperCollins.

Saul, W. E. (Ed.). (1994). *Non-fiction for the classroom: Milton Meltzer on writing, history, and social responsibility.* New York: Teachers College Press.

Sautter, R. C. (1990). An arts education school reform strategy. *Phi Delta Kappan, 75*, 432–437.

Schroeder, A. (1989). *Ragtime Tumpie.* Boston: Little, Brown.

Sebestyen, O. (1985). *On fire.* Boston: Atlantic Monthly Press.

Seixas, P. (1993a). The community of inquiry as a basis for knowledge and learning: The case of history. *American Educational Research Journal, 30*, 305–324.

Seixas, P. (1993b). Historical understanding among adolescents in a multicultural setting. *Curriculum Inquiry, 23*, 301–327.

Seixas, P. (1994a). *Margins and sidebars: Problems in students' understanding of significance in world history.* Unpublished manuscript.

Seixas, P. (1994b). Students' understanding of historical significance. *Theory and Research in Social Education, 22*, 281–304.

Selvin, D. F. (1969). *The thundering voice of John L. Lewis.* New York: Lothrop, Lee & Shepard.

Selwyn, D. (1995). *Arts and humanities in the social studies* (Bulletin No. 90). Washington, DC: National Council for the Social Studies.

Shaara, M. (1974). *The killer angels.* New York: Ballantine.

Shama, S. (1992). *Dead certainties: Unwarranted speculations.* New York: Vintage.

Shemilt, D. (1980). *Evaluation study: Schools Council History 13–16 Project.* Edinburgh: Holmes McDougall.

Shemilt, D. (1984). Beauty and the philosopher: Empathy in history and classroom. In A. K. Dickinson, P. J. Lee, & P. J. Rogers (Eds.), *Learning history* (pp. 39–83). London: Heinemann.

Shemilt, D. (1987). Adolescent ideas about evidence and methodology in history. In C. Portal (Ed.), *The history curriculum for teachers* (pp. 29–61). London: Heinemann.

Shepherd, L. A. (1991). Negative policies for dealing with diversity: When does assessment and diagnosis turn into sorting and segregation? In E. H. Hiebert (Ed.), *Literacy for a diverse society: Perspectives, practices, and policies* (pp. 279–298). New York: Teachers College Press.

Short, K. G., & Armstrong, J. (1993). "More than facts": Exploring the role of talk in classroom inquiry. In K. M. Pierce & C. J. Gilles (Eds.), *Cycles of meaning: Exploring the potential of talk in learning communities* (pp. 119–137). Portsmouth, NH: Heinemann.

Skeels, D. (1989). *Recommendations of the Task Force on Early and Elementary Social Studies.* Presented at the annual meeting of the National Council for the Social Studies, St. Louis, MO.

Sklar, K. K. (1995). *Florence Kelley & the nation's work: The rise of women's political culture, 1830–1900.* New Haven, CT & London, UK: Yale University Press.

Slavin, R. E. (1995). *Cooperative learning: theory, research, and practice* (2nd ed.). Boston: Allyn & Bacon.

Sokoni, M. A. (1991). *Mchesi goes to market.* Nairobi, Kenya: Jacaranda Designs.

Sosniak, L. A., & Stodolsky, S. S. (1993). Making connections: Social studies education in an urban fourth-grade classroom. In J. Brophy (Ed.), *Advances in research on teaching, vol. 4, Research in elementary social studies* (pp. 71–100). Greenwich, CT: JAI Press.

Speare, E. G. (1958). *The witch of Blackbird Pond.* Boston: Houghton Mifflin.

Stanley, D., & Vennema, P. (1988). *Shaka Khan: King of the Zulus.* New York: Morrow.

Stanley, F. (1991). *The last princess: The story of Princess Ka'inlani of Hawai'i.* New York: Four Winds Press.

Stanley, J. (1994). *I am an American: The true story of Japanese American internment.* New York: Crown.

Statni Zidovske Mueum, Prague. (1964). *I never saw another butterfly.* New York: Harpers.

Sternberg, R. J., & Horvath, J. A. (1995). A prototype view of expert teaching. *Educational Researcher, 24*(6), 9–17.

Stock, C. (1993). *Where are you going, Manyoni?* New York: Morrow.

Streitmatter, J. (1994). *Toward gender equity in the classroom: Everyday teachers' beliefs and practices.* Albany: State University of New York Press.

Sturner, F. (1973). *What did you do when you were a kid? Pasttimes from the past.* New York: St. Martin's Press.

Sutton, R. (1990). *Car.* New York: Knopf.

Swales, J. M. (1990). *Genre analysis: English in academic and research settings.* Cambridge: Cambridge University Press.

Takaki, R. (1993). *A different mirror: A history of multicultural America.* Boston: Little, Brown.

Taylor, D. (1993). *From the child's point of view.* Portsmouth, NH: Heinemann.

Temple, C., Nathan, R., Temple, F., & Burris, N. A. (1993). *The beginnings of writing.* Boston: Allyn & Bacon.

Thelen, D. (1995). The practice of history. *Journal of American History, 81*, 933–960.

Thompson, E. P. (1963). *The making of the English working class.* New York: Pantheon.

Thornberg, L., & Brophy, J. (1992, November). *Early elementary students' thinking about Native Americans and their encounters with Europeans.* Paper presented to the annual meeting of the College and University Faculty Assembly, National Council for the Social Studies, Detroit, MI.

Thornton, S. J. (1987). What can children learn from history? *Childhood Education, 63*, 247–251.

Thornton, S. J. (1990). Should we be teaching more history? *Theory and Research in Social Education, 18*, 53–60.

Thornton, S. J., & Vukelich, R. (1988). Effects of children's understanding of time concepts on historical understanding. *Theory and Research in Social Education, 16*, 69–82.

Tierney, R. J., Carter, M. A., & Desai, L. E. (1991). *Portfolio assessment in the reading–writing classroom*. Norwood, MA: Christopher-Gordon.

Todorov, T. (1982). *Theories of the symbol*. Ithaca, NY: Cornell University Press.

Todorov, T. (1990). *Genres in discourse*. New York: Cambridge.

Toolan, M. J. (1988). *Narrative: A critical linguistic introduction*. New York: Routledge.

Traugott, E., & Pratt, M. L. (1980). *Linguistics for students of literature*. New York: Harcourt, Brace, Jovanovich.

Trease, G. (1983). Fifty years on: A writer looks back. *Children's Literature in Education, 14*, 149–159.

Trout, L. (1982). Native American history: New images and ideas. In M. T. Downey (Ed.), *Teaching American history: New directions* (Bulletin No. 67, pp. 91–112). Washington, DC: National Council for the Social Studies.

Tuchman, B. W. (1981). *Practicing history*. New York: Ballantine.

Tunnell, M. O., & Ammon, R. (Eds.). (1993). *The story of ourselves: Teaching history through children's literature*. Portsmouth, NH: Heinemann.

Turner, A. (1992). *Katie's trunk*. New York: MacMillan.

Turner, A. (1987). *Nettie's trip south*. New York: Macmillan.

Uchida, Y. (1985). *Journey to Topaz*. Berkeley, CA: Creative Arts.

Uchida, Y. (1993). *The bracelet*. New York: Philomel Books.

VanSledright, B. A. (1995). "I don't remember—the ideas are all jumbled in my head": 8th graders' reconstructions of colonial American history. *Journal of Curriculum and Supervision, 10*, 317–345.

VanSledright, B. A., & Brophy, J. (1992). Storytelling, imagination, and fanciful elaboration in children's historical reconstructions. *American Educational Research Journal, 29*, 837–859.

Vosniadou, S., & Brewer, W. F. (1987). Theories of knowledge restructuring in development. *Review of Educational Research, 57*, 51–67.

Vygotsky, L. (1978). *Mind in society: The development of higher psychological processes*. Cambridge, MA: Harvard University Press.

Wade, R. C. (1994). Conceptual change in elementary social studies: A case study of fourth graders' understanding of human rights. *Theory and Research in Social Education, 22*, 74–95.

Welch, J. (1994). *Killing Custer: The battle of the Little Bighorn and the fate of the Plains Indians*. New York: Norton.

Wellman, H. M., & Gelman, S. A. (1992). Cognitive development: Foundational theories of core domains. *Annual Review of Psychology, 43*, 337–375.

Wells, G. (1994). *Changing schools from within: Creating communities of inquiry*. Portsmouth, NH: Heinemann.

Wells, G., & Chang-Wells, G. L. (1992). *Constructing knowledge together: Classrooms as centers of inquiry and literacy*. Portsmouth, NH: Heinemann.

Wexler-Sherman, C., Gardner, H., & Feldman, D. H. (1988). A pluralistic view of early assessment: The project spectrum approach. *Theory Into Practice, 27*, 77–83.

Wesniewski, D. (1992). *Sundiata*. New York: Clarion.

White, H. (1978). *Tropics of discourse: Essays in cultural criticism*. Baltimore, MD: The Johns Hopkins University Press.

White, H. (1980). The value of narrativity in the representation of reality. *Critical Inquiry, 7*, 5–27.

White, H. (1982). The politics of historical interpretation: Discipline and de-sublimation. *Critical Inquiry, 9*, 113–137.

White, H. (1984). The question of narrative in contemporary historical theory. *History and Theory, 23*, 1–33.

White, M. (1965). *Foundations of historical knowledge*. New York: Harper & Row.

Whittington, D. (1991). What have 17-year-olds known in the past? *American Educational Research Journal, 28*, 759–780.

Wiggins, G. (1989). A true test: Toward authentic and equitable forms of assessment. *Phi Delta Kappan, 70*, 703–713.

Wiggins, G. (1992). *The case for authentic assessment*. Washington, DC: U.S. Department of Education, Office of Educational Research and Improvement, Educational Resources Information Center.

Wiggins, G. P. (1993). *Assessing student performance: Exploring the purpose and limits of testing*. San Francisco: Jossey-Bass.

Wilde, O. (1982). *The artist as critic: Critical writings of Oscar Wilde*. Chicago: University of Chicago Press.

Wilder, L. I. (1953). *Little house on the prairie*. New York: Harper & Row.

Williams, H. M. (1991). *The language of civilization: The vital role of the arts in education*. Washington, DC: President's Committee on the Arts and the Humanities.

Wilson, A. H. (1983). A case study of two teachers with cross-cultural experience—They know more. *Educational Research Quarterly, 8*, 78–85.

Wilton, S. (1993). Newer biographies are "better than before." In M. Zarnowski & A. F. Gallagher (Eds.), *Children's literature and social studies: Selecting and using notable books in the classroom* (pp. 16–19). Dubuque, IA: Kendall/Hunt.

Wineburg, S. S. (1991). On the reading of historical texts: Notes on the breach between school and academy. *American Educational Research Journal, 28*, 495–519.

Winner, E. (1982). *Invented worlds: The psychology of the arts*. Cambridge, MA: Harvard University Press.

Winter, J. (1988). *Follow the drinking gourd*. New York: Knopf.

Winter, J. (1991). *Diego*. New York: Knopf.

Wright, C. C. (1995). *Wagon train: A family goes west in 1865*. New York: Holiday House.

Yep, L. (1994). *Dragon's gate*. New York: HarperCollins.

Young, C. (1994). Change and innovation in history curriculum: A perspective on the New South Wales experience. In K. J. Kennedy, O. F. Watts, & G. McDonald (Eds.), *Citizenship education for a new age* (pp. 29–46). Queensland, Australia: The University of Southern Queensland Press.

Young, K. A. (1994). *Constructing buildings, bridges, and minds: Building an integrated curriculum through social studies*. Portsmouth, NH: Heinemann.

Zevin, J., & Evans, C. (1993). *Illustrated history of the world*. New York: Kingfisher.

Zhensun, Z., & Low, A. (1991). *A young painter: The life and paintings of Wang Yani—China's extraordinary young artist*. New York: Scholastic.

Zinn, H. (1990). *Declarations of independence: Cross-examining American ideology*. New York: HarperCollins.

Index

ೞഊ